Trails Across America

Trails Across America

Traveler's Guide to Our National Scenic and Historic Trails

Arthur P. Miller Jr.
and Marjorie L. Miller

Fulcrum Publishing
Golden, Colorado

Book and cover design by Alyssa Pumphrey
Cover photograph Copyright © 1996 Joe Cook
Interior photographs courtesy of the authors.
Maps Copyright © 1996 XNR Productions

Logos used in the book are the official trail logos, with the exception of the Potomac Heritage NST, the California NHT, and the Pony Express NHT, whose logos have not yet been created.

Library of Congress Cataloging-in-Publication Data
Miller, Arthur P., Jr.
    Trails across America : traveler's guide to our national scenic
and historic trails / Arthur P. and Marjorie L. Miller.
        p.   cm.
    Includes bibliographical references and index.
    ISBN 1-55591-235-4 (pbk.)
    1. Hiking—United States—Guidebooks. 2. Trails—United States—
Guidebooks. 3. United States—Guidebooks. I. Miller, Marjorie L.
(Marjorie Lyman), 1929- . II. Title.
GV199.4.M55   1996
796.5'1'0973—dc20
                                                                    95-49864
                                                                        CIP
              Printed in the United States of America

        0   9   8   7   6   5   4   3   2   1

                        Fulcrum Publishing
                    350 Indiana Street, Suite 350
                    Golden, Colorado 80401-5093
                          (800) 992-2908

CONTENTS

Dedication

We applaud the efforts of the men and women, both professional and volunteer, who have worked so diligently to create the network known as the National Trails System. It has been an inspiration and privilege for us to share the trails with many of them as they helped us gather the material for these pages.

It has been gratifying as well to be able to forge an agreement whereby the Partnership for the National Trails System will benefit financially from the sale of *Trails Across America*, thus enabling this valuable trail constituency to further expand the national system of trails to which it devotes its efforts.

PREFACE

I WAS BORN AND RAISED IN WESTERN PENNSYLVANIA. IN THE LATE 1950s the Pennsylvania Turnpike was the first piece of an interstate highway system that was eventually to become the largest public works project ever devised by man. What excitement when my father drove it for the first time. "Think of it, son—a mile a minute!"

Little did I realize then how involved I would become in the creation of another interstate system with a vision as far-seeing and with goals just as broad—a national trails system. Like the early days of the Federal-Aid Highways Act of 1956, these are heady times.

By 1998 the federal land acquisition program designed to permanently protect the Appalachian National Scenic Trail should be complete. In June 1993 the last portion of the Pacific Crest National Scenic Trail was dedicated. Rail-to-trail conversions are rapidly accelerating, spurred by the financial muscle of federal grants, which in 1993 totaled $120 million. States like Nebraska, where there had been little interest in the creation of trails, are active now.

Planners envision the day when you will be able to step out of your backdoor onto a local trail that will connect with other trails, ultimately linking neighborhoods, metropolitan areas, states, and regions in an interlocking network of footpaths. It will be a thrill to know that your local pathway connects with one of the national trails designated by Congress as our most significant pathways.

This book is a valuable and much-needed addition to our trails libraries. The backpacker, day hiker, cyclist, horseman, history buff, and auto touring vacationer all will gain insights from these pages. With this guidebook in hand you are ready to step off to new adventures along America's most outstanding long-distance trails. It is important to know the nature and extent of the trail system awaiting us out there. And we can experience my dad's excitement when we use the trails.

—Charles Sloan
President (1989–1993), American Hiking Society

INTRODUCTION

Trails of an Expanding Nation

THE WELL-WORN FOOTPATH WINDS ITS WAY THROUGH THE DIM LIGHT of a forest of sugar maple, yellow birch, beech, and hemlock. It is damp underfoot as you walk through a throng of lady ferns whose dainty fingers reach up to brush your legs. The white blossoms of a carpet of bunch berries polka-dot the forest floor. Evergreen yews arch across the trail. Springtime wildflowers add color while warblers bring their high-pitched songs to the scene.

Short side trails lead to 50- to 200-foot-high sandstone bluffs whose flanks form the corrugated shoreline so characteristic of Lake Superior on Michigan's Upper Peninsula. When the trail swings out to the bluffline, your eyes fill with a widescreen view of this great inland sea and your face feels its breezes. You are walking a section of the North Country National Scenic Trail that runs through Pictured Rocks National Lakeshore in Michigan.

On the North Country there's a good chance you will share your walkway with wildlife. Like humans, animals often choose a trail as the easiest way to get from one place to another. Deer tracks in the damp earth tip you off that white-tailed deer inhabit this area too. So do black bear who may make off with your food unless you string it up on the high poles that park rangers have provided at campsites along the trail. It is not unusual to come upon a porcupine, as two day hikers recently did. Unhurried the porcupine sauntered along the trail ahead of the hikers until it decided it had had enough human companionship and disappeared into the brush.

These are some of the sights, sounds, and smells you will experience along a national scenic trail like the North Country, the longest of the eight national scenic trails that wind across parts of the United States. These congressionally designated footpaths lead through some of America's most spectacular wilderness areas. Of the eight the North Country skirts the Great Lakes while four others lead the hiker north-to-south along mountain ridgelines. Another runs through a tropical lowland, another through a river valley, while the eighth traces the geographic imprint left on the land by ancient glaciers (see map on page 52).

History calls the tune on a second type of nationally designated trail—the national historic trail. Instead of being, like a scenic trail, a continuous footpath through unpopulated areas, each of the eleven national historic trails marks the route followed by those who took part in an epic exploration, migration, military action, or commercial venture.

Each of the chapters will focus on one of these nineteen congressionally designated scenic or historic trails, describing the terrain along the route, portraying its scenic attributes, pointing out its natural history features, and identifying historic sites, regional museums, and trailside visitor centers you will find along the route. Many of these interest points are illustrated on the map that accompanies each chapter.

But travelers should not expect to find each of these designated long-distance footpaths and historic motor routes open before them in an unbroken, continuous ribbon. Although two national scenic trails—the Appalachian National Scenic Trail and the Pacific Crest National Scenic Trail—have been virtually completed end to end, others have not. Of more than fourteen thousand miles designated as national scenic trails approximately eight thousand miles is actually marked and available to hikers. Of twenty-three thousand miles designated as national historic trails some eleven thousand miles is marked to guide travel by auto, water, or on foot. The route shown on each chapter map, therefore, represents both existing and proposed sections of each trail.

National Scenic Trails

National scenic trails often lead through wilderness areas, the last unaltered landscapes in America, the wild places where humans have not reshaped the land or stamped things out in straight lines.

Long-distance backpackers gets satisfaction from venturing into the backcountry where they know they will be subject to the harsh laws of nature and must carry with them everything they need to camp out and subsist on their own. Long-distance hiking is a persevering effort that continues over a number of days or weeks, a series of endurance tests. The successful backpacker gains a great feeling of pride and self-assurance from accepting this challenge and meeting it.

Hikers testify that such a trek reduces life to its essentials: food, shelter, beauty. No longer insulated by the support systems of modern civilization, the hikers have the opportunity to use all of their senses, to feel the raindrops and the sun's heat, to hear the breath of the wind in the pines above their heads, to see the mountain vistas. Hikers find themselves close to nature where curiosity comes into full play and may lead to surprising discoveries. Hikers feel more closely connected to the cycles of nature. Hikers experience delight in learning to identify a new tree or a flower that hadn't been recognized before.

Hiking a trail is also good for your health. There is no doubt, health experts report, that walking or hiking helps a person keep fit. Sagging and expanding body contours are a constant reminder that lack of movement leads to muscular degeneration. Weakness, shortness of breath, aches and pains, tension, and nervousness are symptoms of those who fail to stay active. Consistent exercise is the answer, and walking and hiking are readily available forms of exercise. Hiking is an aerobic exercise that gets the whole body moving; the heart beats faster, breathing becomes deeper. Hiking is known to relieve tension, ease depression, put a person more in control of his or her life, and make him or her more sensitive to the surrounding sights and sounds. Most doctors agree that true health begins with aerobic fitness. The scenic trail corridors that stretch across the country also help preserve wildlife and plant life and thereby help maintain biological diversity. A trail corridor—which is, in fact, a long, linear park—gives animals a natural migration route and protects rare plants, animals, and natural features.

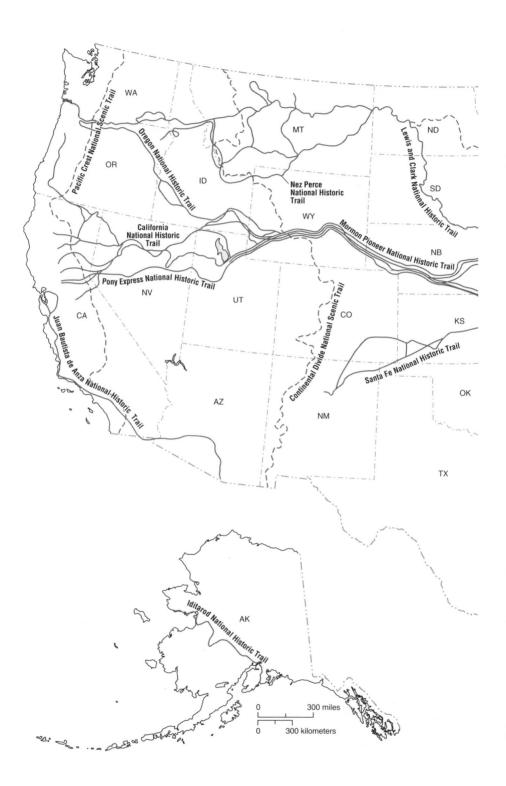

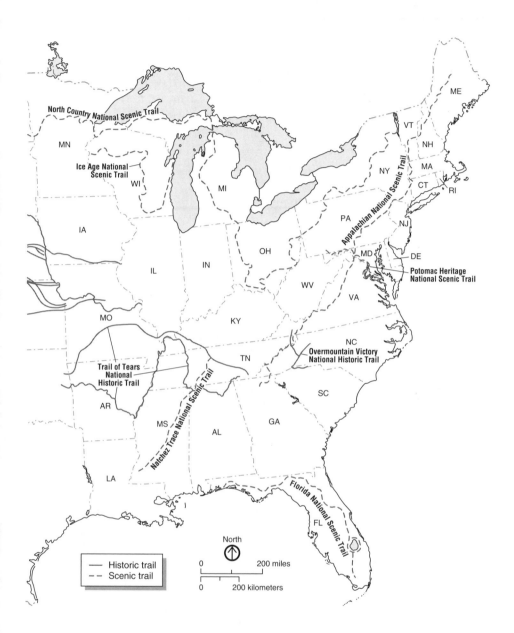

North Country National Scenic Trail

ME

VT

NH

MN

Ice Age National
Scenic Trail

WI

MI

NY

MA

CT

RI

Appalachian National Scenic Trail

PA

NJ

IA

OH

V MD

DE

IL

IN

Potomac Heritage
National Scenic Trail

WV

VA

MO

KY

NC

Overmountain Victory
National Historic Trail

Trail of Tears
National
Historic Trail

TN

Natchez Trace National Scenic Trail

SC

AR

MS

AL

GA

LA

Florida National Scenic Trail

FL

North

0   200 miles

Historic trail
Scenic trail

0   200 kilometers

National Trails System—an overview

Segments of some of these national scenic trails, it should be noted, carry a local name instead of the national scenic trail symbol. This is because national trail planners often incorporated existing trails as part of the designated long-distance national system, maintaining the local trail name and markings. As a result hikers may still see only the local symbol on certain segments rather than the symbol of the national trail.

The planners look forward to the time when these long-distance trails will be interconnected to other short trails, greenways, and parks to form a nationwide network of natural corridors and open spaces that will link city and countryside. With such a network city dwellers will find themselves connected to one or more long-distance scenic trails—and an almost unlimited horizon for outdoor adventure. Already most users of long-distance trails are actually short-trip hikers who enjoy short segments but who relish being connected to a trail that disappears beyond the horizon.

National Historic Trails

In addition to national scenic trails Congress recognized another type of long-distance trail as part of the National Trails System—the national historic trail that identifies and commemorates reminders of the nation's past.

Whereas national scenic trails are interstate recreational trails laid out for hikers, horseback riders, and cyclists, national historic trails are primarily auto tour routes that follow roadways located on or near a historic route taken years before by a courageous explorer, a westward-bound wagon train, or a military contingent. Five of the historic trails pay homage to the westward expansion that peopled the country between the Revolutionary War and the Civil War—the remarkable colonizing movement when ambitious settlers moved to unknown remote places, not to conquer or convert or fortify or even to trade, but to find and make a new life for themselves and their children.

As a commemorative motor route a national historic trail leads you along roadways occasionally marked with a distinctive logo. Interpretive signs erected along the route mark historic sites and explain the events that took place there. Waysides provide auto pulloffs that provide an opportunity to explore a historic structure or walk a side trail that leads to a historical interest point. At other places remnants of the actual trail itself are preserved, such as the wagon ruts that amazingly are still visible along trails like the Oregon and Santa Fe Trails. Some landmarks along a national historic trail, however, are on private land and may not be open to visitors.

Portions of a national historic trail may also offer the traveler the chance to hike, ride horseback, use a four-wheel-drive vehicle, or travel by boat as he or she explores the trail segment. At national parks, national forests, and state parks along the route the visitor will find living history demonstrations, exhibits, and museums that display artifacts recovered by historians and archeologists. At St. Louis, for example, the jumping-off place for many of the wagon trains that led to the settling of the West, is the Museum of Westward Expansion. Beneath the soaring symbolic arch at Jefferson National Expansion Memorial, a national park area, is an underground museum where exhibits dramatically retell the beginnings of the epic marches that took thousands across the unknown spaces.

Leading the visitor through exhibits arrayed in concentric circles that represent time periods, the museum describes the opening of the American West by the explorers, mountain men, trappers, traders, and finally by the overland settlers. Quotations from trail diaries and letters make the events seem as though they happened yesterday.

History comes alive as the visitor follows in the footsteps of the pioneers, crossing the rivers they forded, seeing the natural landmarks they saw, and experiencing the weather conditions they battled—even if he or she is viewing the scene through the window of a comfortable car, motor home, or trailer instead of from the hard seat of a Conestoga wagon. "A long, narrow museum," one trail association member called a national historic trail. A historic trail brings into focus the challenge to those who transformed this nation from a wilderness to a peopled land.

Long-distance Trails and How They Began

The trails of today are the result of an evolution of travel routes that began even before the first Europeans set foot on the continent. When the Europeans arrived they at first followed the trails the Indians had long used, trails that led to sources of water or to deposits of copper, gold, silver, or turquoise. The Indians acquainted them, too, with the use of the canoe. Many early trails were water trails; canoeing down or up a river was easier than bushwhacking your way across country.

But as the country's population increased along the Eastern seaboard and the land available for farming grew scarcer, the colonists and land speculators yearned to move westward beyond the formidable Appalachian Mountain barrier.

In the spring of 1775 Daniel Boone, that experienced backwoodsman and trailblazer, led a group of thirty armed and mounted axmen from Virginia through the Cumberland Gap into what is now central Kentucky, following a trail that had long been used by Indians and was familiar to Boone from earlier hunting expeditions. In two weeks of felling trees and clearing underbrush they cut a rough and rocky trail wide enough for a string of pack horses to make its way into Kentucky with one of the first contingents to settle beyond the mountains.

The same year, on the opposite side of the continent, doubtless unknown to the settlers of the East Coast, another leader was guiding a group of courageous colonists across the deserts and mountains of the Southwest to found a colony for Spain at San Francisco. Juan Bautista de Anza, a Spanish captain, successfully established the seventh in a string of missions designed to strengthen Spain's claim to the West Coast territory. The route he followed is commemorated today as one of the national historic trails.

After the Revolutionary War American settlers spread westward through the Cumberland Gap and other passes through the Appalachians into the lands of the Midwest, lands that they had earned as the spoils of victory over the British or by treaty. By wagon and horseback they followed the newly built National Road that led from Cumberland, Maryland, near the headwaters of the Potomac River, into the new states of Ohio, Indiana, and Illinois. Other pioneers floated their families and household goods by water down the broad Ohio River to the Mississippi.

When President Thomas Jefferson negotiated the purchase of the Louisiana Territory from France in 1803, it spurred exploration and trapping beyond the Mississippi into the Great Plains and onward to the Rocky Mountains. To gather information and report on the resources of this great unknown area Jefferson sent an Army captain, Meriwether Lewis, and a friend of Lewis's, former Army officer William Clark, to explore these new lands and search for a water route to the Pacific Ocean that would open this new territory to trade and settlement. The Lewis and Clark National Historic Trail commemorates their epic journey.

Other Army officers—Zebulon Pike, Stephen Long, and John Frémont—surveyed and mapped parts of the West. Colorful "mountain men" such as Jim Bridger, Kit Carson, Thomas Fitzpatrick, and Jedediah Smith mapped other areas of the Rockies as they trapped the beaver whose pelts brought top dollar in the European fashion market. It was these explorers and trappers who paved the way for the wagon trains of settlers who would soon follow—and left their names behind along today's historic trails. Bridger established a trading post in southwest Wyoming that supplied emigrants on the Oregon Trail, a trading post that has been reconstructed for travelers to see today. Jedediah Smith, who found his way around more of the West than anyone else of his time, was the first of these trailblazers to discover South Pass in what is now Wyoming—the important passage through the Rockies that later proved to be the indispensable entrance gate to the far West and California for thousands of settlers.

Now the powerful westward push across the country harnessed the covered wagon that was pulled by either oxen or mules. Mile after painful mile these sturdy Conestoga wagons hauled settlers and their goods across the wide open spaces that were beyond the reach of the easier river transportation. During the 1820s trader William Becknell blazed the Santa Fe Trail to carry manufactured goods from Independence, Missouri, to what was then Mexico, where the goods were exchanged for silver, furs, and mules. His efforts live on as the Santa Fe National Historic Trail.

Fur traders and missionaries—the latter seemingly always out in front when it came to opening new territories—were the first white settlers to reach the Pacific Northwest. The enthusiastic reports they sent back east of fertile valleys just waiting for a sharp plow encouraged thousands of people to make their way west on the Oregon Trail after 1835. From 1856 to 1860 more than thirty thousand Mormons, fleeing religious persecution in the Midwest, walked across the Great Plains to Utah, some of them even pushing their belongings in handcarts, a scene recalled along the Mormon National Historic Trail. During the 1840s California's mild climate and fertile valleys attracted a steady stream of pioneers but the stream grew into a torrent after 1848 when gold was discovered near Sacramento.

The gold rush brought the "forty-niners" from all over the world. Only a few found their fortunes in the California foothills, but many stayed to become farmers, ranchers, and merchants, contributing to the growth of the coastal region.

This determined push of settlers to claim new lands had tragic effects on the native people who stood in their way. The story of the forced removal of Indians to reservations—the Cherokee from their homeland in North Carolina and Georgia and the Nez Perce from their homeland in the Pacific Northwest—is documented by two other national historic trails.

By 1850 the frontier had been pushed all the way to the Pacific Ocean as vast new lands were opened for settlement. The Pony Express route, now identified as another national historic trail, contributed to a sense of unity in the country as the fast mail cut in half the time it took for messages to reach California from the East Coast. Twenty years later the country was further stitched together with a thread of steel—the transcontinental railroad. New immigrants kept arriving from Europe to fill the railroad cars, lured to the United States by the assurance that they would find land to own and work to do. The government did a "land office business" selling its newly acquired land to the eager newcomers who would populate these empty spaces.

Conservationists vs. Exploiters

By the turn of the century, however, people began to realize that although the continent had been conquered the conquest had been made at a considerable cost. The call of the frontier had stressed free or low-cost land for everyone and abundant resources waiting to be exploited in the name of prosperity. Now attention began to shift toward conserving some of the outstanding natural and historic resources of the country instead of simply consuming them. The word "conservation" began to be heard in the land.

Something had to be done, many people decided, to modify the headlong and reckless exploitation of the country's natural resources—the aggressive timber cutting that had deforested many eastern mountains and woodlands, the scarring of the landscape brought about by the extraction of mineral deposits, the widespread plowing of grasslands, the wholesale slaughter of the bison herds.

Something had to be done as well, they argued, to prevent not only the obliteration of the country's natural heritage but also the loss of the country's manmade heritage. With the American frontier fading, wilderness was seen to be desirable instead of an obstacle to be overcome. Many Americans by this time were working in factories and offices rather than on the farm. In their leisure time many of them wanted to get out of the city and into the great outdoors where they could watch a sunset, swim in a cool mountain pool, or watch a cascading waterfall. Nature and the wilderness, conservationists said, should be their teacher, their companion, their friend.

A yearning for the lost frontier also strengthened this desire to experience the wilderness. In the woods or in the mountains a person could prove himself as self-reliant as were his frontier forebears. When he backpacked down a trail or pitched his camp at night under the stars he could display the same can-do spirit that his pioneer forefathers possessed.

Three wilderness-loving private citizens led the way in translating this longing for close encounters with the wilderness into the concept of a long-distance hiking trail.

In 1910 twenty-three hiking enthusiasts led by John P. Taylor, then principal of Vermont Academy, formed the Green Mountain Club to build a wilderness trail that would run the length of Vermont to the Canadian border. Eighteen years later the Long Trail was completed, its 260 miles constructed almost entirely by volunteers. The first of the long-distance recreational trails, the Long Trail continues as a popular hiking trail today.

Another avid hiker named Benton MacKaye (pronounced ma-KYE) sparked a grassroots movement to lay out a wilderness trail along the ridgeline of the Appalachian Mountains from New England into the South. In an article published in October 1921 in the *Journal of the American Institute of Architects* MacKaye proposed the idea of a hiking trail that would extend from New Hampshire to North Carolina (a concept later extended northward to Maine and southward to Georgia). The purpose of such a wilderness trail, he said, would be to "conserve, use and enjoy the mountain hinterland which penetrates the populous portion of America from north to south" and to thereby open up the countryside "as an escape from civilization."

MacKaye's idea caught on, particularly among hiking enthusiasts in the Hudson Valley of New York and New Jersey, where volunteers had already built some hiking pathways. In 1925 leaders organized the Appalachian Trail Conference, a federation of trail clubs along the route proposed by MacKaye. Members were encouraged to lay out a section of the trail near their home and to build lean-to shelters for hikers that would be spaced about a day's hike apart. By 1928 these volunteer outdoorsmen and women—often working on the trail over weekends and during vacations and donating their own money to the cause—had constructed 500 miles of trail in New England, New York, and New Jersey. The National Park Service, U.S. Forest Service, states, local communities, and the Depression-era Civilian Conservation Corps combined forces with the trail groups in an example of citizen/government cooperation. By 1931 the trail had grown to approximately its present length of 2,160 miles from Mount Katahdin in Maine to Springer Mountain in Georgia. Today the Appalachian Trail holds the distinction of being the first and one of the longest continuous, marked recreation pathways in the world.

In the West, a similar dream of a long-distance hiking and equestrian trail was taking shape. In 1932 Clinton C. Clarke, an executive of the YMCA and outdoorsman from Pasadena, California, proposed a trail that would follow a rugged highland course along the coast atop the ridges of the Sierra Nevada and the Cascade Range in Oregon and Washington all the way from Mexico to Canada.

Clarke visualized a continuous trail "along the summit divides of the mountain ranges ... traversing the best scenic areas and maintaining an absolute wilderness character." In putting forth his trail idea Clarke foresaw the value of such a trail much as MacKaye did. The Pacific pathway, he said, would help preserve wild areas and would encourage people of "our too-artificial civilization" to return to a simple life and gain a deeper appreciation of nature and the outdoors.

In 1932 he organized a group of hiking and riding clubs to mobilize a campaign to develop the Pacific Crest Trail. From the beginning the Pacific Crest Trail Conference had a head start on its dream of a 2,400-mile ridgetop trail that would become the counterpart of the Appalachian Trail of the East. Volunteers in Oregon, a state often in the forefront of environmental innovations, had already constructed 442 miles of the Oregon Skyline Trail along the ridgetop route. In north-central California another segment, the existing John Muir Trail, a 185-mile segment, was incorporated into the Pacific Crest Trail. Trail clubs got busy and connected the Lava Crest Trail segment in Washington, the Tahoe-Yosemite Trail segment in northern California, and the Desert Crest Trail segment in southern California. In 1941 the 445-mile Cascade Crest Trail segment in Washington was added. Finally, in 1993, the completed 2,638-mile Pacific Crest Trail was opened from Canada to Mexico.

A National System of Trails

The successes of the Appalachian Trail and the Pacific Crest Trail led President Lyndon Johnson in 1965 to call for a nationwide trail study "to help protect and enhance the total quality of the outdoor environment as well as to provide much needed opportunities for healthful outdoor recreation."

"We can and should have an abundance of trails for walking, cycling and horseback riding in and close to our cities," he said. "In the back country we need to copy the great Appalachian Trail in all parts of America and to make full use of rights-of-way and other public paths."

The study that followed pointed out that simple pleasures such as walking and cycling had become increasingly limited for the American people as society has urbanized and as economic development has preempted areas that earlier had been devoted to outdoor recreation uses. "With more leisure time and with rising amounts of disposable income available for recreation use, more and more Americans are seeking relaxation and physical and spiritual renewal in the enjoyment of the traditional simple pleasures," it stated. "A surging demand for opportunities to enjoy outdoor activities presses upon natural resources which are shrinking under the impact of our rapidly expanding population and economy."

To meet this need Congress in 1968 enacted the National Trails System Act, which provided for a system of trails throughout the country. It designated the Appalachian and the Pacific Crest Trails as the first two national scenic trails. The act set down the methods and standards for adding new trails to the system and encouraged private, nonprofit trails groups who had shown the way to continue to provide volunteer citizen involvement in the planning, development, maintenance, and management of trails.

The act of 1968 and later amendments established four types of nationally recognized trails:

National Scenic Trail—A long-distance, interstate trail chosen for the nationally significant scenic, natural, and cultural qualities of the region through which it passes. When completed a national scenic trail is a continuous, protected, and marked scenic corridor that provides outdoor recreation and enjoyment of its scenic beauty by those who use it. National scenic trails are often routed through national and state parks, national and state forests, national wildlife refuges, and other public landholdings to take advantage of the scenic potential and interpretive facilities of these preserves and to avoid laying the trail across private lands.

National Historic Trail—A long-distance, interstate marked route that allows the public, usually auto travelers, to retrace a significant route of exploration, migration, military action, or commerce. A national historic trail corridor generally is made up of remnant sites and trail segments and is not necessarily continuous; it preserves for public use and commemoration historic structures, artifacts, and memorabilia that tell the story of the people who made the experiences of the trail an indelible part of the nation's history.

National Recreation Trail—A trail that usually lies within one state, often in or near a city or urban area. National recreation trails are usually multiuse, providing a variety of recreational activities such as hiking, biking, horseback riding, trail biking, cross-country skiing, snowmobiling, roller-blading, or use by those in wheelchairs. They include nature trails, fitness courses, and historic tours. Some are even water routes such as canoe trails. They may be managed by federal, state, county, or local parks and forests, by public utilities, military bases, private agencies, or companies. Some national recreation trails make use of utility rights-of-way; others are trails converted from former logging roads or abandoned rail corridors.

They vary from a trail running through a city park to an integrated trail system within a community. For example, New York's Seaway Trail, the longest national recreation trail in the country, winds for 485 miles along the Great Lakes coast of upstate New York, providing cyclists and motorists with scenic vistas, picnic areas, and views of historic sites. Its initial success led to its extension to Pennsylvania's Lake Erie coast. The Freedom Trail in downtown Boston, on the other hand, is a two-mile stroll along city streets where a trail marked by red footprints on the pavement guides the visitor past such familiar landmarks of the American Revolution as Old North Church, Paul Revere's home, and Old City Hall.

Altogether more than eight hundred national recreation trails have been designated. A complete listing including trail length, types of uses, and administrating agency is available in the publication *Register of National Recreation Trails* (Superintendent of Documents, Washington, D.C. 20402-9328, ISBN 0-16-041664-7).

Side and Connecting Trails—Side trails provide additional points of access for hikers and bikers to national scenic trails, national historic trails, and national recreation trails. Connecting trails provide the connections that link trails together into an expanding network.

Trails are added to the system as national scenic or historic trails through a four-step process. After a trail is identified a study, requested by Congress, determines the feasibility and desirability of the route. Eligibility depends upon the significance, integrity, and potential for public use and enjoyment of the proposed trail. National groups that encourage trail development, such as the National Recreation and Parks Association, the Rails-to-Trails Conservancy, and the American Hiking Society, are consulted. Planning agencies, state and local park agencies, and land managing agencies as well as trail organizations, trail-user groups, and interested individuals are brought in to help define the proposed route. The study, which often recommends alternatives, is forwarded to Congress.

If Congress authorizes establishment of a new national scenic or historic trail, the federal agency to which it is assigned prepares a comprehensive management plan. Workshops are held to get reactions from those affected. Issues, concerns, and opportunities are identified. The effect of the trail on the environment is assessed. The plan then sets down guidelines for the routing, development, management, and protection of the trail and for certifying sections of the trail that fully meet these standards.

National recreation trails have a shorter path to designation. They are designated by either the Secretary of the Interior or the Secretary of Agriculture. Since 1971 more than eight hundred national recreation trails have been approved. To gain recognition as a national recreation trail the trail's managing agency submits information on the purpose, uses, maintenance, police protection, and rules and regulations for the trail to the nearest National Park Service or U.S. Forest Service regional office. If the management, availability, and location criteria are met, the application is forwarded to the Secretary, who establishes the new national recreation trail. The new trail then becomes eligible to share in the funding available through the Land and Water Conservation Act, which helps states complete public recreation projects that fit into their approved state outdoor recreation plan.

In the last 30 years the expanding rails-to-trails movement has brought many additional miles of trails into the National Trails System. Through the efforts of the Rails-to-Trails Conservancy, more than five thousand miles of abandoned railroad rights-of-way across the country have been converted into five hundred trails of all kinds, many of them national recreation trails. Uses vary from walking and jogging to horseback riding to wheelchairs to cross-country skiing and snowmobiling. Hundreds more such "rail trails" are being developed.

Trail Organizations

Volunteers have always played an essential role in the establishment, development, and maintenance of America's trails. Today, organized into thousands of local trail clubs, these enthusiastic volunteers often are the first to envision a trail, help lay out its route, gain landowner cooperation, educate public officials on its potential value, and mobilize a campaign to establish it. Once the trail is established the local trail club does most of the maintenance required to keep it free of obstructions and washouts, its pathway clearly marked, and its shelters in good repair. Trail club members also help resolve right-of-way problems, negotiate with public agencies, buy easements, and persuade local citizens of the trail's value.

To coordinate the efforts of these volunteers most of the national trails have also organized a trail association to promote the trail's improvement, plan outings along the trail, and keep the association members informed of the results of their collective efforts. At the end of each of the following chapters is a description of the association or associations whose mission is improving that trail.

In 1991 sixteen trail associations formed the Partnership for the National Trails System. This partnership represents the collective interests of the organizations of trail volunteers and works with Congress and federal agencies to preserve, protect, develop, and maintain the national scenic and historic trails. The partnership serves the associations of the national trail community by providing a forum; developing collective initiatives; providing advocacy for the trails before Congress and the federal agencies; promoting support for the National Trails System among corporations, non-profit organizations, and charitable foundations; and organizing leadership programs for volunteers. The work of the partnership is guided by a small professional staff and supported through assessments from its member associations, contributions from individuals and corporations, and foundations grants. The partnership is located at 214 North Henry Street, Suite 203, Madison, WI 53703.

This, then, is the story of how the national scenic and national historic trails came into being. It is time now to take a closer look at each of these nineteen outstanding trails. Together they wind their way across forty-five of the fifty states, coming close to many a backdoor of the citizens who will use them.

Use this book as your guide to the wide world of the national trails. Backpackers may find here the challenge of an end-to-end hike on a scenic trail. Families may find a theme for an educational vacation along one of the national historic trails. Travelers may add to their itinerary an interest point along a long-distance trail that crosses their travel route. All should find enjoyment and adventure exploring some of America's best-kept secrets—its national trails.

Section One

NATIONAL SCENIC TRAILS

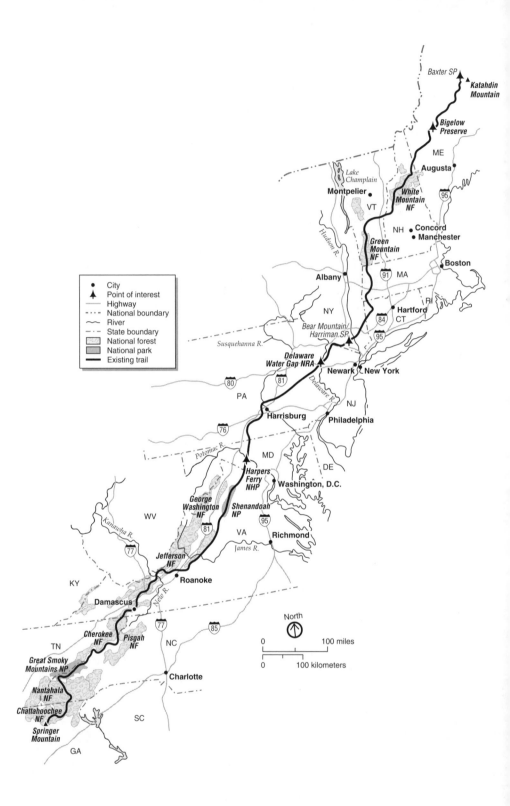

Baxter SP

▲ Katahdin Mountain

▲ Bigelow Preserve

Lake Champlain

ME

Augusta

White Mountain NF

VT

Montpelier

NH ● Concord
● Manchester

Green Mountain NF

MA ● Boston

Albany

NY

Hartford

Bear Mountain/ Harriman SP

Susquehanna R.

CT

Delaware Water Gap NRA

Newark New York

PA

NJ

Harrisburg

Philadelphia

Potomac R.

MD

DE

Harpers Ferry NHP

Washington, D.C.

George Washington NF

Shenandoah NP

WV

Kanawha R.

VA

Richmond

Jefferson NF

James R.

Roanoke

KY

Damascus

New R.

TN

Cherokee NF

Pisgah NF

NC

Charlotte

Great Smoky Mountains NP

Nantahala NF

Chattahoochee NF

▲ Springer Mountain

GA

SC

North

0   100 miles

0   100 kilometers

Chapter 1

APPALACHIAN NATIONAL SCENIC TRAIL

WHEN THE NATIONAL TRAILS SYSTEM ACT WAS ENACTED IN 1968, IT established the first two national scenic trails in the country. One was the Appalachian Trail, the well-known footpath that stretches from Katahdin in Maine to Springer Mountain in Georgia. The other was the Pacific Crest Trail, a north-to-south route that follows high mountain ridgelines in the far West.

The Appalachian Trail took its place as the "granddaddy" of what would become a spreading system of national trails, the model that trail planners looked to as they planned other national scenic trails. Its establishment was an official confirmation of the dream put forward by Benton MacKaye a half-century earlier. MacKaye, the forester, land planner, and visionary, had proposed a long-distance hiking trail whose "ultimate purpose is to conserve, use and enjoy the mountain hinterland which penetrates the populous portion of America from north to south ... to preserve and develop a certain environment and ... to open up a country as an escape from civilization."

Today the Appalachian National Scenic Trail is one of the longest continuous, marked footpaths in the world. Linking peak to scenic peak, the pathway extends for approximately 2,160 miles as it runs along the crests of the washboard-like ridges of the Appalachian Mountains that sweep down the Eastern seaboard. A swath of solitude, the "A.T." winds close enough to major cities to offer the 180 million people who live nearby a long—or a short—hike; as a result, some three million enthusiasts hike sections of the trail each year. The trail threads through fourteen states as it takes advantage of natural sanctuaries offered by eight national forests, six national parks, and numerous state forests, parks, and preserves. It crosses twenty rivers, dips to sea level at the Hudson River, and climbs to its highest point (6,642 feet) at Clingmans Dome in Great Smoky Mountains National Park before reaching its end in Georgia where the Appalachian Mountains dwindle into the coastal plain.

It is natural to speak of the Appalachian Trail, as MacKaye did, as beginning in the north and ending in the south. In fact the first sections of trail were completed in New York and the northern end of the trail developed first. The Appalachian Trail Conference, the long-established organization that manages the trail and informs and assists hikers, numbers its detailed trail guides from north to south.

But most of the "thru hikers"—those persevering outdoorsmen and women who hike the entire length of the trail—do it from south to north, starting at Springer Mountain and ending at Katahdin. Beginning their trek in early spring in Georgia, they try to reach Katahdin before the chill of October.

The trail changes character as it unwinds. In the far south the pathway roller coasters up and down peaks and valleys, then becomes more undulating in the Middle Atlantic states, and finally climbs and descends even steeper inclines in New England. Mixed forests of fir, tulip poplar (yellow poplar), sugar maple, yellow birch, hickory, and oak shade much of the southern segment except where the trail traverses one of the distinctive balds that dot the landscape. A bald is an open summit, bare except for grasses and shrubs, where no trees grow.

In Virginia, a state that holds one-fourth of the Appalachian Trail, the pathway provides numerous viewpoints from the ridgetop to the farmlands below. In Pennsylvania, New Jersey, and New York sharp-edged rocks remind you that the ancient glaciers once ground to a halt here, dropping their load of rocky debris.

In New England the trail leads through forests of conifers and hardwoods such as birch, aspen, and red oak to reach bare rock summits where blasts of wind have reduced the vegetation to a tundra growth of grasses, lichens, mosses, and a few bent-over shrubs.

By 1937 the Appalachian Trail had been blazed as a continuous hiking trail from Maine to Georgia, thanks to the pioneering efforts of a few dynamic leaders and the hard work of hundreds, if not thousands, of volunteer trail builders. The work of these devoted volunteers—still the hallmark of this long-distance trail—is coordinated and directed by the Appalachian Trail Conference, which was organized in 1925.

The Appalachian Trail, and to a lesser extent the Pacific Crest Trail, have received federal funds to acquire land along their routes—a benefit that other national scenic trails have not enjoyed. As part of the 1968 legislation Congress authorized an appropriation of $5 million to purchase land or easements to protect portions of the Appalachian Trail. States were encouraged to protect segments within their borders. By 1978 59 percent of the trail route was protected against nonhiking uses, mostly the sections that ran through public lands such as national forests, national parks, and state forests and parks.

Relatively little private land, however, had been purchased. So in 1978 Congress authorized money from the Land and Water Conservation Act to buy private landholdings along the trail with the aim of protecting the entire length of the trail and preventing potential blockages of the footpath. Funds for the Land and Water Conservation Fund come from royalties paid to the federal government for offshore oil leases and from federal excise taxes; these proceeds are then expended for conservation purposes that benefit the public, including the Appalachian Trail.

By 1993 $150 million from the fund had been spent on A.T. land acquisition by the National Park Service and the U.S. Forest Service. Today all but 40 miles or less of the Appalachian Trail lies on publicly owned land, a greenway preserved as part of our natural heritage for present and future generations. In the near future the entire trail route is expected to be thus protected.

In 1984 the Appalachian Trail led the way in an innovative approach to long-distance trail management. From the beginning the maintenance and upkeep of the A.T. rested in the hands of local trail clubs whose volunteers spend many hours each year looking out for each club's assigned portion of the trail. Volunteers of the thirty-two clubs often spend their weekends clearing trees that have fallen across the pathway, repainting blazes, repairing eroded sections of the trail, and erecting shelters for hikers.

In an unprecedented example of cooperation between a private group and government, the Appalachian Trail Conference in 1984 signed an agreement with the National Park Service, which

5

administers the trail, committing the ATC and its member clubs to provide the stewardship necessary to maintain the trail corridor according to certain exacting standards. To do this each club along the trail route takes an inventory of the natural assets of its stretch of the trail, everything from a virgin stand of trees to an unusual geologic formation. It then draws up a local management plan which the National Park Service approves. The plan spells out how the trail standards will be applied to its assigned segment. As a result the Appalachian Trail, which has been called "the longest national park in the world," is one of the few public natural areas to be managed primarily by private citizens acting as volunteers.

In return for all this maintenance work the National Park Service and U.S. Forest Service provide liability and medical insurance protection to the Appalachian Trail Conference and to the club volunteers who do the day-to-day work on the footpath.

"It's as though a park the size of Yosemite National Park was strung out in a long corridor and was maintained free of cost by expert volunteers," said David Startzell, executive director of the Appalachian Trail Conference. "Our affiliated trail clubs take the responsibility for the care of more than 100,000 acres of federally acquired trail corridor lands that are outside the boundaries of the national forests and national parks. In a recent year 5,700 volunteers donated more than 137,000 hours, a work contribution we estimated to be worth one-and-a-half million dollars."

David Richie, formerly the Appalachian Trail Project Manager for the National Park Service, stated that the transfer of this maintenance responsibility from the federal government not only meant a cost savings to the taxpayers but also reflected a consensus that the potential for doing the best job rested with volunteers rather than with a government-paid workforce. Club maintainers, he concluded, "are the real specialists in trail work and have more of a commitment. These volunteers really want to do the work."

Need a Topographical Map?

Hikers on many of the long-distance national scenic trails find that the well-known "quad maps" published by the U.S. Geological Survey are indispensable. Details shown on these maps include contour lines, elevations, natural and manmade landmarks, towns, rivers, lakes, paved and unpaved roads, and trails.

For an index of the quad maps available for each state call 800-USA-MAPS or write to the U.S. Geological Survey (ESIC), 507 National Center, Reston, VA 22092. Using the index you can then order from the USGS the quad maps that cover your trail route.

Georgia to North Carolina

On a clear day on Springer Mountain, the southern terminus of the Appalachian Trail, a hiker gets a tantalizing glimpse of the hazy mountain ridges that stretch to the horizon. In a clearing, one of the few open vistas in the surrounding forest, is a gently sloping area of grass and flat rock surfaces. Set into one of the rock surfaces is a bronze plaque (see cover image) that declares this spot to be the terminus of the Georgia to Maine trail, "a footpath for those who seek fellowship with the wilderness."

Nearby, in a metal drawer built into a granite boulder, is a trail register that records the heartfelt feelings of the hikers who reach this point.

"This is the perfect place to get away from the daily grind," one wrote. "I consider my trip here a pilgrimage to a sacred place."

Although few hikers end their journey at Springer, many start from here, reaching Springer Mountain by a 2.3-mile approach trail from nearby Amicalola State Park. Most of the ambitious thru hikers—those who intend to hike the entire 2,160-mile length in one season—start here, usually in March or April. With good luck, a sturdy pair of hiking shoes, and plenty of persistence, they will reach the northern end in Maine by October.

The trail is well protected at its southern end since it runs entirely within Chattahoochee National Forest and Nantahala National Forest before entering the Great Smoky Mountains National Park. The Forest Service has further designated the Springer Mountain terminus as a national recreation area. "This means that we manage this part of the forest not for timber sales as we normally do, but to provide the best environment for hikers, hunters and fishermen," said Kent Evans, the Forest Service district ranger. A double-decker shelter for recreationists is tucked away in the woods not far from the trail's end. It is one of some 250 shelters that have been constructed along the trail over the years. A few were erected by the Civilian Conservation Corps, which did yeoman work on the trail during the 1930s; others have been added by the Forest Service, national and state park services, and local trail clubs.

The trail moves into Georgia's northern mountains, surmounting two peaks of more than four thousand four hundred feet. It drops to lower elevations as it dips through gaps, then curves around the headwaters of the Chattahoochee River, which flows from these highlands downslope to Atlanta. In the higher elevations the hiker walks beneath red oaks, white oaks, tulip poplars, and maples; crossing a stream through a valley often brings an eye-catching scene of masses of rhododendrons gracefully draped over the current of a sparkling brook.

Springer Mountain terminus of Appalachian Trail. Joe Boyd of the Georgia Appalachian Trail Club inspects plaque at trail's end.

Then the trail takes the hiker into the Nantahala Mountains, well known to veteran outdoorsmen as the most rugged terrain along the trail south of the Mahoosuc mountain range at the border of New Hampshire and Maine. A steady climb brings you to the summit of Standing Indian Mountain (5,498 feet). Although the trail in the Nantahalas tops 5,000 feet only a few times, the steep mountain flanks and deep-cut valleys require numerous switchbacks, stairsteps, and sidehill trail treads. The hiker climbs a slope only to descend immediately to negotiate another stream. To cross a bridge over the Nantahala River itself—a river famed for its challenging whitewater canoeing and kayaking—the trail drops from 5000 to 1,700 feet within eight miles, a true test of the hiker's physical condition.

North Carolina and Tennessee

After crossing the Little Tennessee River at Fontana Dam, a dam built as part of the Tennessee Valley Authority project which added new lakes, riverways, and electric power plants to this region, the A.T. passes through Great Smoky Mountains National Park, a hiker's paradise. Within the park and onward to the Virginia border, summits of 6,000 feet are the rule rather than the exception; numerous peaks reach 5,000 feet. The highest point on the trail, Clingmans Dome, is near the center of the park.

The trail follows the central spine of the mountains for seventy miles across the park. Few roads interrupt the green wilderness. The Appalachian Trail serves as the backbone of a network of side park trails that make the Smokies a favorite for hikers as well as the most visited national park in the nation. These spur trails offer the Appalachian hiker a potential diversion; many of the side trails lead to an interest point such as a waterfall, a creek, or a historic site. Overnight shelters welcome hikers at 8- to 10-mile intervals. In the Smokies these three-sided shelters have an added feature—chainlink fencing on the fourth side that serves as "bearproofing."

And black bears are here, all right. Park naturalists estimate that from 400 to 600 bears inhabit the park, their numbers depending primarily on the acorn crop in a given year. But despite these numbers hikers rarely see a bear. Bears in the backcountry generally avoid people and pose little threat except to food supplies and packs, which they methodically tear apart if these are not hung at least eight feet off the ground.

White-tailed deer, too, are plentiful. So are wild hogs, introduced early in the twentieth century for a nearby game park. A number of hogs escaped and thrived within the park. They root up the ground in search of roots, mushrooms, and other edibles.

Hikers will probably see areas along the trail that have been "plowed up" by these unwelcome animal immigrants.

Fertile soil and abundant rainfall encourage the development of world-renowned varieties of flora, including about 1,500 kinds of flowering plants, more than 400 kinds of mosses and liverworts, 230 lichens, and some 2,000 varieties of fungus. Broadleaf trees predominate in mountain coves; along the crests grow conifer forests similar to those of central Canada. In fact, you can experience a full range of life zones simply by going from the lower elevations in the park to its highest crests.

Wildflowers and migrating birds abound in late April and early May. During June and July rhododendrons bloom in spectacular profusion. Autumn brings a pageantry of color to the mountains while winter fog rolling over the mountains can blanket the conifers in frost. Each season has its own appeal to those who choose to explore these natural wonders.

The segment of trail through the Smokies is notable also for the system of "ridgerunners" who serve within Great Smoky Mountains National Park. Park Service managers and the Appalachian Trail Conference have worked together to ensure a satisfying experience for hikers while at the same time preserving the wilderness character of the backcountry. Other ridgerunners patrol the trail in Connecticut, Massachusetts, Vermont, and New Hampshire.

For the peak hiking season, from March to October, the Appalachian Trail Conference hires four ridgerunners, knowledgeable hikers who range up and down the 70-mile footpath acting as sort of backwoods ambassadors.

The need for such ambassadors became evident on one occasion when more than a hundred backpackers tried to crowd into one of the park's thirteen shelters. To bring order out of the confusion the park instituted a backcountry permit system and approved hiring the ridgerunners, whose salaries are paid jointly by the ATC, the Park Service, the park's nonprofit Natural History Association, and the Smoky Mountains Hiking Club.

Dennis Fulcher, a ridgerunner, described his job as one part trail companion, one part advisor, and one part trail watchdog. "You never know who you're going to meet on the trail," he said, smiling as he remembered the day he helped avert trouble for a three-generation family of seven who had taken to the woods for its first backpacking adventure with more enthusiasm than camping experience.

Fulcher, a veteran hiker himself, has completed the A.T. from end to end once and is halfway through doing it a second time. Bearded and lean from long hours on the trail, he retired from his job as an instrument technician on aircraft and rocket engines to devote his energies to outdoor pursuits.

"Some of the folks I see are experienced outdoorsmen, others are novices," he said. "We're out there on the trail to provide answers to their questions, to reassure hikers that help is available if they need it, to protect the resource from overuse, and ensure that hikers enjoy a quality experience. We also monitor the shelters to make sure that those with permits get the accommodations they deserve."

In addition to assisting and advising trail users Fulcher and the other ridgerunners notify the park's maintenance crew of any deterioration of the trail such as a toppled tree blocking the pathway or an area made impassable by flooding. He acts as the eyes and ears of the ranger force, maintaining radio contact to notify rangers of any emergency, safety problem, infraction of regulations, or behavior problem.

But mostly he is a friendly counselor, passing out tips on hiking and camping techniques, interpreting the environment, and ensuring that everyone treats the trail and backcountry with respect. He can point out, for example, that two of the most popular day hikes in the park go along the A.T., making use of a trailhead on the only cross-park road, the Newfound Gap Road (Route 441). From the trailhead at Newfound Gap the A.T. goes five miles south to an observation tower at Clingmans Dome and four miles north to a scenic viewpoint at Charlie's Bunion.

Continuing north along the ranges of this extension of the Blue Ridge section of the Appalachian Mountains, the A.T. comes within the protection of two more national forests—the Cherokee National Forest and the Pisgah National Forest, which occupy the upper mountain slopes all the way to the Virginia border. The trail moves back and forth between North Carolina and Tennessee as it follows the state border close to the ridgeline. The pathway unwinds like a roller coaster through this mountainous domain, leading the hiker to several high crests, numerous balds, waterfalls up to forty feet high and two major rivers—the French Broad and the Nolichucky.

The footpath now makes its way to Roan Mountain, an open summit that is covered in pink each June with a sweep of Catawba rhododendrons. A little farther on it crosses the Overmountain Victory National Historic Trail, a route that commemorates an epic transmountain march by a group of frontiersmen during the Revolutionary War (see page 131).

Virginia

Thru hikers on the A.T. sometimes feel they will never get through Virginia. The trail cuts a path for 550 miles diagonally across the state from the southwestern tip to its northern border at the Potomac River. First it follows the westernmost range of the Appalachians—the Allegheny Mountains—which brings it close to West Virginia, then swings to the east to cross the Valley of Virginia and climb to the Blue Ridge, the Appalachian's eastern rampart, to continue the remaining two-thirds of its path across the state.

For much of the way the trail runs through Jefferson National Forest and George Washington National Forest. Farther on it is protected within the boundaries of the Blue Ridge Parkway and Shenandoah National Park.

Near the Tennessee-Virginia border is Damascus, sometimes called "the friendliest town on the A.T." It is the gateway to the Mount Rogers National Recreation Area, where the trail passes directly over Whitetop Mountain, the second-highest peak in the state, and near Mount Rogers, the highest at 5,729 feet. The town is well known for its hospitality to hikers; the route goes right down its main street, past stores, garages, and service stations. Many a thru hiker has picked up his or her mail at the town post office where the postmaster maintains a special shelf for hikers. Long-distance walkers are happy to make use of the town laundromat, add supplies to their backpack, or take a break from the trail to spend a night at a guest house and get a hot bath.

Long-distance hikers even join in a town festival each year when a thousand or more walkers and townspeople get together for "Appalachian Trail Days," a combination reunion and fair that is held for ten days in May. Backpackers camp in a field next to a church, spending their days swapping stories, meeting old hiking friends, eating pancakes and barbecued chicken, attending fishing clinics and slide shows, and dancing to blue-grass music.

The trail meets the Blue Ridge Parkway north of Roanoke and shares the ridgetop with this scenic drive for the next hundred miles. But so well have the trail clubs and their advisers routed the trail within this long, narrow right-of-way through the Jefferson and Washington National Forests that only rarely does the hiker see the roadway. Even when the pathway runs close to the parkway, it is often set back in the forest or behind a rise so that traffic noise is muffled or entirely absent. At several locations, the trails swings away from the parkway to circle the opposite side of a peak.

The backpacker gets his reward for tired feet and aching muscles when the trail breaks out of the forest to give him a wide-screen view of a mountain gap or a valley far below. The steep, tree-covered mountainsides slope down to the piedmont on the east and into broad valleys on the west, valleys dotted with small communities and a checkerboard of farms.

It is no mystery how these mountains got their name of "Blue Ridge." From an overlook the dark green foliage on the near slopes shades into the blues and grays of more distant ranges. It is as though sheer curtains had been dropped between the observer and the next range and the next, each curtain producing a lighter shade. A more scientific explanation is that the mountains appear blue because water droplets are released into the air by the trees. On a sunny day the bright blue sky and white clouds contrast with the muted hues of the mountains and brighten the valleys. On a damp day the scene changes to shades of gray as strands of low clouds and fog fill the hollows.

For most of its run through the Blue Ridge the trail winds beneath a canopy of trees. In the fall dogwood, sourwood, and blackgum turn deep red as the forest is transformed into a blaze of color. Tulip poplars and hickories turn yellow, sassafras a vivid orange, and red maples red or orange. Oaks add a russet or maroon while the evergreen pines, spruces, hemlocks, and firs provide their contrasting greens and grays.

Depending on the season, the hiker here is treated to splashes of color from flowering shrubs which put on a show to rival the trees of fall. Because of differences in elevation, blooming occurs at different times. Azaleas bloom at lower levels about mid-May and at higher elevations in mid-June. Mountain laurels bloom from mid-May to early June. Dense thickets of rhododendrons turn purple in early June while wildflowers pop up along the trail beginning in April.

The Blue Ridge Parkway leads to Shenandoah National Park, where the trail continues along the ridgeline. Hikers proceed from ridgetop to saddle to knob to gap. The only thing that interferes with this bucolic setting is that, as along the Blue Ridge Parkway, the footpath closely parallels the roadway. In fact, when the roadway was constructed here, it displaced the original footpath. But there is an upside to this proximity to both the Blue Ridge Parkway and the Skyline Drive of Shenandoah National Park—day hikers can easily gain access to the A.T. thru hikers, for their part, can take advantage of the park's five developed camping areas at Loft Mountain, Lewis Mountain, Big Meadows, Skyland, and Mathews Arm.

Huts maintained by the Potomac Appalachian Trail Club are located every 10 to 12 miles. The PATC, which draws many of its members from the Washington, D.C., metropolitan area, is one of the largest and most active of the trail clubs along the A.T. The PATC maintains not only the full length of the Appalachian Trail through Shenandoah National Park but also looks after 500 miles of side trails that lead to waterfalls, peaks, lookouts, and meadows. To help train these willing volunteers, the Shenandoah park staff each season hold a two-day workshop to teach the PATC members the maintenance techniques they will need—how to clear away blowdowns, control erosion, construct a trail, and manage vegetation.

The chances of seeing wildlife are good at Shenandoah. Deer, bear, bobcats, turkeys, and other animals that were formerly rare have returned to this second-growth forest. You might even come across a deer standing in the trail ahead of you—animals use the trails as well as humans. Black bears (about five hundred at last count) typically stay to themselves out of sight of hikers. About two hundred species of birds have been recorded in the park. A few, such as ruffed grouse, barred owl, raven, woodpecker, and junco, are year-round residents.

The A.T. passes or closely approaches several of the park's numerous waterfalls. Fed by springs or runoff from the ridgetop, the waterfalls pour over moss-covered rock ledges into fern-filled glades, a delight to the hiker and a good chance to cool trail-weary feet.

At places the trail leads across great jumbles of jagged rocks that cover an entire flank of a mountainside. At Hawksbill Summit (4,049 feet) the trail crosses one of these talus slopes where flights of ravens often circle overhead. At Blackrock Gap the trail leads through a similar jumble of boulders, some as large as boxcars. A glance upslope shows the indentations in the ridgeline where a cliff has collapsed and tumbled downhill. The fact that a level trail now bisects both these areas of upturned rocks is a tribute to the skill of trail club crews who constructed the pathway across these rockslides.

In these exposed rocks can be read the geologic history of the mountains. The jagged boulders are reminders that much of what we know today as the Blue Ridge Mountains was formed as a result of volcanic action millions of years ago. Molten magma from beneath the earth's surface slowly solidified to become the "basement rock" or core of these mountains. For the next 500 million years erosion and uplift of the earth's crust exposed the granite basement rock while even more lava pushed its way to the surface through deep cracks in the granite.

Then, geologists say, some 600 million years ago, a completely different event took place. A huge depression developed that stretched all the way from Newfoundland to Alabama, and an ancient sea flooded the area. Layers of sediment accumulated on the sea bottom. Then, as the huge, unseen tectonic plates shifted far beneath the earth's surface, the seafloor fractured. One plate rode up over another, tilting and folding the terrain above it like an accordion. The action drained the sea and created the sweeping panorama of crumpled landscape that has become the Appalachian Mountains.

Maryland, Pennsylvania, New Jersey, and New York

Along the Virginia portion of the trail hikers from time to time catch glimpses from the overlooks of the Shenandoah River as it winds its way through the valley to the west, accompanying the trail northward. At Harpers Ferry a unique geographic location, the trail meets the river.

Here the Shenandoah River joins the Potomac River—and Virginia meets both Maryland and the easternmost tip of West Virginia. In earlier years hikers had to ferry by boat to get across the Shenandoah. Now the trail leads across a highway bridge and through the interesting, preserved streets of Harpers Ferry, a town renowned as the place where abolitionist John Brown raided the federal arsenal in 1859. Then the route crosses the Potomac on a railroad bridge and continues along the towpath of the Chesapeake and Ohio Canal that runs beside the Potomac River, also part of the Potomac Heritage National Scenic Trail (see page 25).

The crossroads town of Harpers Ferry serves as headquarters for the Appalachian Trail Conference. Leave the trail and walk a few blocks and step into the ATC visitor center and bookstore. In addition to housing the organization that coordinates the volunteer work that maintains the long-distance trail, this rambling stone building and those within it provide trail guides and maps as well as firsthand advice on conditions along the trail. The National Park Service also maintains a project office—the federal management office for the trail—in Harpers Ferry.

The trail, as it crosses Maryland, Pennsylvania, New Jersey, and New York, follows a well-defined ridge of the Appalachians that runs surprisingly straight across the four states. The pathway is sheltered by several state forests and parks as it maintains an elevation of about fourteen to fifteen hundred feet, except for places where it dips into a gap or across a river. Other trail segments are protected by lands purchased to provide a natural right-of-way for the hikers. Most of the distance—260 trail miles—between Harpers Ferry and the Delaware Water Gap to the northeast is taken up by two masses called South Mountain and Blue Mountain, both actually long ridges.

History lies all around. The trail leads past sites of Civil War battles, a state park that commemorates George Washington's early efforts as a surveyor, and Gathland State Park where a ceremonial archway honors foreign war correspondents. The trail leads from Maryland into Pennsylvania across one of the nation's most historic boundaries: the Mason-Dixon Line. In the 1760s two British surveyors named Charles Mason and Jeremiah Dixon laid down this line to solve a dispute between the colonies of Pennsylvania and Maryland. Later the line also became the symbolic division between the southern and northern states—although when the war broke out Maryland remained loyal to the Union.

The ridges of southern Pennsylvania are littered with the remains of the old iron industry—iron furnaces and charcoal pits.

Then the trail descends to the Cumberland Valley southwest of Harrisburg, where it has been relocated from the rural roads it was once forced to follow. Then it climbs back to Blue Mountain and regains the elevated route that takes it through several more state parks and forests.

One of the pioneer trail clubs, the Blue Mountain Eagle Climbing Club, was responsible for completing an early portion of the A.T., the 102-mile section between the Lehigh River and the Susquehanna River. This group, which drew its support from Americans of German heritage who brought their hiking traditions with them from the old country, blazed this section as early as 1930 in response to Benton MacKaye's call to build a long-distance eastern trail.

Just before it leaves Pennsylvania the trail leads into the turn-of-the-century town of Delaware Water Gap, named for the scenic feature that has long attracted thousands of vacationers to the spot where the Delaware River cuts through an Appalachian ridge. A church in town is typical of several churches along the trail that provide not only spiritual renewal to the hikers but shelter as well. The mission of the Presbyterian Church of the Mountain includes serving as "a hospice ministry to travelers and those in need far from home." The church provides bunk space, a shower and bathroom, cooking facilities, and a mail drop in the church basement. The congregation even provides hikers a hot meal once a week. Needless to say, it has become a popular stopover on the trail.

The A.T. crosses the Delaware River on the I-80 highway bridge, swinging past the Kittatinny Point Visitor Center within Delaware Water Gap National Recreation Area, where trail information is available, then regains the ridge once more as it follows the eastern edge of the park in New Jersey for 30 miles to the New York border. It skirts the New York City megalopolis and reaches Bear Mountain State Park and the Hudson River.

It was here that the very first section of the A.T. was laid down by the New York–New Jersey Trail Conference in 1922–1923. Its members had a big incentive to do so because Mary Williams Harriman, the wealthy widow of the railroad tycoon Edward Harriman, had decided to donate many acres of land to form a park along the river. Not only that, but to provide access for herself and to extend the trail to the north, the Harriman family built—

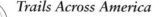

at its own expense of $5 million—the Bear Mountain Bridge that spans the Hudson. Today hikers reap the benefits of these early conservation efforts as they walk through the popular park and across the bridge to continue their way north.

Connecticut and Massachusetts

The hiker finds low, heavily forested mountains along the 50 miles of the A.T. that goes through Connecticut, then the higher, rounded peaks of the Berkshire Mountains in Massachusetts. Greylock State Reservation, which protects 10 miles of the trail, encloses the highest peak in Massachusetts, Mount Greylock (3,491 feet).

The trail clubs in both states belong to a larger organization, the Appalachian Mountain Club, the oldest mountain club in the country, organized in 1876. Even before the Appalachian Trail idea was born the AMC had developed and managed dispersed recreation opportunities such as mountain huts, camps, and hiking and skiing trails.

Like the other trail clubs, the Berkshire Chapter of the Appalachian Mountain Club accepts the responsibility for maintaining its 89 miles of the A.T. in Massachusetts. Ten of its members, for example, spent one Saturday rerouting one-and-a-half miles of the trail within the town of Cheshire, moving it from a public road to wooded land that had been purchased by the National Park Service as part of the natural corridor.

The job on this day was typical of the hard work put in by trail club members. Out of their cars came materials and tools— shovels, Pulaskis, crowbars, axes, and paintbrushes. By the end of the day ten men and women had built 50 feet of bog bridge out of planks and railroad ties to span a wet area, erected a stile to allow hikers to climb over a barbed wire fence, erected a post in a meadow to guide hikers across an open area, and cleared brush and branches from the new trail route. They marked the new path with the familiar white blaze and "blacked out" older blazes that had marked the old route. As a result of the work on this day and other days, the Berkshire group brought up to standard its section of the trail.

One member had driven two-and-a-half hours from his home to join the work crew. Another, Kay Wood, a woman in her seventies, is a story unto herself. For years she and her family lived close to the trail in Cheshire and took an interest in the hikers who came along, sometimes inviting them into their home to share a cool drink or a warm meal. After her children were grown and her husband died, Kay decided she wanted to hike the trail herself.

She began the trek in Georgia and reached Virginia before knee trouble forced her to return home. But the next year she picked up the quest, this time starting from Katahdin at the northern end. "Grandma K," as she was known to fellow hikers, celebrated her 65th birthday on the trail, floating a balloon from her backpack to celebrate. She made it to Virginia, thus completing the other half of the route in one of the more memorable end-to-end journeys on the A.T.

Kay Wood (left) and Helen Monico, of the Berkshire Chapter of the Appalachian Mountain Club, paint blazes on a rerouted section of the trail near Cheshire, Massachussetts.

Vermont and New Hampshire

Two national forests—the Green Mountain National Forest and the White Mountain National Forest—provide a verdant setting for the trail through Vermont and New Hampshire. From the Massachusetts border, the A.T. runs for a hundred miles northward along the Long Trail, a trail that continues the full length of Vermont along the spine of the Green Mountains. The Long Trail predates even the Appalachian Trail; construction began in 1910 and the trail was completed to the Canadian border in 1931.

When the A.T. leaves the Long Trail it swings eastward to enter New Hampshire and head for the Presidential Range of the White Mountains, so named because the most prominent peaks bear the names of former presidents. These rugged peaks are far different from the rounded humps of the southern Appalachians or the rolling ridges of the Middle Atlantic states—these are hulking masses of granite rock often encircled by threatening clouds.

The most impressive, and one of the great challenges of the trail, is Mount Washington (6,288 feet). Its weather is anything but benign. Snow lingers eight or nine months of the year and a wind gust of no less than 231 miles an hour has been clocked at its summit. Its soaring peak shoulders a full thousand feet above treeline, making its flanks the longest open slopes on the entire A.T.

But the Appalachian Mountain Club's hut system—rustic lodges that accommodate from thirty-six to ninety guests each, spaced a day's hike apart—takes some of the risk out of hikes across these windswept and cloud-shrouded peaks. During the

Members of Berkshire Chapter of the Appalachian Mountain Club build a stile to enable hikers to step over barbed wire fence along the Appalachian Trail—one Saturday's volunteer work.

summer season each hut has a staff to provide a hot meal and a bunk for tired hikers.

From Mount Washington the trail crosses peaks named Clay, Jefferson, Adams, and Madison, eventually finding its way to lower elevations where it crosses the Androscoggin River to reach the Maine border.

Maine

After negotiating the difficult Presidential Range of New Hampshire the A.T. hiker must still complete the most remote section of the trail—278 miles across the Maine woods. When the trail was first being laid out planners thought the Maine wilderness so forbidding that they considered establishing the trail's northern terminus at Mount Washington. But a special study in 1933 reported a feasible route using old logging roads and paths that would end at Katahdin.

Now the thru hiker must conquer this final lap across the wilderness to claim Katahdin as his or her prize. One of the toughest miles of the entire 2,160-mile trail lies at the border of New Hampshire and Maine where the trail enters an area of boulder-filled glacial valleys. This is Mahoosuc Notch, where the hiker must carefully pick his way past huge slabs of granite that have fallen from cliffs on either side, walk past gnarled scrub trees, clamber up rock chimneys, and duckwalk through rocky tunnels. Caves abound in the hillsides. It does not help his sore muscles to know that Mahoosuc Notch is such a remarkable piece of geography that it is listed on the National Register of Natural Landmarks.

It is as though the A.T. had a mind of its own and did not want the hiker to complete it. He must climb several mountains that tower over three thousand feet, three of which are higher than four thousand feet, to earn the reward of the view from an alpine summit before descending to the next stream valley to begin yet another ascent. He has to wade through the cold waters of mountain streams at places where no bridge has yet been built.

The Kennebec River, once one of Maine's important logging rivers, is another obstacle. You can schedule a ferry by canoe across the 100-yard-wide crossing, but some hikers decide to wade across. The early morning hours, before an upstream dam releases tons of water, are the time to do it. Even so the water may be thigh-deep to a six-footer. Algae-covered rocks on the bottom make the footing slippery as the powerful currents clutch at the hiker's legs. If he is caught in midstream during a dam release, he could be in trouble. At least one person has drowned at the crossing.

It was here in Maine that the final two-mile link of the original trail route was blazed in 1937, part of the pathway that takes the hiker near the top of Spaulding Mountain. In the 1930s the Civilian Conservation Corps did a lot of the work in Maine, as it did in Virginia and North Carolina. The CCC cleared new sections, brought old trails and roads up to standard, painted blazes, and constructed twenty trail shelters, several of which are still used today by grateful hikers.

Before you reach Katahdin you must walk through the "hundred-mile wilderness," a region of seemingly endless spruce-fir forests. Much of the pathway once ran through land owned by paper companies who harvested the trees to feed nearby pulp mills. Now the National Park Service and the state together have acquired a corridor here for the trail. No towns and only an occasional backcountry timber road interrupt this remote region, which can only be penetrated on foot.

Near trail's end the mountains alternate with lowland lakes and bogs. Maine's bogs are legendary; marshy areas where a 40-inch rainfall and the dam-building tendencies of beavers combine to fill low spots with clinging mud and pools of black water. Stumps ground to a point and mound-shaped lodges rising out of the ponds are common sights, proof of the beaver's presence. The Maine Appalachian Trail Club has put hours of effort into building walkways across these muddy bogs and rerouting the trail around newly dammed areas.

It is hard to imagine a more fitting climax to the long, exhausting journey from Georgia to Maine than the rocky monolith called Katahdin. After a steep woodland trek the trail comes out above timberline, where it becomes a difficult but seldom dangerous rock climb. About a mile from the peak the mountain flattens, giving the hiker a chance to catch his breath and, on a clear day, get a view of the countryside.

Then on up the rocky slope to the end of the trail at Baxter Peak where a large, maroon sign announces "Katahdin—Baxter Peak, 5,267 feet" and lists the distances to various points back down the trail. It is the end of the trail, the hiker's holy grail. Nearby stands a high rock cairn, the accumulation of bits of rock and pebbles that hikers have carried with them the entire trek so they could enjoy the honor of adding their contribution to the cairn.

Is it worth it—four or five months of blistered feet, sore shoulders, hot sun, and cold rain? Here is what one thru hiker wrote in a trail register as he neared the end of the Appalachian Trail:

> Time was no longer measured in minutes, hours and days remaining to the day, and number of miles between town stops.
>
> It was the hardest task I ever tackled in my life, physically and mentally, but because I had wanted to hike the trail, the difficult times were a bit easier. Hiking the A.T. has been a dream of mine for a long time and now it is an array of memories that I will carry with me forever.

Appalachian Trail Conference

Located in a fieldstone building in Harpers Ferry, West Virginia, the headquarters of the Appalachian Trail Conference opens its doors to hikers at a location that is near the trail's halfway point.

Staff workers in the visitor center area offer advice to those following the trail. Visitors also find interpretive exhibits and a well-stocked library. A selection of guidebooks, maps, and other hiking publications are available or may be ordered.

From its headquarters the ATC coordinates the maintenance of the trail through its thirty-two affiliated clubs and four field offices. The backbone of the conference is the confederation of hiking, outdoors, and Appalachian Trail clubs whose volunteer members maintain and relocate segments of the trail, manage surrounding lands, help in land acquisition negotiations, compile and update guidebook and map information, work with trail communities on special events, and recruit and train new volunteers.

For more information write the Appalachian Trail Conference, P.O. Box 807, Harpers Ferry, WV 25425.

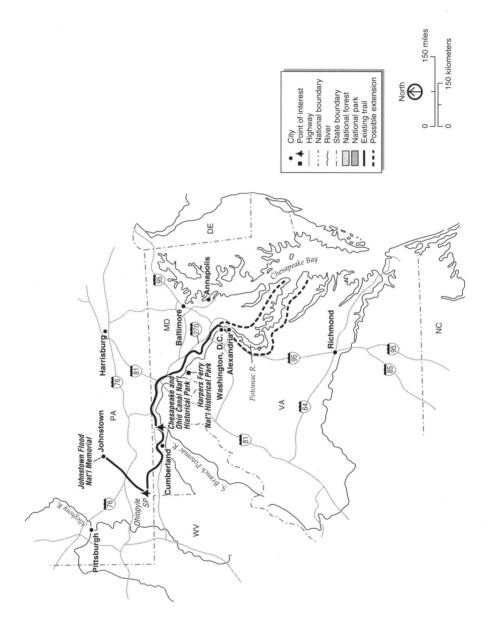

City
Point of interest
Highway
National boundary
River
State boundary
National forest
National park
Existing trail
Possible extension

North

0   150 miles
0   150 kilometers

Johnstown Flood
Nat'l Memorial

Johnstown

Harrisburg

Pittsburgh

Allegheny R.

PA

76

81

76

Ohiopyle
SP

Cumberland

S. Branch Potomac R.

WV

81

Chesapeake and
Ohio Canal Nat'l
Historical Park

Harpers Ferry
Nat'l Historical Park

Washington, D.C.

Alexandria

Potomac R.

VA

64

95

85

Richmond

NC

MD

Baltimore

270

95

Annapolis

Chesapeake Bay

DE

95

Chapter 2

POTOMAC HERITAGE NATIONAL SCENIC TRAIL

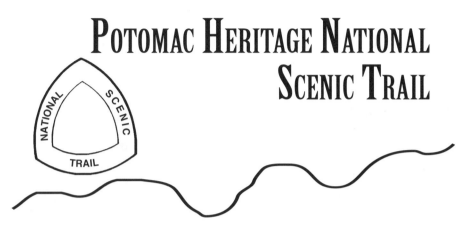

T HE POTOMAC HERITAGE NATIONAL SCENIC TRAIL, AS BEFITS A TRAIL that goes through the nation's capital, owes its existence to a president. President Lyndon Johnson and his wife Ladybird would occasionally ask their driver to pull off the road and stop the car along the Potomac River as they returned to the White House from the airport. For a few moments they would enjoy the view of the capital city from the Virginia side of the river.

To make scenes like this available to more people President Johnson, in a speech in 1965, enunciated the idea of a trail along the Potomac that would bring public attention to the natural resources and historic sites within the river corridor. He formally proposed it as a national scenic trail in 1966, and it was established by Congress in 1983.

If all the sections of this trail are someday completed, an ambitious hiker will be able to trace the Potomac River from its mouth, which empties into the Chesapeake Bay to the river's upper reaches, then swing northward into the mountains to conclude his or her journey in the Appalachian ridges near Johnstown, Pennsylvania.

Although the easternmost part of the Potomac Heritage National Scenic Trail has yet to be planned or laid out, the remainder of the pathway—some 370 of its planned 825 miles—can be hiked or biked. Along the way it passes through contrasting environments: the tidewater Potomac estuary, urban and suburban areas of Maryland and Virginia, the preserved corridor of the historic Chesapeake and Ohio Canal, rural fields and farms of Maryland and Pennsylvania, and wilderness stretches in the mountains.

At present the trail begins at George Washington's classic estate of Mount Vernon on the Potomac River south of Washington, D.C. From there it threads its way past the nation's capital on the 18.5-mile-long Mount Vernon Trail, which runs alongside the George Washington Memorial Parkway. It continues upriver from Georgetown to Cumberland, Maryland, on a 185-mile segment that once formed the towpath of the Chesapeake and Ohio Canal, which parallels the river. The towpath is open to hikers, cyclists, and, in places, horses. At Cumberland the trail leaves the river and follows local country roads and foot trails until it links up with the 11-mile Youghiogheny Bike Trail and the 70-mile Laurel Highlands Hiking Trail, which bring it to its end at Johnstown. The trail user, however, may not realize that he or she is on the Potomac Heritage Trail because few national trail signs have been erected; instead most trail segments bear only their local name.

Along the route hikers, cyclists, and equestrians enjoy many scenic views of the river, features of the coastal plain and piedmont regions, and historical landmarks that reflect man's uses of the river—not to mention magnificent views across the Potomac to the famous marble monuments of official Washington, D.C.

Mount Vernon Trail

The Potomac Heritage Trail begins amidst the beauty and sophistication of Mount Vernon, the ever-popular country plantation of our first president, making use of the local Mount Vernon Trail. On almost any day you will see groups of schoolchildren and their teachers, sightseers, and foreign visitors roaming the grounds of the sprawling white mansion with its red roof and its lawns sloping down to the Potomac River.

Hikers and bikers join them as they pick up the trail, a three-foot-wide macadam pathway that runs along the Virginia side of the river. After leaving Mount Vernon it closely parallels the Mount Vernon Memorial Parkway, a landscaped scenic roadway administered by the National Park Service. The trail winds through woods, marshes, and grassy slopes where fishermen try their luck, and picnicking families enjoy broad views of the river. Hikers and bikers pass several bits of history including remnants of a nineteenth-century river defense fortification at Fort Hunt that is now the focal point of 156 grassy acres of picnic and playing fields.

Six miles from the trail's beginning, where Hunting Creek joins the Potomac River, Dyke Marsh offers a diversion in the form of a nature sanctuary. Years ago colonial settlers of the region built a system of earthen dams to try to convert the swamp to productive farmland, but the tide that moves up the river from Chesapeake Bay defeated their efforts and the swamp reverted to its natural condition. Today trail users may wander through the marsh on a National Park Service side nature trail. Cattails, arrow-arum, sweetflag, and spatterdock grow beside the trail. Bullfrogs, leopard frogs, snapping turtles, even a beaver or a muskrat, have been known to haunt these damp surroundings. The Audubon Society has recorded more than two hundred bird species in the marsh.

Two miles farther the Jones Point Lighthouse provides an example of an inland river lighthouse, a warning light built in 1836 to direct ships away from sandbars in the river; the structure now stands directly beneath the massive Woodrow Wilson Bridge. Jones Point is the southern tip of the 10-mile square that defines the District of Columbia. The trail then follows a carefully laid-out corridor through the busy city of Alexandria, Virginia, skirting office buildings and busy streets. Alexandria, a town that once rivaled New York City as a thriving seaport, was a major colonial shipbuilding and tobacco trading center.

For two miles the Mount Vernon Trail runs close to the runways of National Airport where thundering planes land and take off every few minutes. It passes by the Lyndon Baines Johnson Memorial Grove where pink granite slabs bearing statements of the 36th president stand amidst landscaped plantings of shrubs and trees. Nearby sleek boats glide in and out of the Columbia Marina within the shadow of the nation's military headquarters, the Pentagon.

Cyclists and joggers outnumber the hikers on this part of the trail. Government workers, military men and women, housewives, retirees, and student athletes crowd the paved path on most days and in most seasons. Ambling couples, mothers with baby strollers, kids with their dogs, all find their place on the trail. Hikers should be prepared to stay to the right-hand side to allow room for the cyclists and roller-bladers to roll past.

*Cyclists on the Potomac Heritage (Mount Vernon) Trail
wheel through Belle Haven Park.*

Farther upriver, past Arlington Memorial Bridge, the trail approaches Theodore Roosevelt Island, a natural preserve that lies in the river between the busy metropolitan District of Columbia and the highly developed office center of Rosslyn, Virginia. Bikers leave their bicycles and cross a short bridge on foot to enjoy the two-and-a-half miles of cool, tanbark nature trails that encircle the island. In its center, blending with the natural surroundings, stands a 17-foot bronze statue of Theodore Roosevelt, the nation's 26th president. A terrace and promenade encircle this monumental plaza dedicated to a statesman who was a lifelong admirer of the outdoors.

Chesapeake and Ohio Canal Towpath

The Mount Vernon Trail now links up with the old Chesapeake and Ohio Canal towpath that runs along the north side of the Potomac River from Georgetown in the District of Columbia 185 miles to Cumberland, Maryland. From the end of the Mount Vernon Trail the hiker crosses to the north side of the river on the Francis Scott Key Bridge to Georgetown, then follows city streets until he descends to the canal. Meanwhile a side trail, built and laid out by the Potomac Appalachian Trail Club, continues along the south bank of the river for another 10 miles. This continuation of the Mount Vernon Trail parallels the primary route across the river but does not connect with it. The 12-foot-wide towpath, once trod by mules that pulled towboats on the canal, has been converted to a hiking and biking trail that is outstanding for its historic interest, its old-fashioned charm, and the beauty of its natural surroundings.

Begun in 1828 the canal was designed to open up resources and markets of the Ohio River Valley in the West by creating a flatwater transport route from the East through the Allegheny Mountains. Boats were unable to negotiate the river itself because of its steep shorelines, rocky rapids, and swift currents. The boats, not yet powered by motors, could not overcome the river's current.

Ironically, on the very day that President John Quincy Adams signaled the start of construction on the canal, a similar ceremony launched the construction of the Baltimore and Ohio Railroad, whose goal was also to carry freight through the mountains to the West. In its heyday five hundred boats operated along the canal, but the waterway never witnessed the lasting success envisioned by its ingenious designers. Cost overruns (the first recorded in U.S. history), failing contractors, cholera, Confederate shelling during the Civil War, and riots among the Irish and German immigrants who built the canal all plagued the operation. But even these calamities were not as bad as the competition from the railroad that would eventually prove to be the canal's undoing. Finally a disastrous flood in 1924 literally washed out any hopes for the canal's success.

The C & O Canal, when it was completed, carried boats upstream from sea level to 605 feet elevation and back again through a series of seventy-four lift locks. As each section of the canal was put into operation, it was put to use carrying freight (coal, flour, grain, and lumber) from the West to markets in the East, manufactured goods from the East to the West, and passengers in both directions.

Today, for most of its meandering miles, the once-proud queen of commerce is dry, choked with weeds, and spiked with trees. The old locks that once echoed the shouts of boatmen are sagging and deserted. Roses grow wild around the deserted lock houses that recall the less-hurried life of an earlier-day America.

Eventually the canal was purchased by its archrival, the Baltimore and Ohio Railroad. But during the Depression the railroad itself was forced to sell off assets, and the federal government bought the waterway in order to preserve the achievements of the canal era and with the intent of building a parkway along the river. Later, however, Supreme Court Justice William O. Douglas, a devoted outdoorsman, played an important role in preserving the canal and its towpath. In 1954, when highway advocates wanted to construct the parkway and obliterate part of the historic canal, Justice Douglas challenged thirty-six conservationists and newspapermen, some of whom favored the parkway, to hike the entire length of the waterway with him as he explained the benefits it would have as a protected linear park. As the result of the hike editorial writers changed their minds and became advocates, the historic canal was saved, and the park along the river was preserved. Now hikers and bikers enjoy these benefits as they walk the 12-foot-wide level towpath, enjoy views of the river, investigate the historic locks and scattered buildings, and gain a feeling for what life was like in the old canal days.

The C & O Canal towpath serves as a popular segment of the Potomac Heritage National Scenic Trail. Few people hike the whole 185-mile length each year, National Park Service rangers say, but many do bicycle the entire route. Most cyclists take three or four days to pedal the full length.

For both hikers and bikers alike the towpath trail offers a smooth route, often shaded by trees growing on both sides of the elevated trail. Markers are located at each mile point, although no Potomac Heritage Trail markers are evident. Hiker-biker campgrounds with tent sites, fire rings, and latrines are located about five miles apart along much of the trail. In addition the Park Service provides four drive-in campsites that allow access to the canal for recreational vehicles, cars, and trailers.

One way to experience life along the canal a century and a half ago is to take a ride on one of two replica canal boats that are pulled along two rewatered sections of the canal. From mid-April to mid-October trail enthusiasts can sign up for a boat ride either at the canal's beginning at Georgetown or at the visitor center at Great Falls, Maryland, where the Potomac River surges over a drop in the riverbed known as the "fall line." This is the same fall line that appears on rivers all along the East Coast and defines the locations of cities such as Richmond, Baltimore, and Albany. On the Potomac, as elsewhere, it occurs where the piedmont region meets the coastal plain; one reason the canal was built was to bypass this steep drop of more than one hundred feet that produces swirling rapids.

Each replica canal boat is built to the standard 93-foot length, 14.5-foot width, and 5.5-foot draft of the actual boats. As a passenger you ride the flatwater behind a team of trudging mules and marvel as the boat carefully slips through a lock. The boat captain, crew, and mule tenders, all in period dress, narrate your trip, sing canal songs, and share historical lore about boating days.

Although locking through in the canal's heyday was a relatively simple process lock tenders had to be on duty day and night or make sure someone was on hand to tend the lock. The boat's captain would call out "Hey-y-y lock" or blow a tune on a long brass horn; the tender then readied the lock by opening or closing the gates. A boat heading upstream would move into the lock once the upper gates were closed; the lower gates were then shut behind the boat. The lock tender opened paddle gates or "wickets" at the bottom of the upper gates, admitting a flow of water. When the water had raised the boat to the next level the upper gates were opened and the boat moved out of the lock and continued on. For a boat moving downstream the process was reversed. It usually took about ten minutes for a boat to move through a lock.

Each lock was bypassed by a flume that allowed excess water to flow around it. The water that filled the canal was replenished periodically by river water that flowed in from impoundments where the river had been dammed.

The canal builders also had to negotiate natural obstacles such as rivers and streams that flowed at right angles to the canal route. Culverts carried small streams under the canal. Eleven aqueducts carried the canal and towpath over rivers and streams too big for the culverts to handle.

Trail users learn that most of the boatmen in the old days used four to six mules per trip. One team of two or three mules rested aboard the boat in a small stable that was at the opposite end from the family's living quarters while the other team took the tow. The teams normally alternated four-hour shifts. Boatmen could switch their mules quickly by means of a gangplank they extended to shore and often changed teams while their boat lay motionless in a lock.

Several other interest points may draw the hiker's attention on the C & O Canal portion of the Potomac Heritage Trail. At Harpers Ferry, where the Shenandoah River meets the Potomac, walkers might want to step off the trail to make a side tour of the historic town, now a national historical park. It was here that the radical abolitionist John Brown staged an armed raid in 1859 to try to capture arms from the extensive federal munitions plant with which to arm black slaves and lead them to insurrection against their white masters. After considerable bloodshed, the raiders were captured by U.S. Marines under Colonel Robert E. Lee. Brown and six of his followers were tried for treason, convicted, and hanged. Walking the cobblestone streets of the restored town, visitors see a blacksmith shop, pharmacy, dry goods store, tavern, a U.S. Army provost marshal's office, and the brick fire engine house where John Brown was captured.

At Four Locks, at Mile 110, canal workmen constructed four separate locks close together that enabled boats to take a shortcut across a narrow neck of land where the Potomac River made a tight curve. The four locks were needed to accommodate a steep 32-foot drop in the water level. A lockman's house, a mule barn, and a lock master's shanty for protection in bad weather still survive. One of the seven dams built across the Potomac to impound the water needed to fill the canal is near here; it is still used by an electric power company, channeling water to its generators for cooling.

Farther on at Hancock, Maryland, there is a visitor center where an exhibit portrays the mule stable aboard a canal boat and displays diaries that describe everyday canal life. Other visitor centers are located at Great Falls and Cumberland.

Across the river from Paw Paw, West Virginia, canal engineers cut a 3,118-foot tunnel through a mountain to save seven miles. Using hand tools and black powder, crews painfully hacked through shale at the rate of 10 to 12 feet a week. The tunnel, 24 feet wide and 17 feet high from the water's surface to the crown, ranks as an engineering masterpiece of its day.

As hikers make the 20-minute walk through the tunnel, it seems you can almost hear the muffled footfalls of the mules on the towpath and the drip, drip of water echoing off the walls of the great arch. As daylight dwindles to a pinpoint of light at either end of the tunnel, the sense of being under a mountain heightens. When canal boats traveled through, the steady beat of mule hoofs and the slap of water marked their progress. The sound of music reverberated from the brick walls as the boatman sang a song in order to have the assistance of an echo and to calm children who were afraid of the dark.

The dark tunnel, it is said, witnessed many a fight between brawling boatmen. Lacking room for boats to pass inside, the barges backed up at the entrance like cars waiting to board a ferry. If they were not careful in this dark tunnel, a boat might enter from one end while another boat was trying to make its way through from the other end. Then one canal boat had to back up, a tricky proposition. Diaries prove that fists often decided the right-of-way.

At the end of the line at Cumberland, another visitor center tells the story of how this commercial hub grew at the canal's terminus. At the peak of waterway traffic, Cumberland's boatyards turned out 170 new craft a year. A turning basin, one of several along the canal, enabled the boats to turn around, reload, and head south on the return trip to Washington. Many boatmen and their families wintered over in Cumberland, continuing to live on their boats even when the canal ceased operations for the season.

Allegheny Highlands Trail

At Cumberland, near where the states of Maryland, Pennsylvania, and West Virginia meet, the trail changes character from an easy-hiking river valley trail to a challenging route that strikes out across the corrugated ridges of the Allegheny Mountains. Leaving the level-walking experience of the C & O Canal, the Potomac Heritage hiker heads westward across the Maryland panhandle and southwestern Pennsylvania to the town of Confluence, which gets its name from the joining of the Casselman and Youghiogheny Rivers. Following rural paved roads, backcountry dirt roads, and abandoned wagon tracks, the trail crosses four ridges of the Alleghenies as it winds for 65 miles "against the grain" of the mountainous terrain. It leads past the rounded crest of Mount Davis, at 3,213 feet the highest point in Pennsylvania, where an observation tower provides an excellent view of the surrounding terrain. It goes through forests inhabited by black bears, although it will be the rare hiker who spots one since bears usually keep their distance from people.

The trail here is sparsely blazed; the Potomac Heritage Trail symbol and a white arrow indicate locations where the trail takes a turn. One-third of this section is on public lands such as state game lands and a state forest; the remainder is on public roads and private landholdings including several farms owned by Amish farmers. This segment was reconnoitered, negotiated, and laid out during a three-year effort by a devoted trail volunteer, Thurston Griggs, a retired professor of the University of Maryland. Griggs and a team of hiking colleagues, many of whom had experience maintaining the Appalachian Trail, worked diligently to piece together this cross-mountain segment, which opened as a through trail in 1991.

When this trail segment meets the westward-flowing Youghiogheny River, it makes use of 11 miles of a paved hiker-biker trail. Here a rails-to-trails project converted an abandoned railroad track to the paved trail that leads hikers and bikers into Ohiopyle State Park.

Situated in an area of natural beauty, this park was named from the Indian term "ohio pehhle" which means "white frothy water"—a reference to the large falls on the Youghiogheny. The river drops from an elevation of 1,280 to 980 feet within the park, making it a popular location for some of the best whitewater rafting in the East. Another area within the park has been declared a National Natural Landmark for its variety of wildflowers and plants.

For those interested in innovative architecture a three-mile side trip to Bear Run takes you to an architectural gem, a vacation home designed by the well-known architect Frank Lloyd Wright. The house, called Fallingwater, is constructed of reinforced concrete and native stone and is dramatically cantilevered over a cascading waterfall. The house blends so well with the mountainous terrain that it seems to grow out of the site.

Laurel Highlands Hiking Trail

The final leg of the Potomac Heritage National Scenic Trail is a 70-mile-long footpath that takes the hiker and backpacker along a scenic ridge of the Alleghenies northeastward from Ohiopyle to the upper end of the 1,000-foot-deep Conemaugh River Gorge near Johnstown. This is the same steep-sided gorge that in May 1889 was the scene of the death of more than two thousand persons who were caught in the infamous Johnstown Flood caused when a dam on the Conemaugh gave way during a heavy storm.

The well-developed Laurel Highlands Hiking Trail is protected for almost its entire mountaintop route by a combination of state parklands, state forest, and state gamelands—even a privately owned ski area. It is marked every hundred feet with yellow blazes and offers mileage markers at each mile. Trailheads where major highways cross provide access to the trail.

The Laurel Highlands segment provides a suitable ending for the hiker on the Potomac Heritage Trail. Eight campgrounds are spaced along the well-maintained pathway. Each has tent sites, shelters, water, fireplaces, and latrines. Half of the trail is open in winter to cross-country skiers.

But it is in June and July that this portion of the Potomac Heritage National Scenic Trail comes into its glory. In June the slopes are colored by the pink blossoms of the mountain laurel, Pennsylvania's state flower. In July the rhododendrons take over as the mountainsides provide thickets of white and rose. In the fall you walk beneath a canopy of reds, oranges, yellows, and browns as the deciduous trees produce a symphony of hues that brings to a colorful conclusion a trail that began far to the east in the lowlands and the simple greens of the Potomac valley.

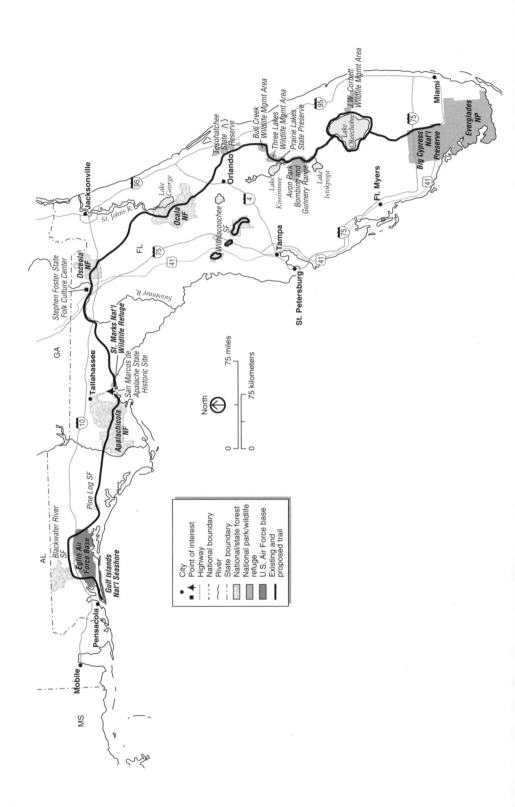

Chapter 3

FLORIDA NATIONAL SCENIC TRAIL

MARJORIE KINNAN RAWLINGS, A POPULAR NOVELIST OF THE 1930S, found the sand pine region of central Florida so enchanting that she lived an isolated life in its backwoods for 25 years, using the locale as the background for her best-selling book, *The Yearling.*

In it she wrote of a 12-year-old boy who lives with his mother and father and a pet deer deep in this Florida scrub country. The story follows the lad as he roams the forest, observes and hunts the wildlife, and absorbs the lessons of nature and of life. Her novel won a Pulitzer Prize in 1938 and was adapted into a motion picture. The book—and Rawlings's other novels, short stories, and poems—explored this sweep of savanna country and its natives who are, as one critic said, "almost part of the soil, the product of their environment."

This area of central Florida that Marjorie Kinnan Rawlings knew so well is part of the scenery hikers experience as they hike the Florida National Scenic Trail. Of the eight national scenic trails that have thus far been designated by Congress, the Florida National Scenic Trail is the only one that transects a subtropical and tropical region. The trail curves in a broken arc from the saw grass marshes and wooded hammocks of the Big Cypress Preserve near the tip of the Florida peninsula to the barrier island beaches of Gulf Islands National Seashore on the Gulf of Mexico at the western edge of the state. In its

1,300-mile length it runs northward through the interior of the state, then westward through Florida's northern panhandle to its end near Pensacola. Along this route the hiker experiences a variety of habitats: sand pine forests and oak hammocks; rivers born of Florida's clear-water springs; swamps darkened to the color of tea by the roots of the bordering cypress trees; prairies and savannas; even huge manmade dikes built to capture water that would otherwise seep across the flat land.

In this flat topography a few feet of elevation makes a big difference. In the savannas, a slight difference in elevation enables a distinct plant community to develop. At the higher and drier end of the spectrum is a forest dominated by longleaf and sand pines, with a dense undergrowth of saw palmettos. As the elevation drops a bit (the gradient is seldom more than 6 feet over a distance of 600 feet), the pines disappear and the wet savanna begins, dominated by grasses and sedges that grow in the saturated or mucky soil. Deeper into the savanna, more surface water accumulates; at a depth of perhaps 8 to 12 inches, the savanna blends into a swampy zone of two- to three-foot-tall, water-tolerant shrubs. Where the standing water reaches one to three feet in depth, stands of pond cypresses grow, forming an island or "dome." The shrubby black gum tree that is found nowhere else in the United States sometimes grows here along with the cypresses.

Most of the Florida National Scenic Trail is a primitive footpath that meanders through the state's interior, a strip of near-wilderness that provides a contrast to the populated urban areas along both east and west coasts. Trail users enjoy the peace and solitude of this "other Florida," a land whose tropical topography includes wetlands, sinkholes, lakes, ravines, salt marshes, swamps, prairies, sandhills, and ocean beaches.

It was an avid hiker who visualized this long-distance trail. James A. Kern, a Miami wildlife photographer and real estate broker, envisioned the Florida Trail in 1964, inspired by a hike he had just completed along the Appalachian Trail.

To dramatize the idea of a long-distance trail for Florida he armed himself with a machete, a map, and a compass and hiked and slashed his way northward for twelve days from the Tamiami Trail, a major east-west road across southern Florida, to Lake Okeechobee, a distance of 160 miles. An article in a Miami newspaper about the machete-wielding hiker included an address to which people interested in forming a trail association could write. Soon a small army of trail enthusiasts responded to his call. Encouraged, Kern turned to a small airplane and flew from one end of the state to the other, reconnoitering for a suitable route for a cross-state hiking trail.

Thus was founded the Florida Trail Association, a group of outdoorsmen and women dedicated to building a trail that they expect will one day run without a break from one end of Florida to the other. Today the association has five thousand members and can lay claim to constructing many miles of trail along the planned corridor. The hardworking club members have also developed a number of side and loop trails that branch off from the main route. For its first project back in 1965, the trail association constructed and blazed a 60-mile segment through Ocala National Forest.

In 1983, at the urging of trail association members, Congress added the Florida Trail to the National Trails System, officially designating it the Florida National Scenic Trail. The U.S. Forest Service, chosen to administer the footpath, in 1986 produced a comprehensive plan that delineated the route the trail should follow and provided guidelines for its planning, development, management, and protection.

Hiking this scenic trail from one end of Florida to the other on a continuous pathway, however, is still a goal to be achieved. To date you can hike certified trail segments for 450 miles of the route. The longest uninterrupted segment stretches some three hundred miles from just north of Orlando to the Apalachicola River in the northern panhandle. The major missing links are between Big Cypress National Preserve and Lake Okeechobee, the corridor east of Orlando, and the gap between the Apalachicola River and Gulf Islands National Seashore.

Much of the completed trail runs across public lands—federal and state parks and forests. Private industrial forest managers such as paper companies have usually cooperated to let hikers cross their land. But ranchers in the state's cattle country in the central part of the state have been less helpful, although they are now beginning to allow the trail to cross their lands. The U.S. Department of Defense and regional water management districts, which historically have not considered public recreation to be a priority, are also beginning to permit the trail on their lands.

One 12-mile segment, for example, skirts the edge of the U.S. Air Force's Avon Park Range, following the Kissimmee River just north of Lake Okeechobee. A well-blazed trail leads through hammocks of live oaks that drip with Spanish moss. Hikers are likely to see wild pigs, armadillos, wild turkeys, and white-tailed deer—as well as herds of cattle that graze on leased plots within the bombing range. Wide burrows in the sandy soil alert the hiker that the gopher tortoise has been at work. This short section of the trail, Air Force officials say, is getting an increasing number of users each year, most of them day hikers.

Avon Park Range on the Florida Trail.

The most popular time to hike the Florida Trail is late fall through early spring when air temperatures are cool, humidity is low, insects scarce, the trail pathway relatively dry, and migrating waterfowl and wildlife abundant.

Big Cypress National Preserve

At its southern end, the Florida Trail winds for 40 miles through Big Cypress National Preserve, a 2,400-square-mile protected area that lies next to Everglades National Park near the tip of the Florida peninsula. This is subtropical Florida and the surroundings reflect it. The trail leads through wet prairies of saw grass and sedge, dry prairies, sandy islands of slash pine, and groves of dwarf pond cypress that border a marshy area or slough. An occasional hammock or tree island of mixed hardwoods protrudes into the flat landscape. Air plants, both bromeliads and orchids, perch on tree branches like strange bird nests. Parts of the trail in this swampy region may be flooded in summer and fall, so hikers need wading boots or to be prepared to get their feet wet.

The southern terminus of the Florida Trail is on Route 94 or Loop Road, three miles west of the Everglades/Big Cypress Interpretive Center; another handy starting point is the Oasis Ranger Station on Route 41, also called Tamiami Trail, an hour's drive west of Miami.

Big Cypress was named for its huge expanse, not for the size of its trees. But a few of the big trees do remain. Hikers may see a few of the giant cypresses in the preserve, trees that were overlooked by the lumbermen who cut over much of the area and sold their cypress wood to make such items as gutters, coffins, and pickle barrels. A few of the giant cypresses still growing are 600 to 700 years old. Their bulbous bases flare downward and outward to root systems loosely embedded in the rich, organic peat of the marsh.

In the dry season, from January to April, water evaporates or flows into estuaries to the south and the swamp's aquatic life becomes concentrated in the remaining pools and sloughs. To these pools come stately wading birds like herons and egrets and the unique wood stork, the only stork that lives in North America.

The alligator plays an important role during the dry season. When the "river of grass" runs dry the alligator wriggles its body and sweeps its tail from side to side, eventually building up the soil into a bowl shape as it excavates a "gator hole" that provides a watery spot to keep itself wet. Other birds and animals often flock to the gator hole, an oasis in the now-dry surroundings.

Far from the fearsome dragon that myths have made it out to be, the alligator is actually a shy creature. Its name is derived from *el legarto,* "the lizard," coined by early Spaniards. Usually dull gray in color, the alligator is most at home in the water, propelling itself by swishing its tail from side to side.

41

For the most part the alligator eats fish, snakes, turtles, and small animals that it catches in or near the water. It has flaps over its ears and a specially adapted respiratory system that enables it to eat while submerged without breathing water into its lungs.

When stalking its prey the alligator lies deceptively motionless in the water, eyes alert. When a fish swims by it opens its huge mouth, then snaps it shut with a force of up to 1,200 pounds per square inch. Surprisingly, the big amphibian eats only once or twice a week. The rest of its time is spent basking in the warm sun or lying in a mud cave.

Although alligators are common in this watery world, you can count yourself lucky if you see one. An even more elusive animal is the rare Florida panther that is known to roam the Big Cypress Preserve and Everglades National Park. The panther, one of thirteen subspecies of cougar, is a cousin of the familiar mountain lion of the West—and has the same sleek, tawny coat. Once both the western mountain lion and the panther of the East were plentiful but hunting disastrously reduced their numbers, and the breed was declared endangered in 1967. Hemmed in by highways, citrus groves, and populated areas, only thirty to fifty panthers are believed to remain in southern Florida.

The panther is shy and avoids contact with humans if possible. A solitary hunter, it does its stalking and hunting at night, then stays secluded in dense cover such as a cypress swamp or a hardwood hammock during the day. Its prime quarries are white-tailed deer and wild hogs. The best chance to see a panther, as is the case with many animals, is an hour or two before sunrise and an hour or two after sunset.

A Florida Panther Recovery Team led by the U.S. Fish and Wildlife Service has been working in southern Florida since 1976 to learn more about this endangered cat, to breed panthers in captivity, and then to release them into the wild to try to save the breed from extinction.

Lake Okeechobee

The view the hiker gets is quite different here where the trail runs atop the huge dikes that encircle the lake. Okeechobee is the largest lake in the southern United States, second only to the Great Salt Lake as the largest body of water located wholly within the country.

The dike around this big lake and a series of canals that carry water away from it were built in the 1950s in response to a perceived need to protect property from the damaging results of flooding during hurricanes and to divert the lake's water to nearby agricultural areas. The dikes are a source of controversy between those who farm the rich soil around the lake and environmentalists who fear that artificially diverting the water in the region through the dikes and canals will do irreparable harm to the Everglades to the south, depriving it of the flow of water it needs.

Before the engineers altered the lake by heaping up the high dikes, water from Lake Okeechobee spilled over and flowed like a "river of grass" some fifty miles wide and less than a foot deep into the Everglades that lie some seventy miles to the south. Now the canals have diverted much of this water flow toward the east and less water reaches the Glades. Without the water they need, many plants and animals of the Everglades are increasingly threatened.

Okeechobee is a Seminole Indian word that means "plenty big water." The lake is about forty miles long and thirty miles wide and is fed chiefly by the Kissimmee River which flows in from the north. Its average depth is only seven feet—wading birds can often be seen as far as a mile from the shore searching for prey in its shallow waters. Hikers have the choice of following a trail around the east side of the big lake or an alternate trail around the western edge. Both trails stay high and dry atop the dikes and both have long, straight stretches that seem to reach to the horizon. Both trails offer beautiful views of the lake and nearby lakeshore and farmlands of sugar cane and vegetable crops but offer few trees for protection against the hot sun. Wading birds are common, especially egrets and herons. Hikers should keep their eyes open also for kites, hawks, meadowlarks, red-winged blackbirds, and wild turkeys. Raccoons, gray foxes, opossums, armadillos, and alligators inhabit the area.

Ocala National Forest

The familiar orange blazes painted on trees along a 66-mile segment of the Florida National Scenic Trail lead across the Ocala National Forest in north-central Florida—the original section of the trail that was laid out by the Florida Trail Association. Here the sand pine, a scrubby tree that often grows only 15 to 20 feet high, and the taller longleaf pine, which grows from 75 to 120 feet, predominate in the forest. The sand pine, interestingly enough, grows only in Florida. Its cones are termed "serotinous," which means that they require occasional high heat in order to open and expel their seeds. For this tree an occasional forest fire is required to produce the intense heat that enables it to reproduce. When such a fire sweeps across a savanna it spares both the sand pine and the longleaf pine which can withstand the heat, but burns up the saw palmettos that grow beneath the taller trees. In the year after a burn, wild grass springs up beneath the pines. In later years the saw palmettos once again grow to regain their place in the understory.

Within the Ocala forest dwarf live oaks also lift their twisted branches. Cabbage palmettos, wild azaleas, holly, gallberry, and blueberry add their presence to the understory. The oaks serve as host to a bird you may observe in the neighborhood—the scrub jay. This jay wears the same colors but not the familiar crest of the more common blue jay; the scrub jay has a white patch on its throat. Hikers recognize it by its raucous, low-pitched call or by its short flights that end with a sweeping glide. The scrub jay is found in the East only in central Florida, although it is common in much of the Southwest and West.

Within the forest boundaries the trail passes some fifty natural springs, ponds, and cypress and gum swamps. Springs are common in Florida, often erupting from beneath the layer of limestone that lies just beneath the sandy surface. Such a spring may spew out millions of gallons of crystal-clear water a day, enough to generate a swiftly running stream. Water plants that grow close to the surface add splashes of color to the depths of a spring. Where the flow is too fast for plants to get a grip, the bare bottom shows white. In some springs white chips of limestone and flakes of marl swirl up from the depths like snow.

As hikers pass Alexander Springs they may wish to take a break and go for a swim or rent a canoe to enjoy the verdant scenery. The spring itself is so clear and deep that scuba divers come here for their certification test. The water in the spring remains a constant 72°F year-round. Could a transparent and productive spring like this, one wonders, have been the inspiration for the explorer Ponce de León's "Fountain of Youth"?

Out on the river canoes drift through a tropical wilderness where tall cabbage palms line both sides of the narrowing creek, and live oaks support draperies of Spanish moss. Fishermen cast their lines for the bass and bream that dart and disappear among the water hyacinths. The water hyacinth, in turn, provides a home for the tiny apple snail, and the apple snail is the sole food for the limpkin, an awkward-looking brownish bird that tiptoes on spindly legs along the water's edge. Snapping turtles balance atop a log as they doze in the warm sun. Shrubs such as wax myrtle, pyracantha, titi, yaupon holly, atamasco, azalea, pitcher plant, and phlox brighten the banks.

Overhead tree limbs bristle with stiff-leaved plants—epiphytes or air plants. Their "roots" anchor these plants to the tree and absorb nourishing minerals from the rainwater as it runs down their branches or trunk. The common Spanish moss is an air plant. So are orchids. Resurrection ferns cling to branches, curled tight and brown; a brief shower brings them to life once again, open and green. Another common air plant, the bromeliad, has spike-like leaves and is related to the pineapple. Bromeliads have an urn-shaped flower in which rainwater collects. In the treetops each bromeliad acts as a small oasis, a water source for tiny tree frogs and insects in a time of drought.

Osceola National Forest

At Osceola National Forest the trail alternates between the slash and longleaf pine uplands and swampy areas where bald cypress and tupelo (black gum) thrive.

It was the rapidly growing slash pine that once provided the main source of revenue for many Florida backwoodsmen, or "Crackers" as they were known. They knew that if you cut the bark of the slash pine, large amounts of pitch or gum would ooze out as the tree tried to heal itself. The backwoodsmen slashed the trunk of each tree in a V shape, then attached a cup to catch the raw gum. They made the rounds of their slashed trees on a regular schedule, emptying each cup, then took the gum to a still where it was distilled into commercial turpentine.

The bald cypress, a truly remarkable tree, is actually not a true cypress at all but a relative of the redwood and sequoia. Like its California cousins, the bald cypress often lives to a venerable age. Some specimens, according to foresters, have been known to live for 1,500 years.

A conifer, or cone-bearing tree, the bald cypress has flat, needle-like, yellow-green leaves that turn orange-brown in the fall. It is unique among southern conifers because it sheds its leaves in the winter. It grows to a height of 120 feet or more, drawing nutrients from the spongy peatlike soil beneath the water. Its buttressed trunk and its long, thick roots anchor it firmly despite its watery, unstable footing.

Its most obvious characteristic, of course, is its "knees." These extensions of the tree's roots protrude upward several feet above the water level and give added support to the rest of the deep root mass beneath.

The Osceola National Forest also provides a home for a bird that is on the Endangered Species List—the red-cockaded woodpecker. The red-cockaded, once common throughout the pinelands of the South, declined in numbers as lumbermen cut down the mature pines where it builds its nest. By 1970 its numbers had declined so greatly that the U.S. Fish and Wildlife Service added its name to the endangered list.

The trail user's best opportunity to spot one of these birds in the forest is from March to July, when they are actively enlarging their treehole nests in mature pines and flying about to bring insects, insect eggs, and larvae to their young. To identify the bird, however, don't look for the red cockade on its head, despite its name. Juvenile birds do sport a small red marking on their heads, but they soon lose it as they grow to be adults. Instead, identify the bird by its zebra-striped back, black-capped head, and large white cheek patches.

Its home may be in a "candle tree," so named because of the whitish resin that drips down the trunk from tiny holes the woodpecker has drilled around the main cavity it has chipped away for its nest. The sticky resin coating the area around the cavity prevents a predator such as a snake from reaching the nest.

The red-cockaded woodpecker nests between April and July. The female usually lays two to four eggs in the roosting cavity which has been hollowed out by the breeding male. Other members of the female's clan then take turns incubating the eggs during the day; the breeding male returns at night to take his turn. The eggs hatch in 10 to 12 days. Nestlings are very vocal, especially during feeding time. Hikers can often hear the bird babies from the ground as they squawk inside the candle tree.

Suwannee River

In this section the trail runs alongside the Suwannee River, a gently flowing stream that is fringed with live oaks, cypress, pines, and palmettos. The trail here is walkable even though the section has not yet been certified by the Forest Service as meeting all standards. The river the trail follows is as scenic as the songwriter Stephen Foster said it was. It rises in the Okefenokee Swamp of southern Georgia and flows through the Florida panhandle to empty into the Gulf of Mexico. Along the way it is fed by some fifty-five springs. At times it passes through stands of head-high bamboo. The bordering cypress trees stain the water the color of tea. Striking white sand beaches occur frequently. Limestone bluffs rise from the water's edge along most of its route. A close look will show small fossil shells embedded in the limestone, evidence that millions of years ago much of present-day Florida was covered by the ocean.

Visitors will learn about the famous songwriter when they drop in at the Stephen Foster State Folk Culture Center along the trail. At an attractive visitor center are memorabilia of this ill-starred artist who, surprisingly, was born in the North. Displays include dioramas that depict scenes from the songs Foster wrote, some of his original scores, antique musical instruments, the piano he played at his home near Pittsburgh, as well as the desk where he wrote his best-known composition, "Old Folks at Home." Other well-loved songs from his pen were "Oh Susannah," "Camptown Races," "Jeanie with the Light Brown Hair," and "My Old Kentucky Home." Sadly, Foster died in New York City at age 37 with just 38 cents in his pocket, probably never having seen the river he made famous. A carillon at the center chimes out Foster's music every half hour. The annual Florida Folk Festival of musicians and craftspeople gather here in Stephen Foster's honor each May.

St. Marks National Wildlife Refuge

A sweep of salt marshes in Florida's panhandle region forms the coastal fringe of the St. Marks National Wildlife Refuge. St. Marks offers the trail user a greater variety of forest types and wildlife zones than any other north Florida section of the trail. Emerging from the forest of longleaf pine, the trail winds through a hardwood forest, cypress and gum swamp, beech-magnolia grove, cabbage palm and live oak hammock, and expanses of salt marsh along its coastal fringe. For part of the way the trail follows a series of dikes built to impound fresh water for the thousands of waterfowl that winter here—redhead ducks, widgeons, pintails, blue-winged teal, mallards, and gadwalls.

These habitats provide food, cover, and protection for a variety of wildlife. Together the salt marshes, tidal flats, and freshwater impoundments attract thousands of waterfowl and other birds. Salt marshes are valuable nurseries for fish, shrimp, and shellfish. Hardwood swamps support nesting wood ducks and night herons and provide a home for black bears, otters, and raccoons. Pine woods offer food and cover to wild turkey, white-tailed deer, fox squirrels, and pine warblers. The open marshes and swamps support a large population of alligators. On a warm day they can be seen sunning themselves at the edge of an impoundment.

Of the more than three hundred species of birds that have been recorded on the refuge, ninety-eight species nest here. Some nineteen species of ducks and two species of geese are seen from mid-November through January. Protected birds such as the southern bald eagle, osprey, and red-cockaded woodpecker find sanctuary in and nest on the refuge. Bald eagles are seen in the winter, fashioning their large nests of sticks in the flat-topped cypress trees and mature pines that favor the hammocks. Herons and egrets are in evidence all year wherever there is water. In June and sometimes continuing well into autumn, the ponds are covered with white-blooming water lilies, hundreds of acres of them. To get the best view of all this activity go to the refuge visitor center with its observation deck.

In the nearby town of Perry the Forest Capital State Museum depicts the development of the forest industry. Exhibits illustrate modern forestry techniques, how pine trees were tapped for turpentine, the wildlife of the area, and the cutting of forests, cypress swamps, and hardwood hammocks. A Cracker homesteader interprets the lifestyle of the backwoods settlers. A Florida Forest Festival celebrating the lumber industry is held on the fourth Saturday of October with events culminating in what boosters allege is "the world's biggest fish fry."

Apalachicola National Forest

As the Florida Trail unwinds through the pine forest of Apalachicola National Forest it skirts around several sinks, geologic features that are the surface evidence of the limestone bedrock that undergirds most of the Florida peninsula. Some sinks drop as much as 75 feet straight down, their sheer walls framing a deep pool of water below.

Sinks are well named. The surface area simply sinks, leaving a yawning hole. The process begins when rain falls, absorbing carbon dioxide from the atmosphere to form a weak acid that attacks the limestone. Over thousands of years this acid seepage eats away at the surface and belowground, excavating voids, channels, and caverns that sooner or later cause the ground at the surface to give way. It is this underground network of channels and natural reservoirs that produce not only the numerous sinks but other manifestations typical of Florida such as free-flowing springs and rivers that appear and disappear.

Day hikers using the Florida Trail.

Gulf Islands National Seashore

The Florida Trail changes character as it reaches its western end on the sandy beaches of Gulf Islands National Seashore near Pensacola. Here the hiker walks along barrier islands that lie between the mainland and the Gulf of Mexico. Leaving the upland longleaf pine and scrub oak forests, the trail stretches over white sand beaches and through the slash pine and palmetto thickets that grow behind the dunes.

Barrier islands are forever undergoing change. Violent storms cause powerful waves to wash over the island and rearrange large amounts of sand. Winds constantly shift and rebuild the dunes. But barrier islands can "roll with the punch" when a storms hits, effectively reducing the destructive force the blow will have on the mainland. The estuary that forms behind such a barrier island becomes a rich nursery for fishes, crustaceans, and shellfish.

As the hiker follows the trail across the beaches he or she begins to see some grasses and plants growing atop the dunes that are different from those he saw inland. Sea oats, in particular, with its elaborate root system, is vital to the protection and stability of a Gulf barrier island.

A wild relative of the cultivated oat grain, sea oats grow on stalks six feet or more in height and form a fringe along the top of a dune. Each stalk bears a brownish seed head. Like beach grass, sea oats spread by pushing out rhizomes under the sand. Its tall height is not a handicap; its flexible stem bends but does not break when buffeted by the high winds that sweep in from the gulf.

Visitors may see what looks like a low-lying bush growing on a dune. Look again; it may be simply the top of a full-sized slash pine or southern magnolia tree that has been buried under the drafting sand.

Hikers who reach the end of the trail at Gulf Islands should not miss the short side trail that leads to the Naval Live Oaks grove. Here are huge specimens of live oaks, big twisted trees that are what remains of a tree farm originally planted at the order of President John Quincy Adams to propagate trees that would assure the United States a supply of wood for the construction of the Navy's sailing ships.

The live oak is a tree with a dual personality. On the barrier islands where it grows in the maritime forest behind the dunes, the live oak is hunched over and bent, shaped and misshaped by the constantly blowing wind into a shrub only a few feet high. It endures the salt spray that kills many another hardwood. But inland, away from the ocean winds and rooted in soil that is richer than the thin soil of the barrier island, the live oak grows into a majestic tree up to 50 feet high and 1,200 feet in branch spread.

At the grove hikers walk beneath live oaks with trunks two feet in diameter, with ponderous branches festooned with Spanish moss, weighed down until they almost touch the ground. Unlike most oak trees, the live oak is an evergreen. Its two- to five-inch leaves are extra hardy and have a glossy sheen that feels leathery to the touch. A waxy cellulose covering protects it against salt spray, sunscald, and an occasional freeze.

Some of these trees grow to be 200 to 300 years old. They are the heaviest of the oaks and produce one of the densest woods in the country. It was this tough, durable wood that made live oaks so important in early shipbuilding. In the era of the great sailing ships, the U.S. Navy used the curved limbs as ribs and knees, hard-to-find construction shapes. The heavy branches and massive trucks provided posts, beams, and many board feet of lumber. The warship *USS Constitution* received its nickname "Old Ironsides" because of its sturdy live oak construction.

This grove of huge live oaks spells the end of the Florida National Scenic Trail, a footpath that offers the hiker the chance to discover the natural beauty of the wild and rural areas of the state. As the outdoorsman walks this trail through the tropics, he realizes that he has crossed the state from one end to the other on what some have called "the flattest footpath in the nation."

Florida Trail Association

The association founded by James Kern is still active, endeavoring to fill in the gaps in the Florida Trail and to provide a variety of outdoor activities for its five thousand volunteer members.

Each of its twelve chapters around the state is responsible for the development and maintenance of a portion of the trail near the chapter. Work hikes take their place in the year-round schedule of some five hundred activities that the chapters plan, activities that range from learning experiences and a leisurely day outing to an extended backpacking or canoeing trip.

Its bimonthly publication, *Footprints,* carries information about hiking, camping, trails, canoeing, and natural history. The association each year sponsors conferences that teach trail skills, nature appreciation, and wilderness ethics. Its trail guidebook provides a detailed description of the Florida Trail.

For more information write the Florida Trail Association, P.O. Box 13708, Gainesville, FL 32604.

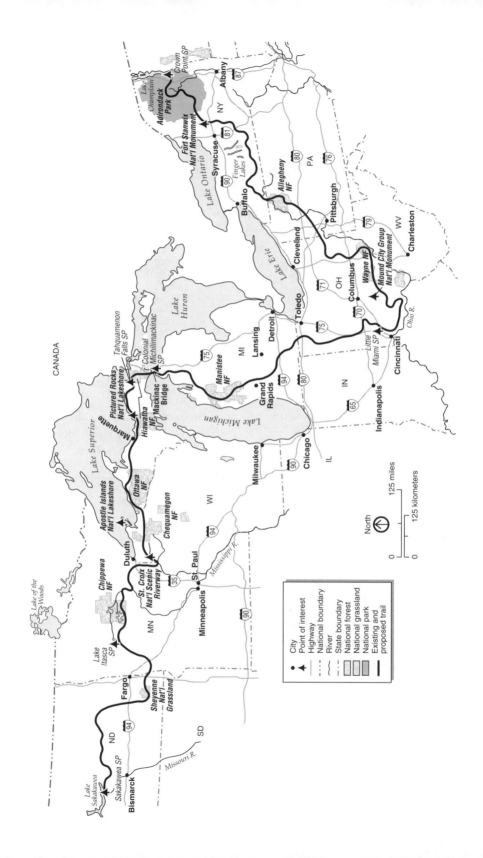

Chapter 4

NORTH COUNTRY NATIONAL SCENIC TRAIL

WHEN IT IS COMPLETED, THE NORTH COUNTRY NATIONAL SCENIC Trail will be the longest of the national scenic and historic trails in the nation—3,200 miles in length.

Unlike the Appalachian, Continental Divide, and Pacific Crest national scenic trails, the North Country does not follow the crest of a mountain range, but instead "cuts across the grain" as it winds through seven northern states. The pathway was conceived by the U.S. Forest Service as a way to link several northern national forests and to give hikers an opportunity to see the Great Lakes landscape. Along the way the trail provides its users with a diversity of terrain as well as scenic, historic, cultural, and recreational features. The North Country Trail has another distinction as well: It lies in the same temperate zone for much of its length, whereas the north-south trails stretch through several different life zones.

The route threads its way past mountain peaks and lakes of the Adirondacks, through the dairy farm country of upstate New York, through the hardwood forests of Pennsylvania, to traverse the flatter, agricultural lands of Ohio and southern Michigan and the evergreen forests of Upper Michigan and Wisconsin. Then it winds along the shores of the Great Lakes and through the lake and forest country of Minnesota until it reaches its end on the prairie of North Dakota, where the terrain is so flat and the trees so scarce that trail builders have to put up posts to mark the route.

But the vision of a continuous footpath that will allow the hiker to walk from one end to the other on this trail through the northern tier of states remains a future dream. Most of the completed segments today lie on national or state forest land where land managers have cooperated to make the trail a reality. About one thousand one hundred miles of the trail has been certified by the National Park Service as fully meeting its scenic trail standards while an additional one thousand miles is usable even though not fully certified.

Much of the remaining route crosses private lands where the goodwill and cooperation of the landowner are a prerequisite. Development of the trail across private landholdings depends largely on the efforts of interested volunteers such as members of the North Country Trail Association and other supporting groups. Their members negotiate rights-of-way and reach agreements with landowners to allow hikers or skiers to cross these private tracts.

The route of the North Country Trail takes it diagonally across New York State to the Pennsylvania border. At its eastern end it begins at New York's Crown Point State Park on the western shore of Lake Champlain and winds across Adirondack Park, the largest scenic park in the country. Although a route across the park has been identified, this initial segment of the national scenic trail has not been laid out.

There are problems at the trail's western end as well. The North Country Trail has difficulty establishing its presence in the North Dakota landscape of sweeping prairies and few trees. In this state, few public lands are available along the trail route. Of the projected 435 miles in North Dakota well over half the land is privately owned rangeland that is fenced, primarily for cattle grazing. Planners and volunteers face the task of obtaining passage for hikers and horseback riders across this fenced rangeland.

But despite these difficulties in North Dakota, the trail ends with an exclamation point. Its terminus at Sakakawea State Park in North Dakota is located on the shore of a huge lake that was formed by damming the Missouri River. Here the scenic trail intersects with the national historic trail that traces the route followed by Meriwether Lewis and William Clark on their epic exploration of the western territories in 1804–1806 (see page 161). Thus the longest national scenic trail in the country crosses the nation's longest national historic trail.

Finger Lakes Trail

After its undeveloped beginning in the Adirondacks, the North Country takes advantage of corridors of public land that remain from the early nineteenth century when a number of canals were built in upper New York state to transport raw materials, manufactured products, and agricultural produce to city markets and to river and ocean ports for shipment.

For example, the trail route runs along the elevated towpath of the Old Black River Canal that parallels the Mohawk River to Rome, New York. Walking the towpath trail, one can visualize the mules pulling the towboats along the waterway, even though the water in the canal has long since drained away, and trees have grown up within its channel. Many of the stone locks that once lowered the boats to the next water level are still standing, testifying to their sturdy construction a century and a half ago.

When the old canal and the trail reach Rome, both are buried beneath the macadam of city streets. The route leads right past the gate to Fort Stanwix, a reconstructed fort that held off a British offensive early in the Revolutionary War. History-minded hikers might want to take a break from the trail to view this National Park Service site. Costumed interpreters describe the defense of the fort, guide visitors through the log buildings of the compound, and relate what everyday life was like for an eighteenth-century soldier.

The trail continues along the canal right-of-way south of Rome, this time the main Erie Canal. The Old Erie Canal linked Albany on the Hudson River with Buffalo on the Great Lakes 363 miles away. It played a crucial role in the development of central and western New York as well as the entire Midwest as it opened up commerce with the world.

Erie Canal Village, a restored canal town, provides a glimpse of how people lived when the "Big Ditch" was in its heyday. A mule-drawn canal boat takes visitors for a short trip on the rewatered canal. Guides in period dress tell about a reconstructed shop, a barn, a train depot, dwellings, and a tavern that now serves soft drinks and ice cream. The trail follows the towpath for another 20 miles through Old Erie Canal State Park.

For the final three-fifths of its journey across New York, the North Country joins the Finger Lakes Trail, a trail built over the past 30 years by volunteers of the Finger Lakes Trail Conference, whose sixteen sponsoring organizations are scattered across the state. The North Country/Finger Lakes Trail runs 350 miles to its termination at the Pennsylvania border. The Finger Lakes Trail also extends eastward, reaching the Catskills along the Hudson River.

More than half of the Finger Lakes Trail lies on private land; the remainder runs through a national forest, state parks and forests, state wildlife management areas, and other public lands. Hikers and skiers will find a number of primitive campsites and shelters along this well-developed pathway.

The trail skirts south of seven of the slender Finger Lakes, providing the hiker some of the most dramatic natural beauty on the entire North Country Trail. In a span of 25 miles trail users walk through or near three state parks, each of which displays evidence of the great glaciers that ages ago bulldozed their way across this landscape. As the mile-thick glacier melted some ten thousand years ago, streams of water poured down the sides of valleys steepened by the passage of the glaciers. Over the years these cascades and waterfalls carved beautiful rugged gorges back into the hillsides.

At Buttermilk Falls State Park what is left from this glacial action is a broad cascade that tumbles down a long rocky slope, giving the appearance of water pouring down a giant stairway.

At Robert H. Treman State Park near the foot of Cayuga Lake, the North Country/Finger Lakes Trail runs the length of the park. It leads along the rim of a gorge through a red pine and hemlock forest, high above the lower gorge trail that most visitors follow as they stay close to the surging waters of Enfield Creek, which cuts through the chasm. The hiker may stop at several overlooks on the rim trail to gaze down at the rushing waters below or walk down the 200 stone steps to get a close-up view of the 115-foot-high Lucifer Falls, the highest waterfall in the gorge.

"Our Cayuga Trails Club, with its 160 members, maintains this 75-mile segment of the trail," said Robin Spry-Campbell, a retired sculpture teacher who hikes the trail regularly with her black Labrador Retriever. "As other trail clubs do, we have monthly work parties and hikes as well as our regular responsibilities of trail cleanup and maintenance, rerouting the trail when necessary, and negotiating with private property owners about trail use and location."

At Watkins Glen State Park, near the foot of Seneca Lake, the trail again runs high atop the rim instead of following the normal visitor route through the lower gorge. Keeping the trail along the rim allows for year-round use since ice and snow block the lower gorge trail in the winter. The rim trail leads through a thick forest of old hemlocks that are guaranteed to keep the hiker cool on even a hot summer day. "These old hemlocks survived when most other big trees in this area were being cut down," explained Tony Ingraham, a conservation educator with the New York State Office of Parks, Recreation and Historic Preservation, "because neither the lumberman nor the farmer wanted to venture into this difficult terrain."

Far below in the gorge, Glen Creek tumbles through the chasm, creating nineteen waterfalls or cascades. They range from straight drops over a cliff to twisted chutes where the rock face has been polished by the running water to the texture and color of mahogany.

Perhaps the most vivid evidence of the erosive action of the ancient river is a series of potholes, symmetrically rounded depressions in the rock floor of the chasm. Many of these depressions, some the size of a wash basin, others the size of a bathtub or larger, were scoured out by stones and gravel that were whirled at high speed by the surging water, a sort of giant augur biting into the surface. Others were fashioned by waterfalls plunging onto the rock surface, eating into the rock to hollow out a depression.

Allegheny National Forest

The North Country Trail leaves New York state at Allegany State Park, where the trail leads hikers across the border to Allegheny National Forest in Pennsylvania. Even though the two states use a different spelling for the word *Allegheny,* the deeply dissected Appalachian plateau characterizes both the state park and the national forest.

The trail winds for 87 miles through the national forest, one of the longest certified sections on the trail, through heavily wooded hills cut by an occasional stream valley. When a hiker approaches the Tionesta Scenic Area he is in for a botanical treat. Here, 2,000 acres in the heart of the forest escaped the woodman's ax and one can see what the primeval forest looked like. Huge hemlocks, some one hundred feet high, shadow the pathway. Beneath the giant hemlocks grow large, old-growth specimens of black and yellow birch, sugar and red maple, white ash, black cherry, basswood, and tulip poplar, forming a habitat rarely seen in the northeastern United States. Even the uncommon cucumber magnolia, whose fruits resemble small green cucumbers, grows in the Tionesta. Ferns and wildflowers such as pink lady's slipper, purple-fringed orchid, white doll's eyes, the delicate starflower, and mountain sorrel bloom here.

A big attraction for visitors to the national forest is the reservoir that backs up behind the Kinzua Dam on the Allegheny River. Boating and waterskiing are popular. Fishermen eagerly try for smallmouth bass, walleye, northern pike, muskellunge, channel catfish, crappie, and yellow perch. A sizable population of black bears roams the forest, underscoring the need for campers to keep their food high enough to be beyond a bear's reach.

After the well-blazed trail goes through the national forest, it continues across the northwest corner of Pennsylvania, making use of several state parks, two additional state forests, and one abandoned as well as one still-active railroad right-of-way.

Buckeye Trail

In Ohio, as in New York, the North Country Trail takes advantage of a partly completed, statewide trail that already exists—the Buckeye Trail, a 1,200-mile loop system that encircles the entire state. For some six hundred miles the North Country coincides with the Buckeye as the trail makes a U-shaped sweep across Ohio. It follows woodland trails, back roads, canal towpaths, and abandoned railroad rights-of-way as it connects a number of state and national parks, state and national forests, wildlife refuges, reclaimed mines, and other conservation areas. It passes prehistoric earthworks of early Indians, covered bridges, old canal locks, wayside inns, and old mills.

It was the volunteer efforts of the Buckeye Trail Association, beginning in 1959, that planned, mapped, and marked the segments of the Buckeye Trail that have now become part of the North Country Trail. Like the associations that lend their help to other trails, the Buckeye Trail Association acquires or negotiates access rights to land along the trail, constructs and maintains the trail, and prepares maps and publications to guide trail users. Various sections of the route are used by different interest groups—equestrians, cross-country skiers, backpackers, and snowshoers. Campsites are available at some points on the trail but they are not located at frequent enough intervals to allow backpackers to camp beside the trail every night.

In southeastern Ohio the North Country diverges briefly from the Buckeye to swing through the Wayne National Forest, which borders the Ohio River. For 35 miles it leads the hiker along a quiet pathway through the forest. It clings to ravines called "runs" where spring rains fill the creeks, cutting deep gullies in the surrounding terrain. At several places it passes caves hollowed out of the underlying sandstone.

"Most of the original forest of oak and hickory was cut by early settlers and used to build houses or to clear the land for farming," explained Ranger Dave Greenwood, noting that Ohio (then known as the "Northwest Territory") began to be farmed as early as 1788. Today, he said, you have a second-growth forest that the Forest Service harvests periodically, contracting with lumber companies to cut the trees either selectively or to clear-cut an area.

"When we clear-cut we leave a buffer of three hundred feet on either side of the trail to keep a natural margin for the hikers," he said. "Even in a clear-cut area we find we do not have to reseed because nature will do it herself." He explained that some seeds remain in the soil, seeds that were dropped earlier by the trees that were cut and removed. Sunlight and rain soon cause the seeds to germinate and grow. The stumps also sprout new shoots that grow into trees. Finally, other seeds blow in from nearby trees, taking root and growing in the newly opened area in the forest.

"There is a natural order of succession as these areas regrow," he continued. First to take root are usually sassafras, locust, sugar maple, and birch. Oak and hickory, slower to grow, eventually overtake the faster-growing species, crowd them out, and produce a new oak-hickory forest. "This natural process will reseed an area and in five or ten years you'll have good tree cover again."

Hikers may be surprised to see the numerous "stripper" oil wells that dot Wayne National Forest. Typically, in a small clearing there will be a rocker arm, collecting pipes for oil and natural gas, and a tank that holds the oil pumped out of the ground. Much of the land in southeastern Ohio is underlain with pockets of oil that have long played an important part in the local economy. This part of Ohio was one of the earliest oil and gas fields in the nation—and continues to produce oil and natural gas today, as does the Allegheny National Forest in Pennsylvania. As the trail passes through the forest it follows a checkerboard pattern of land-ownership. In many cases the Forest Service acquires the surface rights to the land while the owner retains the subsurface rights that permit him to continue to extract the oil and natural gas.

Parts of the trail run along the unpaved roads the townships and county have built in the forest to provide the owners access to their wells.

There is a good chance of spotting wildlife when hiking through Wayne National Forest. White-tailed deer, wild turkey, grouse, woodcock, skunk, opossum, and raccoon are common. River otters have been reintroduced along the Little Muskingum River, a tributary of the Ohio, and seem to be thriving. Coyotes have been seen in the forest, some of the population that is spreading into the midwest and northeastern states.

The rolling hills of eastern Ohio give way to flatter terrain in the western part. Close to the state's western boundary, the trail passes through two of the most extensive urban areas it will meet between New York and North Dakota when it skirts Cincinnati and Dayton. At Little Miami State Park the trail makes use of an abandoned railroad right-of-way that parallels the Little Miami River from the outskirts of Cincinnati to Dayton. The river itself has been designated as both a state and a national scenic river.

Many people use this 50-mile segment. For 22 miles in the suburbs of Cincinnati it is an 8-foot paved pathway with a 12-foot mowed grass fringe along one side that is used by horseback riders. Not only equestrians but hikers, joggers, cyclists, people in wheelchairs, and roller bladers use this popular pathway. Fitness-conscious suburbanites use it regularly. Others use it for an afternoon stroll. Still others rent a canoe at a canoe livery and paddle along the nearby scenic river. In a recent year, 200,000 people used the Little Miami segment, two-thirds of them cyclists.

The North Country/Little Miami is the beneficiary of an active citizen group, Little Miami, Inc., which began action in 1967 to conserve the scenic river valley in its natural state. Its members petitioned to designate the river as a scenic river, thus preserving the valley as a greenway. When a railroad line that had hauled freight ceased operation, the state purchased the abandoned right-of-way and turned it into the recreational asset that exists today.

The trail meanders along with the river through four counties and twelve townships, encountering rolling farm country, towering cliffs, steep gorges, and forests. Outcroppings of dolomite and shale are exposed by the steep cliffs. Mammoth sycamores hang over the river's edge and great blue herons swoop across the water. Eastern hemlock and Canada yew are among the cool-weather plant species that grow in the sheltered climate of the gorge. Virginia bluebells, bellworts, wild ginger, and wild columbine are among 340 species of wildflowers that thrive here.

Heading north the trail once again makes use of an abandoned canal, the Miami and Erie Canal, which once linked southwestern Ohio with Lake Erie. As hikers follow the old towpath, they pass stone locks and reservoirs that once fed the canal as well as a canal museum at Lockington.

Into the North Country

From Ohio the North Country Trail moves northward into Michigan where it fulfills the promise of its name. For some 870 miles as it crosses the state it winds through rolling countryside, passing through three national forests, one national lakeshore, three state forests, and five state parks. Near its midpoint it meets the Great Lakes when its route takes it across the famed Mackinac Bridge and across Michigan's Upper Peninsula to the shore of Lake Superior.

In southern Michigan the trail leads through rural farmland where most of the land is privately owned. Trail development is needed here and anyone hiking the route needs to consult a county map to make his or her way along local roads. After skirting Grand Rapids, Michigan's second-largest city, the trail begins a long, uninterrupted stretch.

A 122-mile segment leads through the Manistee National Forest where the sandy soil makes for easy trail walking. Primitive campsites are available for overnight backpackers. In the spring hikers find succulent morel mushrooms in these woods.

Continuing northward the route reaches the Straits of Mackinac (pronounced "mackinaw")—a good place for a history lesson. This wide strait that connects Lake Huron to Lake Michigan is the site of the well-known bridge, a bridge that carries not only cars but also the North Country Trail to Michigan's Upper Peninsula. Two centuries ago this same strait served as a vital east-west link for another form of transportation, the *voyageur* canoes that linked trading cities of the East like Montreal with the barely explored interior of the country. Fort Michilimackinac, which grew up here in the eighteenth century, was a major depot for the thriving fur trade.

Every winter fur traders set out from Michilimackinac to barter with the Indian trappers who caught the fur-bearing animals.

Returning with their furs to Michilimackinac in the summer, the traders were met by *voyageurs* from Montreal whose 40-foot birchbark canoes were laden with such supplies and merchandise as knives, blankets, clothing, rum, guns and shot, and ironware utensils. After exchanging their trade goods for pelts, the *voyageurs* returned to Montreal with furs destined for the European market. Beaver was the most sought-after item; hats made from beaver pelts were the fashion rage in Europe. Indian trappers also brought in fox, bear, ermine, otter, and muskrat.

Today you get a firsthand feeling for the fur-trading days when you tour Colonial Michilimackinac, an authentically reconstructed fortified fur-trading post located on the shore of the strait at the foot of the Mackinac Bridge, one of the longest suspension bridges in the world. Interpreters in period dress guide you past log barracks, blockhouses, a powder magazine, craftsmen's shops, a blacksmith shop, a guardhouse, a storehouse, and the priest's home. The compound comes to life as the priest leads children in games, a trapper relates his adventures in the woods, a housewife explains her recipes, a fiddler makes music, and soldiers fire muskets and a cannon.

In contrast to the eighteenth-century fort, a trip across the five-mile Mackinac Bridge is strictly twentieth century. No hikers or pedestrians are allowed on the bridge, except once a year on Labor Day morning, when fifty thousand or more people celebrate the "Mackinac Bridge Walk" by strolling across the long span. On other days, a patrol car periodically loads up hikers and their gear and transports them over the bridge for a nominal fee.

Another historical interest point awaits at the northern end of the bridge. Father Marquette National Memorial and Museum depicts the life and work of the Jesuit missionary who established a mission at St. Ignace on the strait. Two years later, with Louis Jolliet, Marquette became the first European to map the Mississippi River. At the contemporary museum visitors discover artifacts from Marquette's journeys and get an impressive view of the arching bridge. An Indian longhouse and a canoe are on display.

Michigan's Upper Peninsula

Once on the Upper Peninsula, hikers get a taste of the true North Country as they commence a 210-mile segment that offers the longest consistently wild environment anywhere on the trail. This segment traverses two separate units of the Hiawatha National

Forest, two state parks, a state forest, and Pictured Rocks National Lakeshore located at the edge of Lake Superior. In the Hiawatha Forest they walk through damp surroundings—almost half of the national forest consists of wetlands, a fact underscored by its 413 lakes. Northern white cedar, aspen, pine, and hardwoods shade the pathway. Traces of old logging camps and pioneer homesteads appear in grassy openings in the forest.

At Tahquamenon Falls State Park is a spectacular four-mile segment of the trail that takes the hiker close to the swiftly running Tahquamenon River between the Upper Falls and Lower Falls. Both waterfalls have an unusual caramel color that the water absorbs from the tannin from cedars that grow along the riverbank. The Upper Falls, 200 feet across, ranks as one of the largest waterfalls east of the Mississippi. The water plunges 50 feet to the pool below, whipping up mounds of white froth that is sticky to the touch. The froth comes not from pollution but from the natural chemical composition of the water.

At Muskallonge Lake State Park the trail reaches the shore of Lake Superior. As hikers walk the rocky shore, they should look beneath their feet for agates and other colorful stones. In addition the lakes in the park produce fine catches of northern pike, perch, smallmouth bass, walleye, muskellunge, rock bass, and bullheads. Wild blueberries and raspberries are abundant along the trail in July and August.

It would be difficult to find a section of the North Country Trail that provides the hiker with a greater variety of scenery than the 43 miles of trail that clings closely to the shoreline of Lake Superior as it passes through Pictured Rocks National Lakeshore.

The first surprise on this "Lakeshore Trail" segment is the sand dunes at the eastern end of the park. About ten thousand years ago, when the last glacier melted, it left behind a deposit of rocks and sand now known as Grand Sable Banks. Atop this ridge, which reaches 300 feet in height, the winds that blow across the lake have built sand dunes, picking up bits of sand from the lakeshore and blowing them inland. The trail runs around the backside of five square miles of these dunes. Interpretive signs teach lessons about what makes a sand dune move, the marram grass that slows the sand's movement, and the "ghost trees" of jackpine that reappear after the moving sand has buried and killed them.

From the dunes the hiker follows the trail to the bluff line high above the chilly waters of Lake Superior. The winding footpath leads through damp forest areas where beech and sugar maple grow, curving from time to time toward the shoreline as it offers spectacular views of the lake 200 feet below. Short side trails extend out to the edge of the escarpment, rewarding the trekker with dramatic views. The sheer multicolored cliffs, which vary in color from gold to yellow to terra-cotta to tan give the park its name. The color of the cliffs reflected by the water changes with the play of light and time of day. Wave action has added beauty, eroding the sculpted cliffs into odd formations, cutting holes and arches into their rocky flanks. Huge chunks of sandstone that have broken away and fallen from the cliffs can be seen in the clear, shallow water close to the shoreline.

Beech, hemlock, pine, spruce, and fir trees grow in the lush forest, while underfoot, ladyferns and white bunchberry carpet the forest floor. At one point the trail leads the hiker through a grove of white birch trees. Chipmunks scamper about the forest floor from tree to tree while noisy ring-billed gulls glide overhead.

Several streams that originate in the marshes and lakes of the interior become waterfalls as they pour over the sandstone cliffs. The trail passes twelve waterfalls in seven miles, including Munising Falls, 50 feet high. Here a short side trail and a set of steps earn the hiker a close-up look at the cascading water. The caramel color of the water is typical of the tannin-stained streams of the Upper Peninsula.

At length the trail moves down off the escarpment into a low-lying marsh at Sand Point. Interpretive signs along the half-mile section of the Salt Point Marsh Trail boardwalk describe the plants and animals that inhabit this wetland area. One of the animal "stars" here is the beaver; no less than three beaver lodges can be seen in a pond encircled by this boardwalk side trail.

"When we planned how the trail would run through the national park, we tried to lead the hiker along the bluffs as much as possible," said District Ranger Fred Young, a member of the team that laid out the North Country Trail route through Pictured Rocks in the mid-1970s. "We turned the trail inland only at places where the cliff erosion made it impossible to continue along the bluff line or where we could take the pathway through a contrasting environment."

History, too, marks the trail. Hikers pause to read wayside exhibits that relate the stories of a log slide, a steep bank where lumbermen once slid huge white pine logs into the lake, and the Au Sable

Light, which was built in 1874 as a navigational aid for ships on the Great Lakes and still thrusts its white tower into the sky.

As a result of its variety, the trail through Pictured Rocks is a favorite with backpackers. Some four thousand to five thousand people hike through on overnights each season, most of them spending two nights in the park. There are thirteen backcountry campgrounds for the overnighters, some with water available, some without, spaced from two to five miles apart along the lakeshore trail. Rangers require backpackers to get a permit at one of the visitor centers at either end of the trail segment so the staff will know who is using it.

Other waterfalls claim the hiker's attention as the trail continues westward toward Wisconsin, crossing a unit of Hiawatha National Forest and the Ottawa National Forest. A state park protects the scenic beauty of Laughing Whitefish Falls, a waterfall that displays the same caramel-colored water and foam-covered plunge pool. The trail passes through the Porcupine Mountains Wilderness State Park, one of the few remaining large wilderness areas in the Midwest, where uncut, virgin timber and secluded lakes, wild rivers, and streams attract vacationers.

Chequamegon National Forest

In the north woods of Wisconsin the hiker reaches the section of the North Country Trail to which it owes its name. Forest Service crews in the late 1960s developed a 60-mile stretch of trail in Chequamegon (pronounced sho-WAHM-e-gon) National Forest as the first segment of the new long-distance trail. The segment relied heavily on old logging roads, spur railroad beds once used to haul logs out of the forest, and already-established trails.

The Chequamegon, like many forests of the Great Lake states, was thoroughly logged over in the late 1800s and early 1900s. Whole hillsides of white pine, hemlock, and other tree species were cut and their trunks dragged to the nearest river to be floated downstream in log rafts or hauled to a rail spur where they were loaded onto flatbed cars.

At Drummond Woods along the trail, interpretive signs tell the story of these massive timbering operations, which provided much of the lumber that built cities like Chicago. A short loop trail takes the trail user to an old-growth stand of hemlock, cedar, and white pine where you have to twist your neck to see the tops of 200- to 400-year-old trees that escaped the woodsman's ax.

In spite of its extractive history of logging, iron mining, and farming, the region is now forested once again, sparsely inhabited, and essentially wild. The second growth of aspen, birch, black ash, and northern hardwoods provides a leafy cover for the trail. Hiking is more challenging in the eastern half of the forest, an area of rock outcroppings and scenic overlooks.

The trail in the western half winds over rolling uplands and through low-lying marshes, tracing a path through two wilderness areas, the Porcupine Lake Wilderness Area and the Rainbow Lake Wilderness Area. These areas, defined by the Wilderness Act of 1964, are "areas where the earth and its community of life are left untrammeled by people; where people are visitors who do not remain." Nearly half of the 4,442 acres of Porcupine Lake Wilderness is covered by sugar maple, red maple, and yellow birch. The hiker will find six large lakes and a number of small ponds that offer canoeing, fishing, wildlife viewing, and "no-trace camping." Farther west, the larger Rainbow Lake Wilderness beckons to the backcountry hiker with six miles of the North Country Trail.

Wildlife thrives in this unpopulated forest. White-tailed deer abound. Black bear roam the woods but keep to themselves in the backcountry. One ranger who had served at the forest for six years stated that during that entire time she had seen only one bear. Smaller mammals include porcupines, bobcats, minks, weasels, beavers, fishers, and the rare pine marten.

The fortunate hiker might see a paw print or hear the howl of the shy and elusive timber wolf. This endangered species is making a strong comeback in Wisconsin and Minnesota, rangers say. "Several new packs have formed in the past fifteen years, making five or six packs of six to eight wolves each in the forest," said Recreation Planner Susan Nelson. "They're migrating eastward from Minnesota, and have probably doubled their numbers in that time. We think this strong comeback is the result of a plentiful food supply of deer and beaver. But hikers need have little concern for wolves because they will normally avoid people at all cost."

Chippewa National Forest

The North Country takes advantage of the protection offered by one other national forest before it comes to its end. At Chippewa

National Forest, midway across Minnesota, the landscape, like Wisconsin's, bears the imprint of the ancient glaciers. The trail route runs for 68 miles along the forest's southern boundary. It unfurls through a watery landscape, climbing gentle hills that are actually moraines deposited many years ago by the glaciers and skirting hundreds of lakes that were formed when chunks of ice melted in the sandy debris left by the ice sheets. It is rare for a hiker not to have a lake or a river in sight; the forest counts more than one thousand two hundred lakes and nine hundred miles of rivers.

Lacy tamarack trees grow with their roots in the marshes that surround many of the lakes. Look for the familiar three-petalled trillium, wild iris, jack-in-the-pulpit, and the showy lady's slipper in these soggy areas. The pink-and-white showy lady's slipper, the state flower of Minnesota, is the largest, and to many, the most beautiful orchid in the country.

Trail users will undoubtedly see some of the birds, reptiles, and mammals that thrive in this damp environment. Ducks, herons, and loons are common. A turtle slithers from a log into the water. Beavers construct their ingenious lodges at the edge of a quiet lake, leaving skid marks on the bank where they have dragged saplings from the forest to the water.

Ospreys and bald eagles are attracted by the plentiful fish. The sharp-eyed hiker may spot the jumbled nest of an osprey atop a dead tree; look for the eagle's nest high in the crown of a tall white pine. Rangers recently counted 186 pairs of eagles in the Chippewa National Forest, more than at any place in the United States outside Alaska. In a recent year, no less than 171 young eagles survived their infancy and fledged from their nests.

You can distinguish among the osprey, the eagle, and the turkey vulture not only by their size and coloring but by their flight patterns. The osprey's wings extend out from its body, sweeping backward at their midpoint. The bald eagle soars with its long wings stretched straight out. The turkey vulture has upswept wings and flies with a wobble as though it were unstable in the air.

In this part of Minnesota the North Country Trail crosses several other long-distance pathways. Together they form a network of pathways that enables a hiker or cross-country skier to switch from one to another. The Heartland Trail, for example, a 50-mile-long trail built by the state on a converted railroad right-of-way, is used by equestrians, cyclists, hikers, snowmobilers, and people in wheelchairs and crosses the North Country near the town of

Walker. The Soo Line Trail, another rail-trail conversion that intersects the North Country, is a 120-mile-long trail that gets year-round use by hikers, all-terrain vehicles, and snowmobilers. The national forest itself offers several intersecting side or loop trails designed mainly for hunters.

To keep the North Country path in good shape for the hikers the Chippewa rangers rely on a platoon of volunteers. "We count on our Adopt-a-Trail volunteers to tell us of blowdowns, beaver activity or wet spots, anything that might make the trail difficult to hike," said Connie Carpenter, a forest technician. "They also check the condition of the blazes and make sure no wheeled vehicles or snowmobiles are using the footpath." Carpenter's volunteers include a local Lions Club, an elementary school class, an Izaak Walton League chapter, a local company, several families, and individual hikers.

"Each of the volunteers takes responsibility for a section of the trail," says Kit Arnquist, who looks after a mile-and-a-half portion. "On this section, the Forest Service seeds the trail with clover to make a soft treadway underfoot. Clover grows slowly and requires little mowing."

"I walk my section two or three times a year, then call headquarters to give my report on the trail's condition." Arnquist, a special education teacher, lives with her husband Tim in a home set deep in the woods, scarcely a stone's throw from her trail section.

Lake Itasca State Park

A notable interest point lies near the trail in Minnesota—the headwaters of the Mississippi River. At this point, the mighty Mississippi begins as a narrow stream on the journey that will take it more than two thousand five hundred miles to the Gulf of Mexico. Its modest beginnings are preserved within the boundaries of Lake Itasca State Park. The trail hiker may join a number of other visitors to step across a line of rocks that span the stream where it flows out of Lake Itasca, its origin.

The North Country Trail extends for 12 miles across this large state park, passing numerous lakes and intersecting several of the other trails in the park's extensive network of hiking, cross-country skiing, snowmobiling, and bicycling trails. A well-developed park, Lake Itasca has a lodge, restaurant, cabins, hostel, campgrounds, and an active activity program.

North Dakota Prairies

As the trail nears its western terminus the forests and lakes of Minnesota give way to the open, grassy prairies of North Dakota. The deciduous forests of the Midwest fade and the gently rolling prairie takes its place. The few trees whose silhouettes interrupt the otherwise endless horizon are the burr oaks that grow in "tree islands" or savannas that dot the open landscape and the cotton-woods, quaking aspen, elms, and basswood that grow in scattered patches. To moderate the sweep of the wind across the prairie, ranchers have planted lines of trees of differing heights across their land. For these "shelterbelts" they often plant Russian olive, chokecherry, green ash, and cottonwood.

For much of its 435 miles across North Dakota the trail follows the Sheyenne River valley, passing two historic forts preserved as state parks, a county scenic area, a reservoir and recreation site, a regional park, a canal, and an Indian reservation. Today, before the trail is fully developed, hikers have to follow local roads much of the way in this region where towns are few and far between.

There are, however, several completed segments. The longest is a 25-mile section across the Sheyenne National Grasslands in the southeastern corner of the state. The grassland consists of former agricultural land the federal government bought from drought-stricken ranchers in the 1930s and restored as productive grazing lands.

The appearance of the North Country Trail here is like nowhere else on its 3,200-mile length. The route is almost invisible as it blends into the prairie grass. To guide the horseback riders or hikers who cross the featureless terrain, rangers have driven fence posts marked with the blue-and-white triangular trail symbol at 500-foot intervals along the way. Out here the fence posts are called "reassurance markers," a welcome sight indeed in this wide-open prairie landscape. Windmills that draw water for the cattle that graze the land also serve as landmarks to guide the rider or hiker through the big bluestem and blue grama grass. The posts and windmill landmarks are designed to mark only a general route across the grassland—thus preventing hikers from laying bare a pathway that would invite wind erosion of the fragile prairie.

Rangers report that more equestrians than hikers use the grasslands portion of the North Country Trail. The grasslands are known for high heat and humidity during the summer, so hikers should carry along a full canteen of water (no drinkable water is available along the trail). Hikers also need a compass for it is entirely possible to lose your way in this endless sea of grass, especially on an overcast day when you do not have the sun as a navigational aid. Taking insect repellent is a good idea to protect against the mosquitoes, wood ticks, and horseflies.

But the rewards are there for those with the ambition to tackle this little-used portion of the trail. Hikers may spot the white blossom of the rare prairie-fringed orchid, a threatened plant that is found only in North Dakota, Minnesota, and Manitoba, Canada.

In the spring those who venture out shortly after daybreak might witness one of the most unusual of animal rituals—the mating dance of the prairie chicken. At a certain location near the trail, a level clearing called the "booming ground," eight to twenty male prairie chickens will gather. Each male takes over a small part of the booming ground, an area he has previously fought for and won.

Then he does his dance—dashing forward, head down, tail high, his wingtips dragging on the ground. He stamps a tattoo with his feet, pivoting, at the same time raising two tufts on his neck that look like horns. Now two vivid orange air sacs balloon outward from the sides of his neck—they are called tympani, or drums. A hollow *whoo-hoo-hoo* booms from the bird's inflated throat sacs, a sound that observers say they can hear a mile away on a clear, calm morning.

The females, seemingly unimpressed, watch from the sidelines. The courtship ritual continues every morning for days until the cocks finally mate with the hens. Then each hen heads for the tall grass cover where she hollows out a well-hidden nest and later lays a dozen brown-flecked olive eggs. The Sheyenne Grasslands is one of less than a dozen places in the country where one can still witness this dance of the prairie chicken.

Halfway across the state the North Country Trail meets the Missouri River—and intersects with the national historic trail that commemorates the route of the Lewis and Clark expedition of 1804–1806 that explored the new lands gained by the Louisiana Purchase. The scene today has changed greatly from the days of Lewis and Clark. The final three miles of the North Country Trail takes the hiker across the huge Garrison Dam, one of six dams that now control the flow of the Missouri River, producing benefits in flood control, hydroelectric power generation, irrigation, water supply, and recreation.

Passing a power-generating station and a national fish hatchery, the trail comes to its conclusion at Sakakawea State Park, a campground and marina on the shore of Lake Sakakawea. The 178-mile-long lake, backed up by the Garrison Dam, is the largest humanmade lake in the United States.

Although only a few hardy outdoorsmen have hiked the entire 3,200-mile length of the North Country Trail from Lake Champlain to Lake Sakakawea because of its disconnected nature, more and more enthusiasts are hiking, biking, or skiing the improved segments. Additional study and planning are needed in the East to fulfill the dream of the trail's planners—to connect the North Country Trail to the Appalachian Trail. In the West, a 200-mile section along the McClosky Canal was added in 1993, providing new hiking miles across the prairie. An average of 60 miles of trail are built and certified somewhere along the trail each year.

Yet few national scenic trails provide a greater variety of hiking experiences than those offered by the North Country. Clearly, the longest national scenic trail has a long way to grow—but bit by bit is stretching to reach its potential.

Hiking in a Wilderness Area

When a trail enters a designated wilderness area, you need to remind yourself that you are walking through a sanctuary where nature calls the tune.

More than eleven million acres of unspoiled lands—large tracts of public land in the mountains, deserts, swamps, and forests and along lakes, rivers, and shores—have been set aside under the Wilderness Act of 1964. Many of these wilderness areas are preserved within national forests, national parks, national wildlife refuges, or other public lands.

For a hiker it is a privilege to enter these untamed spaces, to gaze at uncut virgin stands of trees, to view secluded lakes and wild rivers. In the wilderness you will find no developed campgrounds with water pumps, fire grills, or bathrooms. Nor will you find organized recreation activities such as swimming and boating. Instead you should follow the well-known motto of "leaving nothing but your footprints and taking nothing but photographs." To have a minimum impact on the land, you will be required to backpack in, camp along the trail, carry your own water and food, carefully dispose of your waste, and burn or carry out all your trash.

Rangers at Chequamegon National Forest in Wisconsin, for example, pass along the following tips for the wilderness hiker and camper:

- A detailed map and a compass are a must when venturing into the wilderness.

- Make sure someone knows your travel plans—where you are going and when you plan to return. If it is required, obtain a backcountry permit at a ranger station. Sign all trail registers and thus help others keep track of your whereabouts.

- Plan on bringing plenty of insect repellent during the spring through fall seasons.

- Fuel up on high-energy foods for a quick boost.

- Bring a first aid kit. Include bandages, disinfectant, and moleskin for blisters. Help can be a long distance away. Knowing how to use a first aid kit is vital for you and your companions.

- Keep an eye on the weather and plan for the unexpected. Bring rain gear, layers of warm clothing, and extra socks. Pack a cap or hat to prevent heat loss and sunstroke.

- Carry an adequate supply of safe drinking water. A general rule of thumb is one gallon per person a day.

- Wear comfortable, sturdy, insulated, and waterproof boots. Break in your boots before you use them for extensive hiking.

- Wear sunscreen and sunglasses with ultraviolet protection.

- Pace yourself and be conscious of the physical abilities of your traveling companions. Stop and rest periodically. Guard against exhaustion.

- Lock your car and carry your wallet and checkbook with you. Do not leave any valuables in your car.

- When selecting a campsite, use an existing site to lessen the impact of your visit. Locate your campsite at least 100 feet from water or trails to increase the feeling of solitude.

- Before leaving camp, make sure your fire is completely out—cold. Scatter any rocks and wood you use. Pack out your trash; do not bury it. Animals could dig it up later.

- If you should lose your way, stay calm. Select one direction on your compass and follow it to find your way out. The wilderness is not unlimited and roads surround it. Do not abandon your gear. You may need it.

By following these guidelines, you guarantee that your presence will have little or no effect on the wilderness you pass through and that it will remain as pristine for the next person as you found it.

North Country Trail Association

The nonprofit North Country Trail Association was formed in 1981 to organize and coordinate the volunteer effort necessary to establish and maintain segments of the trail that cross private lands and to assist the U.S. Forest Service and the National Park Service in maintaining the trail on their lands.

The association, along with affiliated organizations such as the Finger Lakes Trail Conference and the Buckeye Trail Association, organizes trail construction and maintenance projects, enlists volunteers, secures the resources needed to build trails, and trains trail workers. Outings, work hikes, and social events help fill out a busy schedule for its members. Some members "adopt" a section of trail that they keep passable.

The association headquarters is in Grand Rapids, Michigan, and sponsors a "School of Outdoor Skills" each year for the camping public. Through its "Trail Shop" it offers to those interested in hiking the North Country Trail maps, route itineraries, and trail guides and publishes a quarterly newsletter for its members. For more information write the North Country Trail Association, 3777 Sparks Drive SE, Grand Rapids, MI 49546.

Hikers following the North Country Trail through Pictured Rocks National Lakeshore get spectacular views of sheer, multicolored cliffs and Lake Superior.

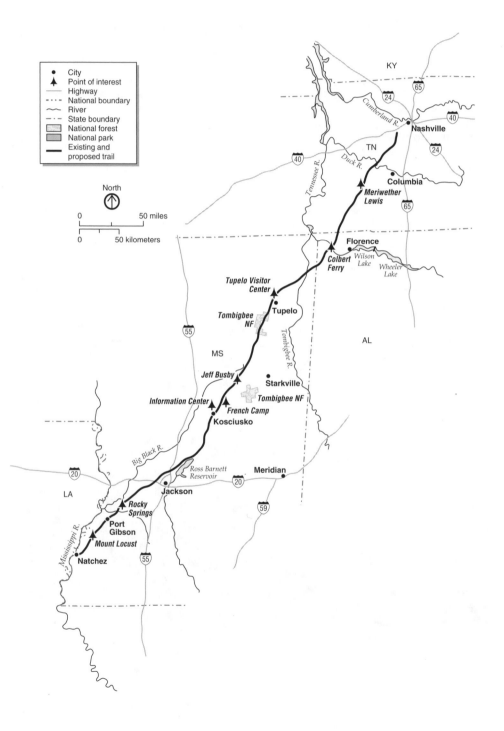

North

0   50 miles

0   50 kilometers

KY

Cumberland R.

65

24

40

Nashville

TN

24

40

Duck R.

Tennessee R.

▲

*Meriwether
Lewis*

• **Columbia**

65

Florence •

▲

*Colbert
Ferry*

*Wilson
Lake*

*Wheeler
Lake*

*Tupelo Visitor
Center*

▲

*Tombigbee
NF*

• **Tupelo**

Tombigbee R.

AL

55

MS

Jeff Busby ▲

• **Starkville**

Information Center ▲

▲

French Camp

Tombigbee NF

Kosciusko

Big Black R.

*Ross Barnett
Reservoir*

Meridian •

20

20

Jackson •

59

LA

▲ *Rocky
Springs*

• **Port
Gibson**

▲ *Mount Locust*

Mississippi R.

Natchez •

55

NATCHEZ TRACE NATIONAL SCENIC TRAIL

T HIS PIONEER PATHWAY, WHICH RUNS DIAGONALLY THROUGH TENNESSEE, Alabama, and Mississippi, owes its early history and period of heaviest usage to the farmers and tradesmen who settled before and after the American Revolution west of the Appalachian Mountains, many in the Ohio River Valley. By 1785 these early frontier settlers had established farms, furnaces, and mills and were reaching out to find markets for their produce and merchandise.

One profitable marketing method was to float their crops and goods down the Ohio and Mississippi Rivers to Natchez or on to New Orleans, where their products could be sold and shipped to East Coast ports or to Europe.

Steering their unwieldy flatboats downriver to the Mississippi Territory was one thing; returning home after selling their cargo was something else again. The big flatboats they used had to be scrapped or sold for lumber after the river trip because the entrepreneurs had no way of getting them back upstream against the stiff Mississippi River current. So the boatmen had to find another way home, and they found it on the Natchez Trace, a rough trail that had originally been beaten into a path by buffalo and Indians.

One farmer who did this and walked back home to Kentucky was Thomas Lincoln, Abraham Lincoln's father. Abe himself later made a similar raft trip down the Mississippi, but

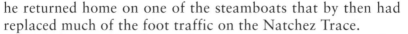

he returned home on one of the steamboats that by then had replaced much of the foot traffic on the Natchez Trace.

French maps dated as early as 1733 identify the route that would later be followed by the trace. It is listed on British maps as the "Path of the Choctaw Nation," referring to one of the two Indian tribes that lived along the route. By 1800 as many as ten thousand "Kaintucks"—the local term for boatmen from anywhere north of Natchez—annually journeyed on the trace, the most direct overland route home.

After bringing their flatboats safely past the shoals and bends of the river and landing at the Natchez waterfront where they sold their trade goods, the Kaintucks purchased supplies for the return overland trip home. Accounts of the time say these provisions typically included a rifle, a pack of cards, and a bottle or two of whiskey. Then began the hazardous journey of 20 to 30 days through the deep wilderness during which the wayfarers had to keep a wary eye out for bandits, unfriendly Indians, and wild animals. The route north took them through territory dominated by two Indian nations, the Choctaw and the Chickasaw, but Indian attacks were actually one of the least of their worries. Those following the trace had to brave exposure to the elements, wade turgid swamps, swim across streams, and watch out for poisonous snakes. The terrain of the trace was rough, and a broken leg could spell death for a lone traveler. The dark dangers of the route earned for the pathway the ominous nickname of "The Devil's Backbone."

For days a venturer on the trace might hike alone along the curving trail. On the few occasions when he came upon a fellow traveler, he probably eyed him warily, at the same time feeling for his rifle. Outlaws were common—the bandits were well aware that many of the travelers carried everything they owned in their saddle bags and purses—the profits from their sale of crops and merchandise. Merchants who had transacted business in Natchez or New Orleans carried their cash proceeds, a tempting target. The few heading south carried money for a stake in a cotton farm or a business in Natchez.

To protect themselves against the highway robbers many of those heading up the trace banded together into groups. But this was sometimes difficult to arrange, and group travel slowed one's progress along the rough road. Consequently some wayfarers, either innocently or carelessly or both, ventured forth by themselves. The result was a saga of bloodthirsty banditry, a story of murder, ambush, and thievery on the road to and from Natchez.

Weather was another enemy. Floods that could turn creeks into torrents, change low spots into bogs, or trap a horse were commonplace. But the trace was the only way home.

In 1801, by order of President Thomas Jefferson, treaties were negotiated with the Chickasaw and Choctaw Indians that granted the United States the right to improve the wilderness road between the Tennessee River and Natchez. The work was done by U.S. soldiers who constructed fords, ferries, and bridges. Even with the improvements, however, this was no carriage road. The soldiers cut trees to clear the right-of-way but left any stump that was no more than 16 inches high. The treaty, moreover, reserved to the indigenous Indians the right to operate any inns along the trace and to operate "necessary ferries over the watercourses crossed by the said road."

The trace was declared a "post road," and mail service by horseback riders was started, providing a connection between the "civilized" area of the nation with its new capital at Washington and the distant frontier outposts in Mississippi and Louisiana. Astute travelers often made the journey in the company of a post rider, feeling more secure in the company of someone familiar with the area.

During these years many inns—locally called "stands"—were built. By 1820 more than twenty stands were in operation. Most of them provided little more than a roof over one's head and plain food—not to mention the risk of being robbed while you slept. Other travelers preferred to sleep in the open, burying their money in the ground, keeping a gun under their arm, and lighting a fire to ward off roaming animals.

From 1800 to 1820 the frontier brimmed with trade and new settlements. The Natchez Trace became the busiest highway in what was then called "the Southwest." But by the late 1820s steamboats had proved their worth and two-way traffic began on the Mississippi River. Steamers called regularly at St. Louis, Nashville, and Louisville. Travelers liked the speed and comparative safety of steamboat travel more than the slow pace of going overland, so travel along the trace grew impractical. The once-busy road slowly blended back into the forest.

The Trace Today

Today the Natchez Trace still fulfills its role as an artery of transportation—but in a way different from a century-and-a-half ago.

Now a landscaped parkway under the administration of the National Park Service, it crosses and recrosses the old trace, adding to the visitor's understanding with historical markers, historic remains, and preserved sections of the old pathway itself. Although it is officially designated as a national scenic trail the Natchez Trace is more akin to a national historic trail because the old trail itself exists only in fragments, and it is best seen by car rather than on foot. The visitor gets a broad slice of history—from prehistoric Indian culture through Spanish, French, and English rule, to American frontiersmen taming the wilderness, to the Battle of Tupelo in our Civil War—all in the 450-mile length of the Natchez Trace Parkway.

The parkway begins at Natchez and stretches northeast to its terminus near Nashville. The only break in the winding, two-lane roadway is a 15-mile uncompleted portion at Jackson, Mississippi. The scenic highway is built within a corridor that averages 825 feet in width and provides land for the preservation of numerous stretches of the original trace, historic structures associated with the overland route and its early history, interpretive wayside exhibits, as well as campgrounds, picnic areas, turnouts, trailheads, and rest areas.

In addition to the parkway the Natchez Trace National Scenic Trail includes three foot and horse trail segments that parallel the parkway. These stretches of hiking and horse trail, which total some fifty miles, have been constructed by volunteers of the Natchez Trace Trail Conference who work in partnership with the Park Service. One hiking segment is near Natchez, one near Jackson, and one near Nashville. Each is marked with the Natchez Trace National Scenic Trail logo and with white blazes. "The hiking trail is usually located far enough from the roadway so you don't hear the cars going by," says Jimmy Hodo, secretary of the trail conference. Where the foot trail segments coincide with the original trace itself, the pathways allow hikers and riders to experience the same feelings the trace travelers must have had two centuries ago.

In addition hikers also have the use of more than 30 miles of side trails and three campgrounds that have been developed within the parkway boundaries. Side trails range from hiking and horseback trails of several miles for day hikers to short nature trails that give parkway motorists a "leg-stretcher" loop trail that starts at a parkway turnout.

Some of these short side hikes also include portions of the old trace. Carved by centuries of wear from footsteps, hoofbeats, and an occasional wagon wheel, remnants of the old trace have sunk as much as 20 feet into the soft loess soil that characterizes the southern portion of the route.

The distinctive loess soil accumulated in this region is the result of glaciers that existed 10,000 years ago in the Upper Midwest. As the glaciers crunched their way along they pulverized rocks and earth into fine particles. As the glaciers receded, this glacial dust was washed down tributary rivers and deposited on the Mississippi River floodplain. From there the soft powder was picked up by the prevailing westerly winds and deposited on the landscape 30 to 60 feet deep as the buff-colored, lightweight soil of southern Mississippi.

Beech, oak, and other hardwood trees arch over the edge of a typical sunken trace segment, over a roadbed that often has sunk deeper than the length of a grown person's head. It gives the appearance of a leafy tunnel through the surrounding forest—a perfect place for an outlaw ambush. Tree roots are undercut by erosion. Wild grapevines swing from the branches. Moss covers the trunk of some of the older trees. Holes in the high banks tell the hiker that mice and other burrowing creatures find a home here. Visitors can walk more than twenty of these preserved segments of the old trace—sharing the experiences of the early travelers.

But the most popular way to follow the trace, other than by car, is by bicycle. In fact, cycling authorities rank the parkway as one of the ten best long-distance bicycling routes in the world with its level or gently rolling terrain, smooth road surface, and low traffic volume. Riders should proceed in the same direction as the flow of auto traffic, maintaining a single file along the edge of the roadway. Cyclists can stay overnight at one of three park campground sites, Rocky Springs, Jeff Busby, or Meriwether Lewis, or at a number of bed and breakfast accommodations and motels located close to the parkway.

"Bicycling on the parkway has become increasingly popular in recent years," said Superintendent Daniel Brown, "and I wouldn't be surprised to see the number of cyclists double in the next five years."

Natchez to Jackson

The logical starting place for either motorist or cyclist—as it was for the boatman of 1800—is Natchez. Reminders of the colorful riverfront town of those days are still evident although they are overshadowed by the mansions and mementos of a later era when Natchez prospered as a river port shipping cotton from southern plantations.

A good way to familiarize yourself with Natchez and the Natchez Trace is to stop in at the storefront visitor center of Natchez National Historical Park, a National Park Service unit that preserves the legacy of Natchez's beginnings as an outpost of the "Old Southwest" and its later heyday as a commercial, cultural, and social center of the South's "Cotton Belt." The ranger at the visitor center on Canal Street near the waterfront can tell travelers the colorful history of Natchez, guide them to the start of the parkway, and inform them about the biannual pilgrimages when visitors flock to see the city's splendid array of antebellum mansions. Be sure to ask for the Natchez Trace Parkway folder, which identifies sites along the route by milepost numbers.

Before the visitor sets out to follow the Natchez Trace, he should take a drive down Silver Street, which descends at a steep grade from the bluff to the river landing with its piers. To the boatmen who floated their rafts down the Mississippi River in the early 1800s this area was known as Natchez Under-the-Hill. The rowdy riverboat landing was once the notorious lair of gamblers, thieves, ladies-of-the-evening—a scandalous embarrassment to the "decent" citizens of Natchez. A Methodist evangelist once called it "the worst hell-hole on earth." Many a Kaintuck boatman set off into the wilds of the trace without the gold he had earned for his cargo, the penalty for too many nights spent in the saloons and gambling establishments Under-the-Hill.

Caves were dug into the steep slope to hold stolen goods. These hideaways sometimes caused landslides in the erosion-prone area. Eventually abandoned after a series of natural disasters, some of the original buildings have now been restored as shops and restaurants. Old brick buildings stairstep down the street, fronted by weather-beaten wood sidewalks. A colorful paddle-wheel steamboat, symbol of the river steamers that gradually spelled the end of the overland traffic on the old trace, is tied up nearby. It offers round-the-clock riverboat gambling on the Mississippi.

A few miles north of Natchez on the parkway is Emerald Mound, at Milepost 10, one of several sites along the route that remind visitors of the Indian tribes that occupied these lands before and during settlement by the Europeans. This large, grass-covered, flat-topped mound, covering nearly eight acres, is said to be the second largest Indian temple mound in the United States. It was used from approximately A.D. 1300 to 1600 by the forerunners of the Natchez Indians, a tribe that was obliterated by French forces in 1729 in retaliation for a bloody attack by the Natchez on French settlers.

A few more miles northward on the parkway, at Milepost 15, is Mount Locust, the only remaining inn or "stand" of fifty that once dotted the Natchez Trace, probably the most significant remaining historic structure along the route. It started as a 16-by-20-foot, one-room log cabin, built about 1780 by Captain John Blommart, a Swiss soldier of fortune who had conducted a group of Swiss Protestants into the colony, which was at that time controlled by the Spanish. In order to earn a grant of 600 acres of land, Blommart had to build "one good Dwelling House to contain at least twenty feet in length and sixteen feet in breadth."

Blommart and later owners of the property made their living as farmers, growing vegetables and fruit and raising animals. To pick up extra income they enlarged the house and opened it to travelers on the nearby trace. By 1779 8,000 to 10,000 people were passing the site each year, and Mount Locust had become one of the best-known stands on the route. It was sometimes filled with as many as 150 guests as wayfarers overflowed onto its porches and grounds.

Now restored by the Park Service, Mount Locust offers a glimpse of the type of accommodations available to trace travelers. Stands were located at 10- to 20-mile intervals, or about a day's walk apart. For approximately 25 cents, the weary traveler could enjoy a supper of mush and milk and the privilege of sleeping on the floor in a room jammed to the rafters with saddles, baggage, and other people. Stands like Mount Locust attracted travelers not only as a place to rest, but also as a touch of civilization in the vast wilderness, a refuge from the hazards of frontier travel.

A Park Service ranger, dressed either as the innkeeper or his wife, today shows visitors around the restored stand. The original structure is notable for its sturdy construction and its excellent carpentry and craftsmanship.

Jackson to Tupelo

Between Jackson, Mississippi's capital city, and Tupelo the terrain consists of gently rolling hills covered with pines, white oak, beech, live oak, and black gum trees and flat prairie lands. Around Tupelo the land changes to "Black Belt" prairie with fertile, black loamy soil that gave rise to large plantations that raised cotton, the South's main income producer for many years. The Black Belt was settled long ago by white planters and large numbers of black slaves; today "Black Belt" refers not only to the soil but to the predominately black farmers who work it.

The motorist must detour around Jackson by taking I-20, I-220, and I-55 before getting back on the parkway again. North of Jackson, at Milepost 122, a boardwalk nature trail winds through a swamp reminiscent of the boggy areas that presented such an obstacle to those who walked or rode the old trace. Accounts tell of man and horse alike getting stuck in these low areas. In such swamps also lurked outlaws who preyed upon the travelers, brigands who sometimes disposed of their victim's body in the murky waters.

Those who stroll the nature trail learn the characteristics of two trees that thrive with their "feet in the water"—the water tupelo and the bald cypress. These swamp trees are easy to identify with their imposing height and enlarged, buttressed trunks that flare out at the base to give the tree support in its wet surroundings. The bald cypress, a truly remarkable tree, is actually not a true cypress but a relative of the redwood and sequoia. Like its California cousins, the bald cypress often lives to a venerable age. Some specimens, foresters say, have been known to live 1,500 years. The bald cypress is becoming increasingly rare, however, because the draining of wetlands has diminished its habitat and commercial lumbermen desire it for its high resistance to rot. An easy way to spot the bald cypress is to look for its "knees," extensions of its roots that protrude several feet above the water level and give added support to the rest of the deep root mass beneath.

French Camp, located at Milepost 180, gets its name from a French settler, Louis LeFleur, who built a cabin at the site in 1812. A reconstructed cabin stands there today, built in the "dogtrot" style with an open breezeway running between the two halves of the house. Inside a craftswoman demonstrates quilt making. Indian and French artifacts from the era of the trace are on display. A cafe for travelers fills a rear cabin. Outside in the fall a mule pulls the long arm of a press around in a circle to crush sorghum stalks into molasses.

LeFleur married a Choctaw woman, and their son, who renamed himself Greenwood LeFlore, became a state senator and chief of the Choctaw tribe. He was instrumental in negotiating terms of the treaty with the federal government that compensated the tribe and resulted in the removal of the Choctaws to new lands given to them in Indian territory that later became Oklahoma.

Farther north, just south of Tupelo, the parkway goes through what used to be the homeland of the Chickasaw Indians, who once inhabited the northeastern corner of Mississippi. An interpretive marker at Milepost 243 notes that the Spanish explorer Hernando DeSoto, the discoverer of the Mississippi River, spent the winter of 1540–1541 near here during the Spaniard's epic march across the southern United States. Nearby, at Milepost 266, the parkway headquarters and visitor center houses a museum that contains items pertaining to the trace and shows a 12-minute audiovisual program that relates the history of the trace and the construction of the parkway.

A short side trip on Mississippi Route 41 brings a follower of the trace to the town of Pontotoc, once the center of the Chickasaw nation. In 1832 the Chickasaw signed under pressure a treaty with the United States, ceding more than six million acres of their land to the federal government. Forced like the Choctaws to leave their homeland, they made the journey to new lands promised them in Indian territory. A federal lands office in Pontotoc handled the sale of the Chickasaw lands. Appointees of President Andrew Jackson were sent from Nashville down the Natchez Trace to handle the transactions. A site marker notes the land office's location.

Back on the parkway at Milepost 261 is the site of a Chickasaw village with outlines of the Indian houses and fortifications. Archeologists believe that more evidence of other structures in the village still lies beneath the ground.

A nature trail winds from the village site into the woods. Interpretive signs inform the visitor of the ingenious uses for food and medicine the Chickasaw discovered from various plants and animals. From the acorns of chestnut oak, for example, they ground flour for cooking. They boiled the tender shoots of the greenbrier shrub as a vegetable, made baskets from wood split from the dogwood tree, and applied the sap of the sweet gum to heal wounds or ease a cough.

Tupelo to Nashville

The parkway develops more twists and turns as it heads north from Tupelo, cutting across the northwestern corner of Alabama. Pine and hardwood forests cloak the hilly terrain.

At Milepost 293 the parkway crosses the Tennessee-Tombigbee Waterway, a remarkable engineering achievement. This extensive inland waterway allows ships to sail from the Gulf of Mexico through Alabama on the Tombigbee River and a canal to reach the Tennessee River. The Tennessee and other rivers, in turn, enable ships to continue to the Mississippi, thus opening up a widespread network of some sixteen thousand miles of navigable waterways of the South and Midwest. A few miles off the parkway is the Divide Cut, where a channel was excavated through the rolling hills; its construction rivaled that of the Panama Canal as a massive earth-moving feat. A U.S. Army Corps of Engineers visitor center portrays the construction of the Tennessee-Tombigbee Waterway.

Thirty-four miles farther, at Colbert Ferry, a bridge carries motorists over the Tennessee River where a Choctaw chief once operated a ferry. On the banks of the river the National Park Service has developed a swimming beach, boat launch, picnic area, and ranger station. The widened river has drowned the site where George Colbert operated his ferry from 1801 to 1819, but an interpretive trail leads along a section of the old trace to a point near the ferry crossing. It is reported that Colbert charged General Andrew Jackson the princely sum of $75,000 to ferry his forces across the river during the War of 1812. Colbert, as a Chickasaw chief, also negotiated the treaty in 1801 that permitted the U.S. government to improve this part of the old trace across Indian lands.

As the parkway nears its end in Tennessee, at Milepost 386, another site underlines the tragedies that haunt the trace. In an open grass area near a log cabin is a monument that recalls the death of Captain Meriwether Lewis. Lewis was the co-commander of the Lewis and Clark expedition, the trailblazing group of explorers who spanned the continent in 1805 to reach the Pacific Ocean (see page 161). Lewis, who was later appointed by President Thomas Jefferson to be governor of the Louisiana Territory in recognition of his accomplishments on the Expedition of Discovery, died here in 1809, a probable suicide. He had been making his way along the trace to the new capital in Washington to defend some of the expenses he had incurred while administering the territory. The monument—a broken shaft that symbolizes a life prematurely ended—marks where the brave captain is buried. Exhibits in the log cabin, a cabin later built at the site of Grinders Stand, one of the inns along the trace, depict Lewis's life.

The final leg of the Natchez Trace takes the traveler across a graceful new bridge. Its innovative design relies on two long arches to span a broad valley. Five miles beyond the bridge the parkway ends at Tennessee 100 on the outskirts of Nashville. On the high south bank of the Cumberland River, near the center of the "Music City," sits a reproduction of the humble blockhouses and log stockade of Fort Nashborough, the frontier fort that marked the traditional end of the old trace.

The traveler in the old days was fortunate indeed to reach the end of his trip in good health—and with his money belt as full as when he left Natchez. But despite the risks of the road the Natchez Trace during its two decades of use fulfilled its purpose.

In the beginning it provided a way for Mississippi boatmen to find their way back home. Any pathway, of course, provides an invitation to travel in two directions, and the Natchez Trace was no exception. Soon mail carriers, traders, real estate speculators, government officials, circuit-riding preachers, salesmen, soldiers, and an increasing stream of settlers on foot and on horseback were moving south. The rough-hewn trace not only provided a pathway to the North, but also opened a way for others to venture south in search of new opportunities in the lower Mississippi valley.

Natchez Trace Trail Conference

The Natchez Trace Trail Conference promotes the development, maintenance, and enjoyment of the Natchez Trace National Scenic Trail. Two constituent groups are the Trail Dusters, a group of equestrians in the Vicksburg, Mississippi, area and the Natchez Trace Trailblazers, an equestrian group at Franklin, Tennessee.

Organized in 1973, the conference coordinates its activities closely with the National Park Service staff of Natchez Trace Parkway. Its three hundred members perform trail maintenance work on the hiking and riding path that parallels portions of the paved parkway, clearing brush from the trail, repairing eroded portions, erecting trail signs and blazes, and building bridges as needed. It encourages other groups such as Boy Scout troops to undertake projects to benefit the trail. The conference educates the public about the trail by arranging for speakers for groups and schools and publishes a quarterly newsletter to inform members of its current activities.

For more information write the Natchez Trace Trail Conference, P.O. Box 1236, Jackson, MS 39215.

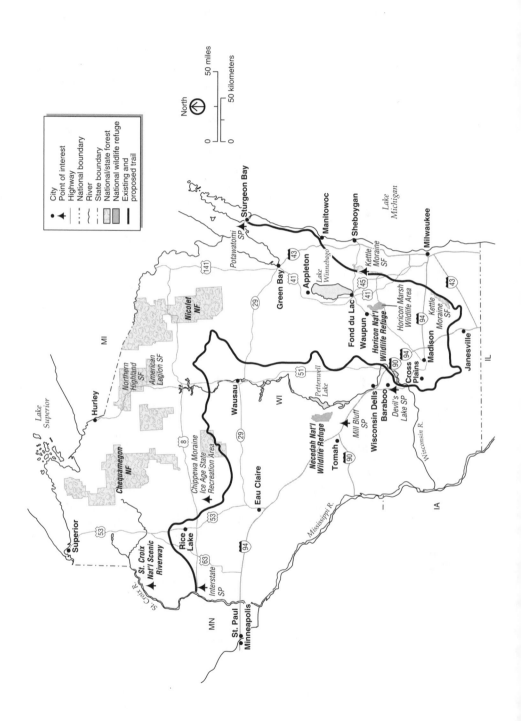

Legend

- City
- Point of interest
- Highway
- National boundary
- River
- State boundary
- National/state forest
- National wildlife refuge
- Existing and proposed trail

North

0   50 miles
0   50 kilometers

MN
WI
MI
IA
IL

Lake Superior

Superior
Hurley

St. Croix Nat'l Scenic Riverway
St. Croix R.

Chequamegon NF

Northern Highland SF
American Legion SF

Interstate SP

Rice Lake

Chippewa Moraine Ice Age State Recreation Area

Eau Claire

Wausau

Nicolet NF

Mississippi R.

Tomah

Necedah Nat'l Wildlife Refuge

Mill Bluff SP

Wisconsin Dells

Devil's Lake SP
Baraboo

Pettenwell Lake

Wisconsin R.

Cross Plains

Madison

Janesville

Green Bay

Appleton

Lake Winnebago

Fond du Lac

Waupun

Horicon Nat'l Wildlife Refuge
Horicon Marsh Wildlife Area

Kettle Moraine SF

Kettle Moraine SF

Manitowoc

Sheboygan

Milwaukee

Lake Michigan

Sturgeon Bay

Potawatomi SP

St. Paul
Minneapolis

141
41
29
45
41
94
43
90
94
51
8
53
63
94
90
29
53
43

Chapter 6

ICE AGE NATIONAL
SCENIC TRAIL

THOSE WHO HIKE THE ICE AGE NATIONAL SCENIC TRAIL AS IT WINDS its way for 1,000 miles through Wisconsin learn a whole new vocabulary—a vocabulary that reflects the Ice Age geology that makes this a unique pathway of the National Trails System.

Take, for example, the first time the hiker finds himself on the top of an esker. An esker, he soon learns if he hasn't already made its acquaintance, is a narrow, gravelly ridge formed approximately ten thousand years ago, one of the distinctive landforms left behind by the gigantic glacial sheet that once shaped the northern half of North America, including most of Wisconsin, and lowered the level of the ocean by hundreds of feet.

As the huge glacial mass melted, meltwater ran in torrents through tunnels that burrowed beneath the thick ice sheet. The torrents carried with them rocks that tumbled along, grinding themselves into smaller and smaller stones and gravel that piled up in the bed of the watercourse as it ran under the ice. When the glacial mass above eventually receded and disappeared this strand of gravel remained, an upside-down, elevated streambed, a rocky ridge left behind by the glacier.

As you walk the trail atop an esker you will note that many of the stones beneath your feet are rounded and smooth—stones that were worn smooth by the rushing glacial stream that ran here thousands of years ago.

It is at moments like this that the Ice Age Trail user comes face-to-face with the dramatic reminders of the great ice mass that once held a large part of North America in its frozen grip. The ancient glaciers that made up this ice mass formed when snow compacted and turned to ice in its central Canadian birthplace. Fostered by the continental climate that existed then—colder and wetter than the climate today—the ice mass moved slowly southward.

As it scrunched along like a giant snowplow, the ice sheet gathered up and entrapped trillions of tons of soil and stones that became its tools for gouging, grinding, and polishing anything that stood in its way. Highlands were scraped low and valleys deepened by the ice mass that at its center sometimes reached 10,000 feet in thickness, almost two miles in depth. Boulders and loose rocks embedded in the moving ice scratched the underlying bedrock like a giant rasp, leaving clear marks of its passage. The grinding action of silt particles polished rock surfaces; the same particles produced "rock flour" that gave a milky cast to the streams of meltwater.

Nowhere is the mark of the glaciers upon the land more impressive than in Wisconsin, which presents today an outdoor museum of glacial remains. The Ice Age National Scenic Trail serves as a window on this ancient world. It traces an S-shaped course across the state that follows the glacier's terminal moraines. A moraine consists of the mounds and heaps and piles of debris left behind on the landscape as each lobe of the huge ice mass receded. As it follows these moraines across the state, the Ice Age Trail links six of the nine scientific reserve units that the Secretary of the Interior designated in 1971 to "assure the protection, preservation and interpretation of the nationally significant features of the Wisconsin glaciation."

At its eastern end the trail begins at Potawatomi State Park on the Door Peninsula, which protrudes into Lake Michigan, then curves south across the long moraines of Kettle Moraine State Forest and turns north past Madison along the edge of the "driftless area," the terrain that lies just beyond the farthest reach of the glacier. The trail then curls through the wilds of Chequamegon National Forest and ends where the melting glaciers carved the dramatic Dalles of the St. Croix River at Wisconsin's western border. The trail traverses relatively level terrain—its highest point is less than two thousand feet.

The concept of the Ice Age National Scenic Trail grew out of an idea proposed by a Milwaukee attorney and outdoorsman. Like the imaginative originators of the Appalachian Trail and the Pacific Crest Trail, Ray Zillmer in the mid-1950s had a bold idea. An avid hiker, he proposed a continuous footpath similar to the Appalachian Trail that would be the central feature of a national park that would preserve the glacier's terminal moraines and display their beauty. By following this pathway, he envisioned, visitors could explore and enjoy the glacial landscape at their own pace.

Congress responded to this desire to save the prehistory of the region by establishing in 1964 the Ice Age National Scientific Reserve, composed of nine separate units, each of which holds some outstanding evidence left by the glaciers; these units are jointly administered by the State of Wisconsin in cooperation and with the financial assistance of the National Park Service. In this early legislation, introduced by Wisconsin congressman Henry S. Reuss, Congress recognized the value of a continuous footpath between the scientific reserve units, but offered no federal assistance to Wisconsin to build it.

Shortly thereafter a group of Wisconsin citizens got behind the idea and built the first segment of what would later become the national scenic trail. With the formation of the Ice Age Trail Council in 1975 these efforts accelerated. Within a few years, the members of the council were successful in establishing several major segments of the trail. In 1980 Congress designated the Ice Age Trail as a national scenic trail.

Through its local chapters, the Ice Age Park and Trail Foundation, which merged with the council in 1990, today continues to work cooperatively with public agencies and hundreds of private landowners to fill in gaps in the trail. Existing segments are maintained by the U.S. Forest Service, the Wisconsin Department of Natural Resources, county and municipal park and forestry departments, and many private volunteers.

Kettle Moraine State Forest

Currently hikers and cyclists can use some of the 450 miles of the Ice Age Trail; 225 of these miles have been certified by the National Park Service and Wisconsin as being fully up to the standard of a national scenic trail. From its eastern end at

Potawatomi State Park the trail route generally follows the shoreline of Lake Michigan, guiding the hiker along the crests of several eskers and beside several bogs. It passes Two Creeks Buried Forest, one of the nine scientific reserve units, where a spruce and hemlock forest was long ago covered and preserved under a layer of glacial clay, sand, gravel, and boulders as the glacier slid over it. Scientists have determined through radiocarbon dating that the ancient tree trunks here are more than eleven thousand years old.

Farther on, after traversing a section where the trail route has not been developed and must follow public roads, it comes to Kettle Moraine State Forest, which displays the greatest variety of glacial landforms anywhere along the statewide trail. At this location, two lobes or tongues of the ancient ice sheet squeezed together, the convergence causing a pileup of glacial debris. The landscape is sculpted into a panorama of rounded domes, conical peaks, winding ridges, and lakes. A visitor center of contemporary design gives the observer a good view of several features of the landscape from its viewing platform. Diagrams mounted on the deck identify several glacial features that are apparent in the nearby landscape. The visitor center itself is built atop one of the terminal moraines.

"You'll see examples of most of the major topographic features left by the glaciers," said Roger Reif, Kettle Moraine's knowledgeable park naturalist. "When you take this hike back in time, you'll begin to recognize these distinctive geological shapes. Then you'll be better able to read the landscape of other areas and realize what occurred at these locations during glacial times."

The Henry S. Reuss Ice Age Visitor's Center at Kettle Moraine is one of three visitor centers located along the trail. These centers, with their displays, films, publications, and explanations, play an important role in helping the trail user comprehend the imprint of the glaciers. Glacial features, one soon learns, are not spectacular. The gentle mounds and sloping ridges look like many another landscape—until one realizes how they were formed.

A segment of the trail takes the hiker along a wide grassy path, marked with the triangular Ice Age Trail symbol, that leads through meadows, old orchards, and patches of forest. Maples, oaks, quaking aspen, red and white pine, and red cedar grow in the thin soil of the moraine. The soil is very shallow, with many feet of sand, gravel, and cobblestones beneath it. Wildlife that inhabit the area include white-tailed deer, wild turkeys, sandhill cranes, and badgers.

The trail leads along the narrow ridge of an esker and passes Butler Lake, an example of another glacial feature—the kettle lake. Here water has filled the depression that remains from long ago when a huge chunk of ice was left behind by a retreating glacier. Covered with debris that slowed its melting, the chunk sank slowly into the surrounding silt as meltwater filled the depression. What remains is a lake—its ancient depths now providing a popular fishing spot in the park. Kettle lakes seldom have inlets or outlets and therefore often slowly evolve into bogs.

At one point along the trail the visitor can see four different glacial features at the same time—a moraine, an esker, a kettle lake, and a kame (pronounced "came"). The kame is a conical, gumdrop-shaped hill that was formed when a vertical shaft or hole opened in the glacier. Rocks and gravel embedded in the ice were washed down the shaft and heaped into a pile at the bottom. When the glacier later melted back, the cone-shaped mound of debris remained as a bump on the landscape.

Two other reminders of glacial action along the trail are drumlins and erratics. A drumlin is an elongated, tapering hill that was scraped up beneath a moving glacier. Some drumlins are up to two miles long and one hundred feet high. Drumlins line up in the direction the glacier came from.

The erratic is an individual rock that was carried along by the glacier as a "hitchhiker" and deposited wherever the glacier happened to drop it. Erratics, also called "wanderers," may be as small as a watermelon or as big as a truck. Since an erratic is geologically different from the bedrock of the surrounding area, you can often tell from its composition where it came from and how far the glacier transported it before dropping the hitchhiker off at its new site. Large erratics were dropped first when the force of the ice could move them no farther; smaller erratics were ground to a smaller size by the glacial action and carried a greater distance before being deposited.

From the northern Kettle Moraine area the trail loops southward, then swings northward again as it traces the glacier's edge. Hikers use public roads that alternate with several short, completed trail segments. The trail winds through Pike Lake State Park where it skirts a kettle lake that now provides swimming and boating opportunities. It passes Holy Hill, so named because a monastery, built atop a high kame, commands a magnificent view of the surrounding countryside. The monks willingly granted permission for the trail to go past the monastery, thus giving the hiker a glimpse of not only geologic but also cultural interest. The trail user may enjoy a panoramic view of the countryside from the monastery's tower.

A 28-mile segment of certified trail takes the hiker through South Kettle Moraine State Forest where several campgrounds and a natural history museum add to the experience. Farther on the route joins the Sugar River State Trail, a rails-to-trails project, for 17 miles, the route leading across the flat landscape of a glacial outwash plain. The meltwater from the ancient glacier deposited extensive stream sediments, leaving behind a fertile soil that has benefited many of Wisconsin's dairy farmers.

West of Madison, at Cross Plains, another of the scientific reserve units, visitors see a striking contrast between glaciated and unglaciated terrain at a site where the glacier came to a halt. On one side are erratics, moraines, and a gorge cut by glacial meltwaters. On the other side, on land left untouched by the glacier, the landscape is very different: irregular bluffs, steep cliffs, and deep valleys.

Devil's Lake State Park, another of the scientific reserve units, provides insight into a different type of glacial effect. Here, in one of its final thrusts, the glacier pushed up tons of rocks at two locations across a deep gorge. The two rock dams effectively plugged the gorge at both ends, creating the deep lake nestled in a gorge that you see today. At the same time the glacier forced the river to make a big bend to the east. The Ice Age Trail circles the deep lake, giving hikers a good view of the two rock piles.

Chequamegon National Forest

The trail now swings to the north on its reverse-S course as it follows moraines through the center of Wisconsin to the north woods. Much of the trail in this region still awaits development. Turning westward, it crosses a landscape full of lakes and bogs born of glacial melt. Entering the forested backwoods of Chequamegon National Forest, the pathway crosses numerous glacial ridges and kames as it skirts the many small kettles and bogs that characterize the north woods. Part of this 42-mile certified segment of the trail may be difficult for hikers because they must cross streams and bogs where there are no bridges.

Wildlife is abundant in this unpeopled part of the state. Few backpackers try this section of the trail. White-tailed deer, black bear, porcupine, skunk, squirrel, ruffed grouse, bobcat, waterfowl, and many varieties of hawks and songbirds fill the hiker's binoculars. Pine snakes and other reptiles are frequently observed, and trail users may even catch sight of a coyote or bald eagle. Blue flag (wild iris), arrowhead, and bunchberry grow here.

This is second-growth forest; trees have been harvested since the timber boom of the late 1800s. In many areas of northern Wisconsin the glacial soils are ideally suited for trees, especially maples, which thrive in the heavy, moist moraine earth. First the timbermen felled the giant white pines to provide lumber for local use and to build the frame houses of settlers on the prairies. Hemlocks were taken and stripped of their bark for tanning leather. Next the hardwoods were cut for the woodworking industry, and finally the aspen for pulpwood. Wisconsin was the leading lumber-producing state from 1899 to 1904 and is the leading state today in paper production.

"About one-quarter of what we cut today in the forest is aspen for pulpwood," Chequamegon District Ranger John Vrablec said. "About seventy percent is hardwoods and the remainder softwoods like pine and spruce."

The Forest Service limits its clear-cutting of trees close to the Ice Age Trail, thus helping to maintain the trail's wilderness setting. But every hiker sees large stumps that recall the once mighty stands of white pine that were taken out years ago. The second-growth trees that replaced them are largely aspen, birch, maple, ash, white spruce, balsam fir, and swamp conifers.

On the eastern side of the forest the trail circles around the Mondeaux Flowage, a dammed portion of the Mondeaux River. The water backed up behind the dam forms a lake that in earlier lumbering days provided water to propel rafts of logs down the river to mills. Now that the log drives are a thing of the past, the Forest Service operates four developed campgrounds near the lake. A nearby lodge offers interpretive displays that tell how the Civilian Conservation Corps of the Depression years built the recreation area, constructed the dam, laid out roads into the forest, and planted trees.

For half of its way across the Chequamegon forest the Ice Age Trail makes use of old logging roads and deer trails. In other narrower sections, rangers have placed the yellow diamond-shaped plastic trail markers close together, 60 or 70 to the mile, because the bushes and trees grow so rapidly in this productive forest.

Beaver also present a problem, building their dams at spots where they flood out the trail. At some places the rangers have found the best solution is to let the trail run across the top of one of these beaver dams. "At other places we will trap and relocate a beaver in the hope that he will build his dam somewhere else," explained Vrablec. "But experience has taught us that it is often easier to reroute the trail than try to move a beaver. The animal will often come right back to the same location and build a new dam." The backpacker in this boggy environment will likely see numerous examples of beaver dams and lodges as well as groves of black ash trees that have been flooded and killed by the beavers.

Chippewa Moraine

Farther west the trail passes through the Chippewa Moraine Scientific Reserve Unit, an area with lessons to teach about "stagnant ice," a phenomenon that occurred when a vast dirt-covered portion of the glacier stopped moving. A dozen different "stagnant ice" landforms are visible in this area. A contemporary visitor center is the centerpiece for 23 miles of the Ice Age Trail that is considered one of the most scenic trail segments in the state.

The center is actually built atop one of the glacial features it is designed to explain—an ice-walled lake plain. This feature developed when meltwater collected in a depression atop a glacier to form a lake surrounded by walls of ice. Often such a lake remained for many years, possibly thousands, while sediment accumulated on its bottom. When the surrounding glacial mass eventually melted away, the accumulated sediment settled onto the earth's surface like a thick pancake, forming a plateau that now stands above the surrounding landscape.

The trail crosses another stagnant ice feature—a debris-filled crevasse. As the glacier ceased to move, fissures appeared in its surface. Debris fell into these cracks. When the glacier receded the accumulated rocks and stones remained behind as a sharp ridge running across the landscape.

Today the trail winds across these glacial ridges as it follows logging and forest roads and leads the hiker over fence stiles and across privately held lands. On this segment it crosses numerous streams, passes eskers and kames, and goes past scores of large and small kettle lakes. The hiker walks by twenty-one glacial lakes on a six-mile segment of the trail. The lakes are full of northern pike, largemouth bass, and smaller panfish. Shorelines provide habitat for mallards, wood ducks, blue-winged teal, mergansers, and muskrats.

Interstate State Park

The last of the scientific reserve units to be linked by the Ice Age Trail is located at the western boundary of Wisconsin on the St. Croix River. The hiker who follows the trail to its western terminus arrives at The Dalles of the St. Croix, a deep gorge where the river slices between high basalt cliffs. "Dalles" is the French word for "gorge."

These black cliffs and the river that swirls between them offer the visitor a popular recreation spot. Climbers rappel down the steep flanks of the gorge. Daredevil divers plunge from the clifftops into the churning water below. A brightly painted sternwheeler takes sightseers on an excursion trip through the canyon. Hikers walk the trails along the tops of the bluffs while picnickers enjoy the spectacular views and watch the activities around them.

This fun-filled scene is in stark contrast to the momentous glacial event that transpired here eons ago, the cataclysm that carved this deep gorge. A huge glacial lake to the north, a forerunner of the present Lake Superior, filled with meltwater and eventually overflowed like a dam bursting. The rushing water powered its way down the valley, carrying with it stones and debris. The deluge carved a channel through the hard basalt, creating a waterfall when it reached the softer sandstone downstream. As the torrent continued to pour over the falls, the lip of the waterfall receded back upstream, eroding the basalt even further and creating the deep canyon.

This dramatic scene at The Dalles puts a fitting exclamation point to the Ice Age Trail at Wisconsin Interstate State Park. The 1,350-acre park provides miles of trails for the hiker and jogger and in winter for the cross-country skier.

The final one-half mile that completes the 1,000-mile route of the Ice Age Trail is known locally as the Pothole Trail. It gets its name from yet another glacial phenomenon. The smooth, rounded holes the visitor sees climbing over the basalt cliffs were created years ago by eddies swirling in the glacial torrent. Some small ones are the size of a bowling ball; larger ones are as big as a barn. Sand and silt in the water, whirled around by the eddies, acted like a drill, biting into the basalt. If a rock called a grindstone fell into the hole, it too was spun around, enlarging the pothole and smoothing the sides of the grindstone. When the raging glacial river flow finally diminished, the wearing process stopped, and the pothole and accompanying grindstone were left behind.

Wisconsin's Interstate State Park and a companion Interstate State Park just across the river in Minnesota contain more potholes in a smaller area than any other location in the world. The deepest one to be measured accurately is over 60 feet deep and 12 to 15 feet wide; it is called "The Bottomless Pit."

Filling in the Gaps

It is no simple task to hike the entire length of the Ice Age Trail because numerous segments of the trail are disconnected from the others. At some places trail users need to take to local roads to find their way to the next section of marked trail.

Only a few determined hikers have followed the long route all the way from Lake Michigan to the St. Croix River. The first to do it was Jim Staudacher, a student at Marquette University who completed the trek of 1,000 miles in 1979. Carrying a 50-pound backpack, this trailblazer hiked the route in 66 days—taking another 11 days for brief stops and rainy-day rest periods. Although the trail is not clearly defined in some places, he reported, it is "basically followable."

Reflecting on the reasons he decided to hike the trail end to end, Staudacher said he was looking for something that would challenge him and at the same time provide him an opportunity to see more of Wisconsin.

"Backpacking is a tremendous way to learn more about the area and get to know a little more about the people," he told reporters at the conclusion. "You can stop when you feel like it and, if you want, get involved with people along the way.

"My decision to be the first person to hike the entire Ice Age Trail was a little selfish," he admitted. "I'd like to be remembered as somebody who got out and tried something a little different."

To try to connect the gaps in the trail is the mission of the Ice Age Park and Trail Foundation. Since only 450 miles of the trail is either hikable or fully certified by the National Park Service, that leaves 550 miles of the 1,000-mile route where no marked trail yet exists.

The foundation's more than two thousand five hundred members are devoted to the trail's completion. Chapter members negotiate easements or "handshake agreements" that permit the trail to cross private land, work out purchase agreements of land to add to the protected corridor, accept land donations, raise funds, help plan new segments, and maintain their assigned portion of the trail by mowing it, removing branches that have blown down, and replenishing markers and blazes.

Adding miles of protected pathway to the Ice Age Trail takes cooperation between the private citizens and government. While the foundation has purchased several critical trail segments, the

Marker along the Ice Age Trail.

State of Wisconsin also has provided funds. Wisconsin currently appropriates funds each year that are used to match privately raised money on a fifty-fifty basis and are put toward the purchase of land or easements for the trail. The federal government, meanwhile, has the responsibility for overall planning and coordination of the trail route.

In some areas protecting the trail corridor may involve staying one step ahead of a developer who has his eye on the same open land. The foundation looks for innovative ways of doing this. In at least once instance, it found that working hand in hand with a developer offered the best way.

Trying to extend the trail through a suburban region west of Milwaukee, the foundation raised the money and purchased 80 acres of land along the trail route, thus preventing a prospective developer from building a community that would have blocked the trail. The foundation then sought out a second developer who was willing to develop a residential community that would allow the trail to pass through it. The new developer succeeded in obtaining a zoning variance from the county, which allowed him to build on three-acre instead of five-acre lots on the condition that he would dedicate the remainder of the land as open space. When he produced a plan that set aside enough land for not only the trail corridor but for other community open space as well, the foundation enthusiastically sold him the land. Today the owners of the newly built homes at "Hawksnest" are pleased to have a segment of the Ice Age Trail running through the woods behind their upscale homes, and the developer proudly advertises that a segment of the national scenic trail is part of the neighborhood.

"Financial arrangements like this are innovative tools we can use in the future for trail development," said Gary Werner, the former trail implementer and land acquisition specialist for the foundation. "The day of the informal handshake agreement to allow a trail to go across private landholdings is probably on its way out."

By using methods like these more hiking miles are being added to the Ice Age Trail each year. And just in time, said experts like Dr. Adam Cahow, professor of glacial landforms at the University of Wisconsin at Eau Claire, who has long been a supporter of the Ice Age Trail.

"In Wisconsin, these glacial features are endangered, just like some plants and animals have become endangered," he said.

"People have long made use of glacial remains as gravel pits, clay for bricks, or rocks for construction work. Now it's time to preserve the remaining glacial landmarks for the geological story they tell.

"There is a certain mystique to hiking the Ice Age Trail. It is more than just a hiking trail. It is a heritage trail, the only national scenic trail that is devoted to a single theme. People from all over the world and other parts of our country come to see these rare reminders of the glacial age."

John Muir, the proponent of saving wilderness areas of the United States, spent his boyhood days in the glacier-shaped Wisconsin countryside, near where the Ice Age Trail runs today. He once wrote of the legacy of the great ice sheets: "Glaciers ... crushed and ground and wore away the rocks in their marches, making vast beds of soil, and at the same time developed and fashioned the landscapes into a delightful variety of hill and dale and lordly mountain that mortals call beauty."

Those who have hiked the Ice Age National Scenic Trail find those words still ring true today.

Ice Age Park and Trail Foundation

The Ice Age Park and Trail Foundation is dedicated to preserving and extending this trail, which traces the farthest reaches of the last Ice Age glacier into Wisconsin, and to improving the trail for the education and enjoyment of the public.

The foundation works with the National Park Service and the Wisconsin Department of Natural Resources to protect the resource, develop materials for trail users, organize local volunteer chapters, build and maintain the trail, and identify areas that are threatened by conflicting land use. The foundation has more than three thousand members and publishes a quarterly newsletter, *Mammoth Tales,* for its members.

Chapters, organized by counties through which the trail passes, send out regular work parties to maintain the trail. The foundation purchases land for the trail corridor using both privately donated and publicly appropriated funds. It raises funds through an annual "Hike-a-thon," which draws some two thousand hikers; hikers vie for prizes as they hike miles along the trail, then collect pledged donations from sponsors for the miles walked. The funds collected are shared with all county chapters.

For more information write the Ice Age Park and Trail Foundation Inc., P.O. Box 423, Pewaukee, WI 53072-0423.

Chapter 7

CONTINENTAL DIVIDE NATIONAL SCENIC TRAIL

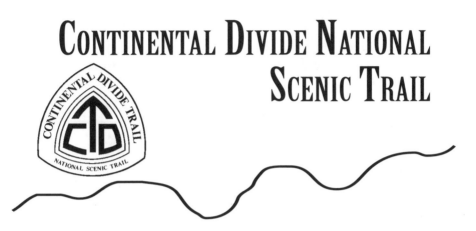

THOSE WHO DRIVE THE EAST-WEST INTERSTATE HIGHWAYS THAT SPAN the United States note with interest a sign located atop a mountain crest in the Rocky Mountains that proclaims that the motorist on I-70 has just surmounted the Continental Divide— "the Backbone of America," where the waters divide, draining one way to the Atlantic, the other to the Pacific.

An accompanying interpretive historic sign points out that this formidable mountain barrier stood in the way of the early trappers, explorers, and mountain men who were faced with finding a way through the Rockies. This massive mountain chain hunches its broad shoulders across the western part of the United States. The Continental Divide was an obstacle overcome only when the thousands of canvas-covered emigrant caravans discovered they could successfully conquer the mountain chain at the low saddle of South Pass in what is now Wyoming.

The emigrants noted as they toiled toward South Pass that the creeks ran east; after crossing the summit, they noted that the creeks ran west. From their crossing they learned that the Continental Divide determines the flow of the creeks, streams, and rivers throughout the western half of the United States. Rain and snow that fall to the east of the Divide trickle into creeks and streams that grow into rivers like the Missouri and Arkansas that flow into the Mississippi River and thence to the Gulf of Mexico. Precipitation that falls west of the Divide gathers in rivulets and streams that feed rivers such as the westward-flowing Colorado and Columbia, which discharge into the Pacific Ocean.

The Continental Divide is actually a hemispheric divide, splitting watersheds from Alaska's Brooks Range through the Rocky Mountains and the Andes to the tip of South America. The Blackfeet Indians of northern Montana, perhaps sensing the continental significance of the Divide, called it the "Center of the World."

Now, in another day and another age, the Continental Divide is not so much an obstacle as an opportunity. Americans today view the Rocky Mountains and the Continental Divide not as an almost insurmountable barrier, but as a stretch of undeveloped mountain and desert terrain that provides a rejuvenating outdoor experience for hikers, horseback riders, and mountain bikers.

In 1978 Congress designated a route from Canada to Mexico along the Rocky Mountains as the Continental Divide National Scenic Trail, thus adding a third north-south scenic trail to the well-established Appalachian Trail in the East and the Pacific Crest Trail in the West.

This vision of a long-distance trail through the Rockies is being translated into a trail on the ground under the lead of the U.S. Forest Service, the agency assigned the responsibility for the Continental Divide Trail, in close cooperation with the Continental Divide Trail Society and the Continental Divide Trail Alliance. But whereas a hiker can walk the Appalachian Trail from one end to the other and can follow the entire length of the Pacific Crest Trail with little concern about getting lost, he or she cannot yet do the same on the Continental Divide Trail. The trail route itself must still be defined at many places. At other places the route has been agreed upon, but the hiker finds no tread to walk on. Nor is the trail marked yet with the scenic trail symbol along most of its length.

To lay out the route between Canada and Mexico, recreation specialists stitched together the public lands preserved primarily within national forests and national parks, passing through private land only where they had to in order to provide continuity for the trail. On some stretches the route runs along rural roads; on others, hikers and horseback riders must leave the trail or road and trek across country. In the high country of Colorado, Idaho, and Montana, the trail route makes use of mining roads, Forest Service roads, and logging roads. It is sometimes a multi-use trail; on many sections a person is as likely to see a mountain biker, an all-terrain vehicle, or a snow-mobile as a backpacker.

The Continental Divide Trail, then, is still a work in progress. When it is completed—probably well into the twenty-first cen-tury—it is expected to stretch some 3,100 miles, almost 1,000 miles longer than the Appalachian Trail, 700 miles longer than the Pacific Crest Trail. The preferred route extends through three national parks, twenty-four national forests, three Indian reserva-tions, and Bureau of Land Management acreage devoted to graz-ing and timber-growing, as well as wilderness areas, state lands, and privately owned lands.

The trail rarely coincides exactly with the Divide itself, but for the most part meanders within a few miles of the geographic divide, crossing back and forth from watershed to watershed. The planners found that in practice it was not always feasible or even desirable to follow the geographic divide too closely. They had to skirt chasms; they needed to avoid endangered species of animals and plants. They knew that a trail that runs high above treeline for a long distance could leave the user without water sources, protected campsites, and towns to replenish supplies. A trail run-ning high atop a mountain range in the alpine region also exposes a hiker or rider to high winds, snow or sleet, and sudden, poten-tially violent thunderstorms—lightning often strikes the highest object around, which could very well be a hiker in the treeless alpine tundra.

Most users of the Continental Divide Trail venture out from a convenient trailhead for only a few miles or a few days and nights. To hike or ride the entire length of the "trail" takes a tremendous sustained effort, a commitment that has taken the few who have accomplished it up to six months.

In addition to the usual preparations every long-distance hiker must make—food supplies, clothes for changing weather condi-tions, physical preparations for the hike—the adventuresome per-son who wishes to hike the length of the Continental Divide Trail must choose the actual route he or she will take over the un-charted portions of the trail, using the best maps and the best advice he or she can get.

No full-length trail map similar to ones for other national trails exists. The Continental Divide Trail Society, however, pub-lishes a pocket-size, mile-by-mile description of the route (see page

114). Even the detailed maps of each national forest do not identify the Continental Divide Trail. The well-known U.S. Geological Survey topographical maps are a must for most sections of the
route, but even with a topo map and a compass the thru hiker
finds himself on an exploring adventure. Despite these drawbacks
and the gaps in the trail route, a half dozen or so hardy adventurers complete the entire route each year—most of them starting at
the Mexican border, usually in May, and reaching the Canadian
border about October.

These thru hikers are convinced the experience is worth it. "It
allows you to become absorbed into the trail and the region," one
woman hiker said. "Words cannot tell you just how beautiful it
was. I went close to twelve hundred miles without seeing another
backpacker. It's so peaceful. You can't even see a hint that anyone
has been there."

New Mexico

The Continental Divide Trail through New Mexico is largely
a do-it-yourself trail. The Divide itself runs for about eight
hundred miles through the state; the few stretches of trail are
in the three national forests that lie along the Divide. Interven-
ing lands that account for most of the mileage are ranches,
other public lands, and Indian reservations. The "trail" starts
at the border with Mexico near Antelope Wells. A hiker starting out from here may be the only person that day to pass by
what has been called the "loneliest border station of the U.S.
Customs Service."

As the backpacker crosses the ranchland that fills the southwestern corner of the state, he or she may see not only herds of
beef cattle grazing on the flatland but also a variety of desert wildlife
and vegetation. Jackrabbits, cottontails, coyotes, javelinas,
pronghorns, white-tailed and mule deer, and rattlesnakes announce their presence. Green mesquite adds some color to the
buff landscape. One of the most dramatic species of cactus, the
Spanish Bayonet, points its narrow, daggerlike leaves toward
the sky.

Crossing I-10, which runs east and west between Lordsburg
and Deming, the long-distance hiker or rider comes upon a
well-cleared section of blazed trail that skirts Silver City, then
begins an ascent into the Black Range Primitive Area at the eastern

edge of the Gila National Forest. As the trail climbs the vegetation changes with each biological life zone. Pinyon pine and juniper trees prevail at about six thousand feet; ponderosa pine becomes dominant from seven thousand to eight thousand feet, while oak and aspen mix with the ponderosas from eight thousand to ten thousand feet. Above ten thousand feet is the spruce-fir zone inhabited by Engelmann spruce, subalpine fir, and Douglas fir.

A short detour off the trail from Silver City provides a fascinating glimpse of Gila Cliff Dwelling National Monument. The people who lived here seven hundred years ago, thought to be ancestors of present-day Pueblo Indians, built their homes in caves 175 feet above the canyon floor. About a dozen families lived, worked, and played in the forty rooms hollowed out of the cliffs. To hunt, gather edible plants, and grow maize, beans, and squash, they descended to the valley floor. To cook their food, eat, and sleep, they climbed back up to their protective cave dwellings. The National Park Service and the U.S. Forest Service jointly operate a visitor center at the historical park.

As it extends through New Mexico the Continental Divide Trail passes near several Indian reservations—the Ramah Navajo, Jicarilla Apache, Zuni, and Acoma reservations. No hiking trails or facilities are developed on these Indian lands, but hikers who request permission in advance may be permitted to cross the reservation lands.

Of all the national scenic trails the Continental Divide takes the prize for the most dramatic changes of scenery en route. One of the most surprising occurs as the trail leaves the forested mountains of southern New Mexico and enters the badlands near Grants. A visitor center at Grants, jointly operated by the National Park Service, U.S. Forest Service, Bureau of Land Management, and State of New Mexico, provides an orientation to this volcanic area for hikers as well as for the auto tourists who pass through on I-40.

The trail follows the edge of the volcanic field preserved as El Malpais National Monument, taking the hiker across rubble fields and past cinder cones, spatter cones, sinkholes, a 17-mile lava tube system, bat caves, and fragile ice caves.

"It's best to wear long pants, heavy-duty shoes, and even gloves when you hike through this lava field," warned Superintendent Doug Eury as he explained the sharp-edged footing in this desolate setting. "Remember, there are only two kinds of hikers here—those who have fallen and those who will fall." He warns hikers in this forbidding terrain to bring along three sources of light and a canteen of water.

A seven-and-a-half-mile segment of the trail through El Malpais runs along the Zuni-Acoma Trail, a traditional trade route used by the Native Americans for seven hundred years to travel between their two pueblos. In its path across the park, the Continental Divide Trail crosses four of the five ancient lava flows that cover the area, crosses several lava "bridges" built by the ancestral Zuni and Acoma, and leads past stark volcanic features.

Trail users see giant lava tubes formed when molten lava crusted, leaving the inner lava still flowing and creating a pipeline as large as a subway tunnel. Next to the Bandera Crater, a cinder cone with a 750-foot-deep crater, the visitor is surprised to discover an ice cave. The temperature stays at 30°F in this ice cavern, where the 20-foot-thick icy floor never melts, even in the hot New Mexican summer. The thickest ice, formed about A.D. 170, bears a green tint from Arctic algae embedded in it.

Trees growing in this lava field find it hard to establish deep roots in the thin soil; instead they grow to be twisted and gnarled like overgrown bonsai trees. Hikers may also admire one of the oldest trees in New Mexico, a Douglas fir believed to be 800 years old, which has grown to only 35 feet in height. Observers also marvel at tree molds formed when a lava flow surrounded, then incinerated, a tree, leaving behind a rocklike mold the exact size and shape as the original tree trunk.

Colorado

For its 753 miles along the Rocky Mountain spine of Colorado the Continental Divide Trail climbs to some of its highest elevations and offers some of its most spectacular views. Staying close to the geographic divide, the trail is almost entirely on public land, most of it national forest land. Since national forest boundaries usually meet atop the Divide, the trail crisscrosses between forests. As it extends across Colorado it passes through the Rio Grande, San Juan, Gunnison, San Isabel, Pike, White River, Roosevelt, Arapaho, and Routt National Forests. Major rivers also rise here—the Rio Grande, San Juan, North and South Platte, Colorado, and Arkansas. This high country is studded with old and new mines, ghost towns, and celebrated ski resorts. All 753 miles are open to hikers and horseback riders and is marked. One-third of the Colorado segment may be used by mountain bikers; one-fifth may be used by all-terrain vehicles and snowmobiles.

This sky-high trail through Colorado can pose problems for some. "About a third of those who hike this part of the Continental Divide Trail have trouble with the altitude," said Les Russell, a district ranger of the Leadville District of the San Isabel National Forest. "Shortness of breath and dehydration are the most common symptoms.

"High elevations decrease the amount of oxygen in the air, making it more difficult to breathe," he said. "It's a good idea to first spend some time at an altitude of ten thousand feet or above to acclimatize your body before you start a hike," he counseled. "Drink plenty of water both before and during your hike to prevent dehydration. Eat light, nutritious meals. Acute mountain sickness can cause nausea, headache, insomnia, lethargy, and loss of appetite.

"Hikers also need to be aware of hypothermia," Russell continued. "If your body loses heat faster than it produces it, you must exercise more to stay warm; this in turn drains your body of its energy reserves. Surprisingly, most cases of hiker hypothermia develop at temperatures between 30 and 50°F, not at subfreezing temperatures. Keep yourself dry and beware of a wind that pulls the heat from your body."

The trail enters Colorado along the San Juan Mountains where many volcanic peaks exceed thirteen thousand feet and the passes are higher than ten thousand feet. Much of the trail runs above timberline, averaging eleven thousand feet in elevation as it crosses the state. It is an austere and windy land, once roamed by prehistoric hunters, more recently by miners, and now worked by geologists, outfitters, fishermen, hunters, skiers, and sheepherders. Krummholz, or stunted trees, speckle the windy heights.

As the trail swings close to Silverton, whose name reflects the bonanza in silver ore that once brought opulence to the city, it coincides with the Colorado Trail. Half of the Continental Divide Trail across Colorado makes use of this pathway already laid down. A small army of volunteer hikers and riders spent their summers for 15 years beginning in 1973 constructing this 470-mile trail from Denver to Durango.

Both Colorado and Continental Divide hikers thrill to the rugged scenery of the Sawatch Range. They walk through lodgepole pine (8,500 to 10,000 feet), Engelmann spruce and subalpine fir (10,000 to 11,500 feet), and alpine tundra above that.

Several of Colorado's famous "fourteeners," peaks that rise above 14,000 feet, lie close at hand. Just east of the Divide at Independence Pass is Mount Elbert, at 14,433 feet the highest in Colorado, the second highest in the lower forty-eight states behind California's Mount Whitney. Nearby Mount Massive is 14,421 feet. The Collegiate Peaks live up to their name, including Mount Harvard (14,420 feet), Mount Princeton (14,197 feet), Mount Yale (14,196 feet), and Mount Columbia (14,073 feet).

Several interest points enliven the trail experience. At Twin Lakes, the Forest Service has restored a 100-year-old log house into a do-it-yourself visitor center. Trail users enter to view exhibits that describe the mining and resort history of the region and to enjoy a wildlife viewing area. At Vicksburg the trail leads by an old mining village of log homes set deep in the forest. The structures have been restored to their original appearance by their owners. The one-street town even has its own museum of mining history.

Near Tennessee Pass hikers and riders who make advance arrangements may take advantage of several overnight huts similar to the huts one finds in New England on the Appalachian Trail. The huts are the result of the enthusiastic efforts of veterans of the U.S. Army's tenth Mountain Division, which trained for mountain warfare in Italy during World War II in nearby Camp Hale. Each hut sleeps sixteen people in three or four bunk rooms, offers a water source, and provides a wood-burning stove for heating and cooking.

The trail skirts Leadville, often following old mining roads that crisscross these mountains. Since the beginning of the silver boom in the late 1800s, Leadville District mines have provided nearly two billion dollars in gold, silver, lead, zinc, copper, iron, bismuth, manganese, and molybdenum. To get to the ore, miners fanned out into the hills. Hikers, although grateful for the roads left by the miners, need to be alert for abandoned mine entrances and hidden pits that invite injury.

Les Russell, USFS district ranger, checks trail register in San Isabel National Forest (Leadville District). Here the trail follows old mining roads.

Many of Colorado's historic mining towns—Aspen, Breckenridge, Crested Butte—have evolved into ski resorts, and the big boom now is in winter recreation. I-70, which crosses the Continental Divide Trail near Loveland Pass, brings hordes of skiers to these slopes each winter weekend.

The Continental Divide Trail merely nicks the corner of Rocky Mountain National Park but the short, 10-mile segment gives hikers and horseback riders another contrast. Unlike most other segments of the trail, the route here follows a shoreline—the edges of one lake and two reservoirs. As one ranger at the park joked: "It's the only place on the Continental Divide Trail where you can sail your boat along the trail!"

The lake and reservoirs are part of a complex system that collects rain and snow that falls on the west side of the Continental Divide and transports and distributes it to the east slope. Not far from where the trail crosses the narrow beginnings of the Colorado River, a tunnel 13 miles long diverts water from Grand Lake to the eastern side of the Divide, where it flows eastward to irrigate fields, produce hydroelectric power, and provide water for cities such as Denver and Pueblo.

As the trail leaves the park it passes by the Never Summer Mountains, then proceeds west. Near the ski mecca of Steamboat Springs, the Divide heads north through the Mount Zirkel Wilderness. As in other wilderness areas, only hikers and horseback riders can use the trail. At about ten thousand feet the trail passes into Wyoming.

Wyoming

In southern Wyoming the trail leaves the mountain greenery to make its way across the sagebrush flats and dry gulches of the Great Divide Basin—the longest part of the trail not within national forests, although two-thirds of it is on public grazing land. Formed by a split in the Continental Divide, the basin, or Red Desert, sprawls across more than two million acres. It receives little precipitation and its sunbaked floor hides a wealth of energy sources—coal, oil, natural gas, and uranium ore. It is nearly treeless and can be very hot or very cold. Winds blow incessantly.

The trail follows a low range of mountains that rims the eastern edge of the huge basin, much of which is utilized as ranchland. The region may be dry, but it holds a variety of wildlife: pronghorns, mule deer, coyotes, sage grouse, prairie dogs, and wild horses. To prevent the roaming herds of wild horses from consuming all the good grazing grass the Bureau of Land Management captures more than a thousand of them each year and offers them to public buyers through its Adopt-a-Horse program.

After curving around the Great Divide Basin, hikers traverse South Pass, a high, sagebrush-covered mountain saddle that enabled thousands of emigrants to cross the Rocky Mountains as they sought land, gold, or freedom in the West. A few miles to the east is South Pass City, a gold-mining boomtown a century-and-a-half ago. It once boasted five hotels and thirteen saloons. Only some fifteen year-round residents are left to profit from the steady stream of tourists who drive through on Wyoming 28 and the few who hike through.

Continuing northward into the Bridger-Teton National Forest in the Wind River Range, the hiker realizes how fortunate the old emigrants were to discover the low-lying South Pass. For the next hundred miles the Wind River peaks define the Continental

Divide as a jagged wall. The trail touches or comes close to the highest summits in Wyoming, including Gannett Peak (13,804 feet), as it skirts a number of glaciers.

In the Bridger Wilderness more than one thousand three hundred lakes, soaring granite peaks, and glaciers greet the long-distance hiker. More glaciers exist here than in any other stretch of the Rocky Mountains—more than sixty. The trail dodges numerous ponds and lakes, weaves through boulder fields, and makes its way through scattered chunks of glacial debris.

As the trail approaches the northern end of the national forest, it leads through Two-Ocean Pass. Here a cold forest stream divides into two creeks that flow in opposite directions, a dramatic example of the effect of the Continental Divide. A sign on a trailside tree tells the story: "Parting of the Waters. Atlantic Ocean 3488. Pacific 1353." The numbers refer to the miles water has to travel until it reaches the respective oceans.

Traversing the Shoshone National Forest, the trail cuts across the southwest corner of Yellowstone National Park. Following the Continental Divide Trail through this popular park bestows on the hiker sights and sounds that other visitors to Yellowstone rarely see. The trail crosses a little-visited part of the park, passing through a variety of environments including pine and fir forests, open meadows, and brilliant blue lakes.

Volcanos that erupted 600,000 years ago have made Yellowstone what it is today—a wonderland of steam and heat and vivid colors and pungent smells. The geysers, fumaroles, hot springs, and paint pots are the surface manifestations of the pressure built up from water seeping beneath the earth and coming in contact with an underground sea of red-hot magma.

The national scenic trail route relies on the park's own trails. Orange metal tags tacked to trees or posts show the way, and signs point out destinations and distances, but nowhere is the trail identified with the Continental Divide symbol or name. Before taking the Divide Trail across Yellowstone, the hiker should obtain the park's backcountry permit and ask a ranger to point out the park trails comprising the 74-mile cross-park route.

Nevertheless a special thrill comes from witnessing some of the lesser-known thermal features in the park. In the Heart Lake Geyser Basin the smell of sulfurous vapors leads the hiker to Columbia Spring, Rustic Geyser, and other thermal wonders in a large meadow filled with caldronlike features. Yellowstone's 200 to 250 active geysers equal more than the sum of all the other geysers in the world.

The trail crosses the park's south entrance road and continues past large Lewis Lake. The backpacker comes to Shoshone Geyser Basin, a moonlike display of steaming fumaroles, hot pots, and geysers near the shore of a brilliantly blue lake. At Shoshone, one geyser has three cones that erupt at the same time.

When the trail emerges in the Upper Geyser Basin the hiker suddenly finds himself caught up with the throngs that come each day to see Old Faithful and the other fascinating thermal features that dot the landscape. Here boardwalks and railings guide the visitor; in the backcountry, on the other hand, the trail user must use caution. The thin crust of a hot spring may give way beneath heavy hiking boots. A breakthrough into the steaming water could be fatal.

The hiker sees plenty of evidence of the 1988 fire that ravaged Yellowstone. About one-third of the trail goes through burned areas. But conifer seedlings are growing into trees that will eventually create the lodgepole pine, spruce, and fir forests that covered the landscape before the big burn.

Montana and Idaho

All but a few dozen miles of the trail through Montana and Idaho are enclosed within the green preserves of nine national forests—Targhee, Gallatin, Salmon, Beaverhead, Bitterroot, Deerlodge, Helena, Lewis and Clark, and Flathead—and Glacier National Park. So remote are some wilderness areas that one writer noted that here "a stretch of wild land survives in which a man can walk north for two hundred miles and cross pavement only twice." Through this rugged terrain the hiker finds mostly improved trails and primitive forest roads.

After crossing into Montana the backpacker heads due west along the crestline of the Centennial Mountains, which straddle the Divide as they form the boundary between Montana and Idaho. The windswept terrain is partly forested, with rocky outcrops and grassy meadows. The views down into the Centennial Valley to the north are spectacular.

The trail continues northward along the crestlines of the Beaverhead Range and Bitterroot Range. Jeep trails and forest roads provide the route although clear-cutting of large acreages in these forests occasionally makes the trail hard to find. At Elk Mountain the trail tops 10,000 feet, reaching its second-highest point in Montana and Idaho. It leads across Lemhi Pass, the notch in the mountains that Lewis and Clark struggled through in 1805; the explorers were following an Indian trail that led across the range between Idaho's rivers full of salmon and Montana's bison country.

Mountain goats cling to the rocky flanks, black bears roam the forest, and elk herds and mule deer forage in the meadows. The backpacker is rewarded not only with sightings of wildlife but also with great views of the surrounding peaks and valleys on both sides of the ranges. When the trail intersects the Nez Perce Trail near Gibbons Pass, it winds above the Big Hole Valley where the Nez Perce fought a desperate battle (see page 265).

In an eastward jog from the Bitterroots the trail loops around Anaconda, Butte, then Helena, as it passes through gold and copper country. Beyond Helena it swings close to Marysville, a ghost town of gold rush days where remnants of saloons, shops, and broken sidewalks still line a forgotten main street.

Northward the Continental Divide Trail winds through the Lewis and Clark and Helena National Forests and the Bob Marshall and Scapegoat Wilderness Areas which lie within Flathead National Forest. This vast reserve, part of it named for the Forest Service official and prominent conservationist who helped preserve it, is a region of snowy peaks, alpine lakes, mountain valleys, meandering streams, waterfalls, towering trees, and abundant wildlife. The trail passes directly beneath the magnificent Chinese Wall, a rocky escarpment of limestone a thousand feet high, a cliff embedded with fossils of sea creatures half a billion years old, fossils that reflect the region's ancient history as a sea bottom.

The route through Waterton-Glacier International Peace Park on the United States–Canada border brings this long-distance trail to a spectacular end. The hiker finds his way across the park through glacial valleys and towering peaks on a zigzag route that makes use of some of the 750 miles of trails that crisscross Glacier. The route stays close to the Divide, which is often a forbidding succession of sawtooth peaks and impossible vertical drops that only a mountain goat could love.

The trail in this northerly region is usually passable at lower elevations by mid-June, but many of the high-country passes are not free of snow until late July. When the snow finally leaves, these alpine areas provide the setting for some of the best wild-flower displays in North America. A few of the colorful members of the cast for this short-lived summer spectacle are heather, gentian, beargrass, false dandelion, and glacier lily.

The Continental Divide Trail coincides with the park's popular Highline Trail, which closely parallels the Divide on the home-stretch to the Canadian border. Many short-distance hikers walk this portion of the trail from Logan Pass eight miles to Granite Park Chalet, one of two rustic lodges that offer hot food and bunks to trail users. The visitor center at Logan Pass is a gathering place for hikers and day trippers alike; it is strategically located atop the Divide on the Going-to-the-Sun Road, which transects the park.

For its final miles the epic trail leads mercifully downhill—to the lowest point in its entire length, 4,200 feet, at Waterton Lake. Oddly enough the northern terminus of the long trail is lower in elevation than the southern terminus in the flatlands of New Mexico—by 1,500 feet. At trail's end a boat waits to take the foot-weary traveler across the lake to Canada.

Waterton-Glacier forms a fitting climax to the Continental Divide Trail, this mountainous route linking three nations. Without a doubt hiking or riding horseback the length of this 3,100-mile ribbon of wilderness through the Rocky Mountains is challenge enough for an outdoorsman of any nation.

Continental Divide Trail Society

The Continental Divide Trail Society is dedicated to the planning, development, and maintenance of the Continental Divide National Scenic Trail as a "silent trail," a trail that provides its users with a largely wilderness experience.

To support the trail society members scout the terrain to identify possible trail locations, collect bibliographic and photographic material on the route, and monitor the actions of government agencies responsible for planning and maintaining the trail. It reviews forest management plans, wilderness and scenic river studies, and proposals for railroads and power transmission lines to assess their effect on the natural environment of the trail.

It cooperates with local and regional organizations, encourages volunteer efforts to improve the trail, and serves as a clearinghouse for suggestions from trail users.

The society publishes the five-volume Guide to the Continental Divide Trail. These pocket-size guides provide a thorough mile-by-mile description of the route as it is currently defined. The society also publishes a twice-yearly newsletter, *DIVIDEnds*. For more information write the Continental Divide Trail Society, 3704 N. Charles Street, No. 601, Baltimore, MD 21218.

Continental Divide Trail Alliance

Organized in 1995, the Alliance seeks to mobolize volunteers and out-door-oriented companies into "partnerships" to assist land management agencies such as the U.S. Forest Service in constructing, maintaining, and preserving this "back-country trail along the full length of the Continental Divide from Canada to Mexico."

It aims to develop "an appreciation and enjoyment of America's natural lands through education and the opportunity to experience the Continental Divide National Scenic Trail."

The Alliance brings together individuals with an interest and businesses with a stake in the Continental Divide Trail to discuss and resolve issues about the trail in their state. The Alliance cooperates with existing organizations such as Volunteers for Outdoor Colorado, Colorado Mountain Club, and the Student Conservation Association to carry out volunteer trail work, training, and educational programs for the public. For more information write the Continental Divide Trail Alliance, P.O. Box 628, Pine, CO 80470.

Chapter 8

PACIFIC CREST NATIONAL SCENIC TRAIL

THE PACIFIC CREST TRAIL IS THE COMPANION LONG-DISTANCE pathway of the West to the Appalachian Trail of the East. As with the A.T., the user finds a right-of-way for almost the entire route—with few detours onto paved roads or gaps to interrupt his progress.

On National Trails Day in June 1993 this western long-distance scenic trail was officially declared to be "completed," a continuous trail marked and ready for use by backpackers and equestrians alike. The event took place 25 years after the Pacific Crest had been officially designated as a national scenic trail.

This ribbon of wilderness unravels for 2,600 miles through the high country of the far western mountains—the Sierra Nevada and the Cascade Range—and links the three countries of Mexico, the United States, and Canada. It passes through some of the most scenic areas of California, Oregon, and Washington. Elevations along the trail range from 13,180 feet at Forester Pass, near Mount Whitney in the Sierra Nevada in California, to near sea level, where the trail dips low to cross the Columbia River which separates Oregon and Washington; the altitude of the trail averages 6,000 feet in California, 5,000 feet in Oregon, and 4,000 feet in Washington.

The Pacific Crest Trail negotiates 19 major canyons, passes 1,000 lakes, and climbs through 57 mountain passes. The thru hiker experiences temperatures that range from well above

100°F in areas such as the Mojave Desert of southern California to well below freezing in the high mountains. Sudden drops in temperature are not uncommon—as drastic as from the nineties to below freezing in a single day. The trail as a whole is usually determined to be "passable" from about the beginning of July to the middle of October, but is often completely free of snow only during August and September.

On its way along the ridgetops it goes through 24 national forests (including more than 30 wilderness areas), 7 national parks, 5 state parks, 4 Bureau of Land Management resource areas, and numerous private landholdings.

The fact that this high-country trail extends from border to border would have immensely pleased the man who had the original concept—Clinton C. Clarke, an executive of the YMCA from Pasadena (see page xx). It was Clarke who in the 1930s organized the group of hiking and riding clubs that took the first steps toward developing what would become this spectacular western trail. Clarke even mobilized youngsters from his own YMCAs, sending them out in relays to explore the route he had mapped, each group walking a few days, then passing along a canvas-bound logbook to the next group.

Most of those who take to the completed trail today either backpack or ride with packhorses for a weekend or a vacation of a week or two. A few hardy men and women—only a handful each year—have conquered its entire length. It takes a well-conditioned, well-prepared hiker five months to accomplish this feat, pushing along at a steady pace. Many others have hiked the full length in segments over a number of years. Dr. Ben York, one of the few to ride horseback the entire length of the trail, stressed the self-sufficiency required: "I rode days without seeing another soul," he wrote. "Though I saw some horse tracks, I saw very few riders on the whole two thousand, six hundred thirty-eight miles."

The trail is administered by the U.S. Forest Service as separate segments divided by states. For a general map of the trail through California and brief descriptions of various California segments, write to the USDA Forest Service, Pacific Southwest Region 5, 630 Sansome Street, San Francisco, CA 94111. For maps of the trail in Oregon and Washington, write to the USDA Forest Service, 333 SW First Avenue, P.O. Box 3623, Portland, OR 97208.

California

The southern starting point for the Pacific Crest Trail lies at the Mexican border amid privately owned ranchlands where beef cattle graze. The U.S. Forest Service has negotiated rights-of-way across the ranching country to the Laguna Mountains, where the route climbs into the Cleveland National Forest, its pathway dotted with sagebrush and prickly pear.

The trail continues across the desert-dry washes of Anza-Borrego Desert State Park where it crosses the Juan Bautista de Anza National Historic Trail (see page 273). In the San Bernardino National Forest, the pathway takes the hiker through dry country chaparral: manzanita bushes with their twisted red trunks and sticky red berries; chamise, also called ribbonwood because its bark peels off in strips; and the tall yucca plant with its sword-sharp spiky leaves and huge root that the Indians roasted and ate as food. California live oaks, their shiny, dark green leaves resembling holly, grow among tall pines and scrub oaks, adding variety to the vegetation. Mount San Jacinto (10,804 feet) is the first of many snow-covered peaks the northbound hiker or horseback rider sees.

After winding through the southern section of the forest, the trail dips beneath U.S. Highway 10, connecting Palm Springs with Los Angeles, a roadway that makes use of the same low pass through the mountains that early settlers found to guide their wagons to California.

The San Bernardino National Forest is one of the most heavily visited national forests in the country due to its location near both metropolitan San Diego and Los Angeles. The trail, well marked here with the Pacific Crest Trail symbol and maintained by local trail club volunteers, unwinds through high mountain meadows, steep slopes with awesome boulders, glacier-carved basins, and bubbling streams. A distinctive phenomenon is the pea-soup fog that often settles in the valleys below the trail, even when the atmosphere is clear up on the mountain ridges. The fog, pushing its way inland from the Pacific Ocean, is trapped by the mountains, creating long fingers of white vapor that extend into the mountain valleys.

As the hiker continues northward he or she crosses the Mojave Desert, the biggest interruption in the chain of national forests that provide the green corridor for the trail. Largely uninhabited, the desert sustains sparse vegetation such as the creosote bush and the Joshua tree, a type of yucca that grows taller than a man.

Small mammals such as lizards, ground squirrels, horned toads, jackrabbits, and tortoises all find their own ways to adapt to this environment of extremes.

The hot, dry temperatures in this forbidding landscape can get the best of unwary travelers. Temperatures can reach 120°F, and people have been known to die when deprived of water after only 90 minutes of exposure. Rangers advise all hikers to carry an extra supply of water and to notify friends of their travel plans before they cross this hot, windy expanse.

From the desert the trail climbs back into the mountains, passing through the Domeland Wilderness Area of Sequoia National Forest, which gets its name from the distinctive barren domes of granite that hump up above the trail. Surprisingly, the giant sequoia trees that give their name to this national forest grow far below the trail on the western slopes of the Sierra.

Beyond, in Sequoia National Park, the Pacific Crest Trail links up with one of the best known of the nation's wilderness trails, the John Muir Trail, and makes use of its treadway for nearly two hundred miles to Yosemite National Park. The Muir Trail was completed in 1938.

The trail's namesake, the famed explorer, naturalist, and writer, campaigned tirelessly for forest conservation and was influential in the efforts to preserve Yosemite and Sequoia as national parks. In 1892 this ardent conservationist organized the Sierra Club, still today an effective national environmental organization.

Following the Muir Trail the route skirts the flank of Mount Whitney (14,495 feet), the highest mountain in the lower forty-eight states (the Muir Trail begins at the summit of Mount Whitney), and leads through Forester Pass, the highest point on the Pacific Crest Trail. It winds through the twin parks of Sequoia and King's Canyon past other snow-covered mountains, across streams chilled by meltwater, around ice-choked lakes, through pine forests, and across meadows filled with mountain heather.

From the trail backpackers can spot more than two dozen peaks that rise above 12,000 feet. Occasionally the trail goes through an area of flattened trees, the result of an avalanche that has scoured the mountainside. Avalanches occur when multiple layers of snow fail to bind together to hold the accumulation, allowing the mass to lose its grip on the slope and sweep down the mountainside. Hikers may see avalanche areas several yards to a mile or so in width.

During the summer months the hiker here may meet one of the backcountry rangers who spends the season living in a cabin near the trail, where he or she is ready to warn of any hazards and assist hikers who get lost or need help.

Nearly 170 kinds of birds find a home in these twin parks. Golden eagles nest on the mountain crags. Deer are common, and black bears, mountain lions, bobcats, coyotes, marmots, and smaller animals inhabit the parks.

The Pacific Crest–John Muir Trail then traverses Sierra National Forest and Inyo National Forest before it enters the eastern side of Yosemite National Park, making its way up Lyell Canyon to Tuolumne Meadows. This meadow is the largest subalpine meadow in the Sierras. Because conservationist John Muir feared overgrazing of this meadow by ranchers with their sheep, he launched the campaign that led in 1890 to the establishment of Yosemite as a national park.

Rangers at the Tuolumne Meadows visitor center are glad to guide hikers to see the colorful wildflowers, the wildlife, and the beauty of the region. Here too, outdoor enthusiasts may book a horseback ride of several days. The ride will take them over part of the Pacific Crest Trail, and they may stay overnight at permanent camps set in areas of scenic beauty along the trail.

The scenic trail, in its wilderness setting, is a big contrast to the popular and crowded Yosemite Valley fifty miles across the park to the west, where thousands of walkers, bikers, horseback riders, and sightseers arrive annually to admire the glacially rounded peaks, spectacular waterfalls, and giant sequoias and to watch for deer and black bear.

In the subalpine backcountry where the trail runs, it is a different story. "Of eighty thousand hikers we issued permits to in a recent year for all the park's trails, only eighteen thousand of them used some part of the Pacific Crest Trail," said Ron Mackie, wilderness manager for the park. "The vast majority of these hikers used the two segments of the trail where you have easy access from Tioga Road, the cross-park road."

By routing the trail along the already-existing John Muir Trail, park managers avoided cutting a new trail through the wilderness. No Pacific Crest symbols appear on the route segment through Yosemite, however; follow the local park trail signs instead.

Past Yosemite the Pacific Crest Trail continues through a series of national forests—Stanislaus, Toiyabe, Eldorado, Tahoe,

Plumas, Lassen, and the Tahoe Basin Management Unit—that provide a verdant natural environment for the pathway. As it passes high above the western shore of Lake Tahoe, it intersects the routes of two other national historic trails—the California Trail (see page 211) and the Pony Express Trail (see page 241), both of them making their way over the Sierras from east to west.

The trail runs through the Desolation Wilderness, part of Eldorado National Forest, where the hiker or rider can look down from trail viewpoints to see beautiful, blue Lake Tahoe far below. This segment of the trail, accessible from U.S. Highway 50 at Echo Summit, is one of the most popular sections of the Pacific Crest Trail in California. The 100-square-mile wilderness area encompasses 3 mountain ranges, about 130 lakes (many stocked with trout), and some 70 miles of trails that include 9 miles of the Pacific Crest. This is a land of stark contrasts. Warm summer days, mild falls, and relatively low elevations belie its barren rocky terrain, its harsh, windswept alpine winters, and its sudden summer storms.

Lassen Volcanic National Park in northern California provides a fitting entry for the trail into the Cascade Range, which stretches through Oregon and Washington. Its mountains were born of the volcanic action that still seethes far beneath the surface to this day. Within the park the Pacific Crest Trail runs approximately parallel to the cross-park tour road that leads motor visitors past the impressive collection of thermal phenomena that characterize this miniature Yellowstone—steaming fumaroles, lava plateaus, mudpots, boiling waters, and sulfurous vents. Lassen Peak (10,457 feet) dominates the park and is the southernmost of a chain of volcanos that extends nearly seven hundred miles northward into British Columbia.

For much of its way through the park, the trail winds through a mature conifer forest where western white pine, Jeffrey pine, lodgepole pine, ponderosa pine, and red fir trees lift their crowns overhead. But the underlying volcanic features are never far away. Boiling Springs Lake lives up to its name; hot vapors gurgle upward from mudpots that edge the lake's turbid waters.

A two-mile side trip over an east-west trail once used by pioneers headed for California—the Nobles-Emigrant Trail—brings the hiker to the Cinder Cone, a nearly perfect cone formed a half century ago when molten rock from beneath the earth exploded and sprayed the surrounding landscape with red-hot lava and cinders.

A trail leads up the steep, bare sides to the top of the cinder cone, a 750-foot climb. At the top the hiker gets a look into two or possibly three craters. Willow, western white pine, and lodgepole pine trees have established precarious footholds within the craters. Eventually the trees will fill these depressions unless the volcano erupts once more.

In the area that surrounds the cinder cone volcanic ash has accumulated up to eight feet in depth. Lava flows from the base of the volcano have solidified into a jumble of lava chunks, while at other places fallen ash has created dark dunes painted in a variety of colors. Farther away a shallow blanket of soil built up by dying pine needles and deteriorating trees covers the cinders. The pines that grow in this thin soil—sometimes to surprising heights—have adapted to the poor soil, water, sunlight, and temperature conditions. Their shallow roots, long-lived needles, and overall shape make the most of their opportunity to survive in the poor soil, short growing season, and deep snows they endure.

At McArthur-Burney Falls Memorial State Park, north of Lassen, Pacific Crest Trail users come upon an oasis surrounding a cool stream and waterfall that seem out of place in this terrain, which owes its origin to fiery volcanic eruptions. The trail follows a rim route within the park that leads through a ponderosa pine forest high above the rushing waters of Burney Creek, a stream that emerges from beneath the earth's surface from reservoirs of cool, pure water that have accumulated in great voids that were formed long ago by cooling lava. At spectacular Burney Falls, an underground stream pours out of a stratum of basalt and cascades into a vivid blue pool at the base of a cliff, then flows through a canyon it has cut for itself through the rock.

Trail users get a close-up look at basalt cliffs that look like so much black Swiss cheese. As the lava cooled many years ago, gas bubbled up from inside the lava in much the same way that bubbles do in yeast-filled bread dough. Visitors today see the pockmarked results, now turned to basalt rock and frozen in time.

As the Pacific Crest reaches the northernmost part of California, it curves westward, swinging within 50 miles of the Pacific Ocean before it straightens out once again to follow the Cascade Mountains into Oregon. A familiar landmark here is snow-covered Mount Shasta; the 14,162-foot peak can be glimpsed by hikers along 350 miles of the route.

Oregon

Snaking through the Rogue River and Umpqua National Forests, the trail enters Crater Lake National Park. Here backpackers and equestrians alike get the opportunity to see one of the most breathtaking views along the trail—the brilliant blue lake that fills the caldera that resulted when a volcanic eruption collapsed the top of a mountain.

The cataclysmic eruption that forever changed the topography of Crater Lake occurred more than seven thousand seven hundred years ago. The mountain, Mount Mazama, sustained a climactic series of eruptions that produced a huge cloud of gas, smoke, ash, and debris that spread over what would become eight states and three Canadian provinces; some five thousand square miles were covered with six inches of ash, including the park's Pumice Desert, which the trail goes through. These eruptions are estimated to have been forty-two times greater than those of the formidable eruption of Mount St. Helens in 1980. As Mazama's magma chamber belowground rapidly emptied, the entire 12,000-foot volcanic mountaintop collapsed, leaving the bowl-shaped caldera for visitors to see today.

When the volcanic activity gradually ceased the caldera slowly filled with rain and melted snow. At a later time, another small cinder cone within the caldera erupted, pushing its conical shape above the water level to form what is now called Wizard Island.

Users of the Pacific Crest Trail get the same opportunity to view this spectacular scene as do other park visitors, since the trail closely skirts the caldera for six miles. At trail overlooks, hikers gaze down the steep slope from the rim to the blue lake 1,000 feet below, the seventh-deepest lake in the world. Horseback riders take an alternate trail inland, but can use a spur trail that brings them to a hitching area close to the lake so they too can admire the magnificent view.

Crater Lake's beauty, however, is available to hikers for only three months of the average year because of the heavy snows that cover this 7,000-foot mountaintop. More than five hundred inches of snow falls in an average winter, making this one of the snowiest places in the country. When the weather clears, skiers replace hikers on the trail.

Three national forests—Umpqua, Willamette, and Mount Hood—spread their green woods to allow the trail to twist northward through the volcanic Cascades. The pathway passes through four wilderness areas within these forest boundaries, pristine areas where man's touch is light and Forest Service rules are strict. As they tread the rumpled ridges, hikers on a clear day can catch sight of no fewer than nine snow-covered peaks between 7,800 and 11,000 feet high between Crater Lake and Mount Hood.

At Mount Hood itself, near the northern border of Oregon, the trail circles the huge mountain's southern and western flanks at about treeline, leading through groves of Douglas and red fir, mountain hemlock, and ponderosa pine, across alpine meadows, and past cascading waterfalls. Hikers stay under tree cover most of the way, avoiding the snowfields and glaciers that extend their white fingers toward the trail even during the summer months.

On Mount Hood's south flank, the Pacific Crest Trail intersects yet another historic trail, the Barlow Road cutoff of the Oregon Trail (see page 207). This rough road, hacked through the dense forest, allowed the trail-weary pioneers on the Oregon Trail to avoid a treacherous ride with their wagons on rafts through the Columbia River rapids. Today signs mark a quiet crossroads created by the meeting of the scenic trail and the venerable east-west wagon road. Motorists driving over Mount Hood on Oregon 35 can turn off, drive a short distance, and view this trail juncture. Leaving a parking area, travelers may walk a section of both the Pacific Crest National Scenic Trail and the Barlow cutoff of the Oregon National Historic Trail.

The hiker is guaranteed company on the trail when the path reaches the famed Timberline Lodge, a rustic hotel built on the slopes of Mount Hood in 1937 as a project to provide jobs during the Depression years. Some 450 men labored to raise it; more than 100 artists and artisans embellished it with paintings, panels of wall carvings, mosaics, woven draperies, and hooked rugs. Today the big lodge is a mecca for skiers, hikers, rock climbers, and snowboarders who schuss down the slopes above the lodge— one of the few places in the country where people can ski year-round. Mount Hood serves as the summer home for the U.S. Ski Team. Hikers who make a short detour from the Pacific Crest may join the climbers to register at the U.S. Forest Service registration point at the lodge.

Washington

Crossing the Columbia River Gorge on the Bridge of the Gods at Cascade Locks, Oregon (the lowest point on the entire route), the trail moves into Washington state, climbing rapidly back into the Cascade Range. Passing over the western shoulder of Mount Adams, at 12,307 feet the third-highest peak in the Cascades, it continues to Mount Rainier National Park.

Rainier, a gleaming landmark, is visible for hundreds of miles when the weather is clear. It is the loftiest peak in the Cascades (14,410 feet) and rises higher above its base than any other mountain in the lower forty-eight.

The trail traces creek valleys through the eastern section of the park, where heavy precipitation spurs the growth of dark, cathedral-like forests—Douglas fir, western hemlock, western red cedar, Sitka spruce, and Pacific silver fir. Miles from the trail, in the center of the park, climbers carefully work their way up the glaciers that lead to the snow-covered summit. The glaciers of Mount Rainier comprise the most extensive "single peak" glacial system in North America outside of Alaska.

From Snoqualmie Pass, where the Pacific Crest Trail crosses I-90, the final segment of the long-distance trail twists toward the Canadian border. The hiker finds tough going as he or she negotiates the ridges and valleys of Washington's North Cascades, passing through Snoqualmie, Mount Baker, and Okanagan National Forests and North Cascades National Park. Heavy snows close off most of the route through these mountains until July. The trail circles the flank of Glacier Peak (10,568 feet), a peak that is appropriately named for the glaciers that cover its slopes.

It is a challenging ending to the trail. Storm clouds often sweep across the jagged peaks. The trail zigzags past lakes that remain icebound throughout the year. Severe storms make trail conditions "subject to change without notice."

A bronze obelisk marks the end of the Pacific Crest Trail at a location that is just a few miles from the Trans-Canada Highway in Canada's Manning Park. Those who reach the terminus often leave a note about their adventure for the hikers who follow after them. The rare individual who completes this 2,638-mile journey will have experienced a splendid tapestry of landscape—desert and mountain, meadow and forest, lake and glacier, valley and peak—the inspiring scenery that characterizes this western mountain rampart traced by the Pacific Crest Trail.

Pacific Crest Trail Association

The Pacific Crest Trail Association is an organization of trail enthusiasts—those who hike it, those who guide their horses over it, and those who help preserve and protect it. Trail users make up the bulk of the membership, and they come from all over the country, Canada, Alaska, and many other countries.

The association coordinates an "Adopt-a-Trail" program wherein specific trail segments are adopted for maintenance and improvement by individuals or organizations such as the Back Country Horsemen, outdoor clubs, and Boy Scout or Girl Scout troops.

It provides and maintains more than forty registers along the trail, in which hikers and riders jot down information about trail conditions and events to exchange with other trail users. The registers also help officials locate a traveler on the trail in the event of an emergency. The association publishes a current list of post offices and other locations near the trail that are willing to hold mail and provisions for thru hikers.

PCTA links up through a matching process people searching for someone to accompany them on a hike or a ride. It maintains a roster of those who complete the entire length of the trail, awards completion certificates, and publicizes their accomplishment.

It publishes a bimonthly newsletter about trail activities, *The Communicator,* which provides information to the public about the trail, publishes a bibliography of guidebooks and trip accounts, and sends delegates to represent the membership at trail conferences and legislative hearings.

For more information, including a three-page illustrated brochure that describes the trail and includes a map of the entire trail length, write the Pacific Crest Trail Association, 5325 Elkhorn Boulevard, Sacramento, CA 95842. A more detailed information packet is available for a nominal charge.

Section Two
NATIONAL HISTORIC TRAILS

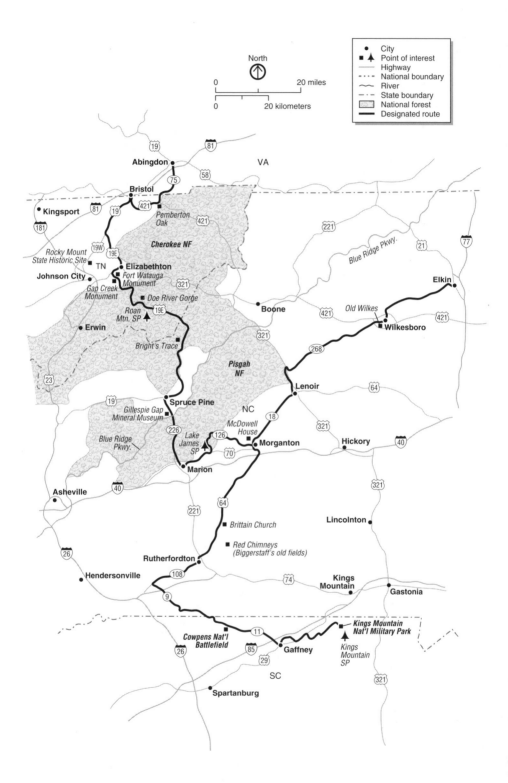

Chapter 9

Overmountain Victory National Historic Trail

T HE OVERMOUNTAIN VICTORY NATIONAL HISTORIC TRAIL, WHICH TRACES its route from the valleys of Virginia across the Appalachian Mountains to South Carolina, has several distinctions from other national historic trails:

- It is the only national historic trail that lies entirely east of the Mississippi River.
- It is the only one to commemorate the route of march of a military campaign.
- It springs to life dramatically each fall when a close-knit group of history buffs duplicates the march their frontier ancestors made over these mountains, a campaign that resulted in a convincing military victory over British forces at the Battle of Kings Mountain during the Revolutionary War.

Each September volunteers of the Overmountain Victory Trail Association turn back the clock to the days when the American colonies were fighting for their political freedom against the oppressive rule of England. Dressed in frontier buckskins and homespun outfits and carrying their trusty Pennsylvania long rifles, the marchers reenact the historic trek, which lasted from September 23 to October 7 and resulted in a critical victory for the patriot cause, a victory that historians say was as decisive to the outcome of the war as the more widely heralded victories at Lexington and Saratoga.

These latter-day marchers know the story well. The events they commemorate took place in 1780 when the war between the thirteen rebellious colonies and England had been going on for five weary years. After years of seesaw battling to a near-stalemate in New England and the Middle Atlantic states, the British had invaded the southern states. King George's generals were convinced that "large numbers of the inhabitants would flock to the King's standard" because the southerners were dependent on England for much of their trade.

British forces had captured the important seaports of Savannah and Charleston, and under the command of Major General Charles Cornwallis they were sweeping northward through South Carolina and Georgia into North Carolina, endeavoring to link up with the main British army in New York. To protect his left flank, Cornwallis ordered Major Patrick Ferguson to make a wide western sweep, recruiting southern loyalists to his side and subduing any troublesome inhabitants along the frontier.

Moving into North Carolina, Ferguson attempted to intimidate the western settlers known as the "overmountain men." These settlers lived in the valleys west of the Appalachians, disregarding an earlier Proclamation Act by the king, which had established a line along the ridge of the mountains. No Indians, the king had decreed, were to live east of the ridgeline and no settlers were to live west of the line. The act was designed to ease tensions among the Indians, the loyalists, the patriots, and the British. But settlers moving down through the Shenandoah Valley seeking good farmland had settled west of the line, placing themselves outside both the protection and approval of the crown.

Ferguson, derisively referring to these settlers as the "backwater men," threatened to march into the mountains and "lay waste the country with fire and sword" if the overmountain men did not lay down their arms and pledge allegiance to King George III.

Ferguson's threats, rather than intimidating the overmountain men, acted as a spur to action. Until now these western settlers had been little threatened by the war, but this was different. The frontiersmen reacted almost spontaneously to the threat, mobilizing their volunteer militias in the same way they had mobilized at other times when Indian attacks threatened.

Farmers left their plows, artisans foresook their workbench, hunters and trappers came in from the woods. Many left their families to carry on without them while they responded to the emergency call.

The patriot contingents assembled from two directions: Militiamen under the command of Isaac Shelby, John Sevier, William Campbell, and Charles McDowell came from what is now eastern Tennessee, southwestern Virginia, and western North Carolina, while troops under Benjamin Cleveland and Joseph Winston marched in from the northern border region of North Carolina. The two contingents came together and consolidated forces at McDowell's farm at Morganton, North Carolina.

Instead of waiting for Ferguson to come to them, these men of action determined to make a preemptive strike and to pursue Ferguson before he could attack them.

Leaving the few wives and families who had accompanied them this far, as well as a herd of cattle, they marched into the Blue Ridge mountain range of the Appalachians. They followed obscure Indian trails through the mountain gaps as they made their way across some of the most rugged terrain of eastern America. Sometimes they had to leave the trail entirely and strike out overland across the steep and rocky, forest-covered slopes.

The overmountain men caught up with Ferguson and his loyalist troops atop a ridge known as Kings Mountain just over today's border in South Carolina. Here Ferguson and his forces were confidently dug in, occupying the high ground in a classic defensive position. In one intense hour of battle the overmountain men fought their way up the slopes to defeat the loyalists—and the momentum of the war shifted in the South. The overmountain patriots, far from being intimidated, had turned on the British, dealing them a crushing blow, killing Ferguson, demolishing Cornwallis's left flank, and scoring the first major victory in the South for the colonists. Never again would the British be able to recruit an easy following of loyalists to fight against the patriots. The victory of the overmountain men forced the British to retreat and gave the Continental Army a much-needed boost in morale. It became the first victory in a campaign that presently would push the British out of the Carolinas, a campaign that led to the surrender of the British forces at Yorktown one year later. Thomas Jefferson later called the Battle of Kings Mountain "the turn of the tide to success" in the American Revolution.

The visitor who comes to Abingdon, Virginia, south of Roanoke near the southwestern tip of the state, on September 23 each year will find gathering there a group of hardy members of the Overmountain Victory Trail Association, volunteers ready to once again reenact the 310-mile march of the overmountain men.

The marchers, all of whom have an abiding interest in history, come from a variety of backgrounds. On one recent march there was a technical writer for a high-technology firm, a 77-year-old retired teacher, a grandfather and his teenage granddaughter, a tobacco farmer, a retired engineer, a former Marine colonel, several women members of the trail association, and a retired gentleman of 78 who flew in from Florida so as not to miss the event. "We welcome everybody to come and join us," said Bob Sweeny, a president of the OVTA. "They may march for a day or two or for the entire two weeks if they wish."

Occasionally a teacher will join the march for a day with some of his or her students. On one reenactment, parents of home-study students used the march as a field trip experience for the young people.

Those not up to marching long miles of county roads, walking mountain foot trails, fording waist-deep streams, and sleeping in the spartan accommodations, as the reenactors do, may follow the route by auto through the four states of Virginia, Tennessee, North Carolina, and South Carolina. Each state has marked the historic trail with brown-and-white identification signs and occasional historical interpretation signs. Some of the signs spell out "Overmountain Victory Trail" while other, smaller signs simply bear the likeness of a militiaman with his rifle outlined in white on a brown background. Signs have been erected on interstate highways so motorists can tell where the historic trail crosses the interstate.

An indispensable aid to anyone following the trail by auto is the folder entitled "Overmountain Victory National Historic Trail, Commemorative Motor Route," which is published by the National Park Service and is available free of charge. The illustrated guide depicts the historical route, shows federal and state highways that cross it, and includes the dates of events that occurred during the march, along with their significance. To get a copy of the folder write to the National Park Service, Southeast Field Office, 75 Spring Street SW, Atlanta, GA 30303.

You might also want to write for a slim, fourteen-page book-let that is available from the Overmountain Victory Trail Association. The "Overmountain Victory Trail Reenactment Almanac" describes the events that occurred on each day of the march in 1780 together with details about what normally occurs during each year's reenactment march: the terrain to be walked, the distance to be covered each day, the campground site, customary ceremonies to be observed, and historic sites along the route. To obtain a copy write to the Overmountain Victory Trail Association (see page 143).

Virginia

The reenactment got its start in 1975 as part of the celebration of the bicentennial of the American Revolution when a number of descendants of the overmountain men organized and retraced the steps of their forebears. They carried petitions and collected thousands of signatures requesting Congress to designate the route as a national historic trail. In September 1980, just before the 200th anniversary of the Battle of Kings Mountain, they got their wish when Congress approved the trail designation.

A typical day's hike for reenactors near Rocky Mount, Virginia.

The march is precisely duplicated; the reenactors spend each night close to the location where the 1780 militiamen originally camped. The gathering point for the first night of camping is "Dunn's Meadow," an open field along a stream in Abingdon. Many reenactors come dressed for the time period; the contingent was "an army without a uniform," in contrast to the colorfully clad loyalist troops they opposed.

The original militiamen were almost completely independent of the usual royal authority in the eastern colonies. They were of Irish, Scotch, Welsh, English, French, and German ancestry. Most were hardy, diligent hunters, small farmers, herdsmen, and artisans. If he was a farmer the militiaman left his fields for his family to till; if a tradesman, he turned the shop over to his wife. Each man provided his own clothing, his own horse, his own rifle, and often much of his own food. The officers, who were elected by their units, were expected to provide gunpowder and supplies.

Like their forebears today's marchers wear hunting shirts of fringed buckskin or homespun linsey-woolsey (a combination of wool and linen). The shirt, made more like a loose blouse, reaches to the knees. The shirt was cut long so the frontiersman could gather it up at the ends to make a pouch, put a quarter bushel of corn or other produce into the pouch, then tie the shirt ends around his waist to carry his load home.

Breeches and gaiters to protect against the underbrush were made from rough, homespun cloth and were worn above high-topped shoes of cowhide or leather moccasins. Some men let their hair grow long so they could tie it in a queue that hung down their back under a broad-brimmed hat. The hat and a blanket provided the overmountain man the only protection he had from rain or snow. Each man carried his own cup, knife, perhaps a pipe and tobacco, and a wallet of provisions—often parched corn mixed with maple sugar. These he carried in a "possibles bag," which hung from a strap over one shoulder.

The frontiersman's prized possession was his Pennsylvania rifle (or Kentucky rifle, as it was sometimes known). Remarkable for its precision and range, this weapon was also known as the Deckard or Dickert rifle after its maker in Lancaster, Pennsylvania. Its spiral (rifled) bore gave it far greater accuracy than the smoothbore muskets the British used. From its curly maple butt to the tip of its octagonal barrel, the Pennsylvania rifle measured 48 to 62 inches and weighed from 8 to 12 pounds. Each militiaman carried a powder horn slung around his neck. Powder horns were often individualized, bearing carvings that the owner had whittled during long winter nights, and most of the rifles bore names given them by their owners.

Getting right into the spirit of the event at a recent reenactment, the reenactors ate a first meal of beef stew cooked in an iron kettle over an open fire, then sat around under a tent telling stories of earlier reenactments and listening to the music of a hammered dulcimer and a harmonica played by Virginia friends who come out every year to entertain the marchers at their first evening campsite.

A number of each year's marchers have family connections to the event and want to learn as much as they can about their ancestors. Short side trips during the two-week march add historical sidelights. One visitor to Abingdon from nearby Johnson City, Tennessee, joined the group around the campfire to learn any details the others might know about his family's participation two centuries before.

Each September 24 the overmountain trek begins. The "core marchers," those who will walk the entire route, take to the secondary roads that overlie most of the historic route. Others who cannot walk the entire way follow in their cars. At the head of the column marches the safety marshal, who guides the group and warns of approaching traffic. The grand marshal brings up the rear, checking for stragglers. If there is a young person in the marching group, he or she is usually chosen to carry the red, white, and blue Overmountain Victory Trail banner at the front of the day's procession.

The marchers average 15 to 20 miles a day. Occasional stops are planned to let the participants catch their breath, take note of a historic marker or gravesite, or simply talk to a farmer or landowner. Reenactors have one advantage their predecessors did not have: Lunch and dinner are usually provided by a patriotic, civic, or church group that volunteers each year to feed the hungry marchers. The resulting meals are a lot better than the parched corn and dried beef the original militiamen carried with them or the occasional pumpkin, apple, or nuts they might pick up along the way.

Over the years the Daughters of the American Revolution chapters have been particularly active in feeding and providing for the reenactors, as have most of the towns along the route. For example, two rural property owners built a new gate in their fence line so the annual marchers could more easily use their pasture as a campsite.

On the first day of the march the reenactors come face-to-face with a reminder of the Revolutionary War days—a venerable old tree. The huge white oak grows near the site just over the border in Tennessee where Captain John Pemberton mustered seventy-five men into the expeditionary force in 1780. Even then, the "Pemberton Oak" was several hundred years old; today it is a patriarch of more than five hundred years whose twisted limbs sweep upward and whose trunk is so large four men cannot reach around it. It is listed on the National Register of Historic Places. "It's one of the few participants of the battle that is still living," one reenactor commented. Each year the marchers fire a volley as a salute to the tree and to the volunteers who mustered here.

Tennessee

Sycamore Shoals on the Watauga River poses a challenge for the marchers, as it did for the original militiamen who had to guide their horses across this shallow ford. The cool water is a welcome relief to sore feet, but the algae-covered rocks that line the bottom make for treacherous footing as the marchers wade across the 50-yard-wide stream. Although the water is usually at midcalf level, it can be higher if the marchers arrive later than the normal 2 P.M. release of water from an upstream dam.

Changing their shoes after wading the stream, the reenactors explore a replica of Fort Watauga, part of Sycamore Shoals State Historic Area located near Elizabethton. The original fort was constructed here to protect the overmountain settlers from hostile Indians. In 1780 Sycamore Shoals served as a major rendezvous point for the various contingents: 200 Virginians under William Campbell; 240 Tennesseans under Isaac Shelby; 240 Tennesseans under John Sevier; 160 men who had already been fighting the British east of the mountains; and 200 more Virginians under Arthur Campbell.

During the march the latter-day Revolutionary War militiamen share their knowledge with the public along the way. They give evening programs at parks and historic areas, including talks about colonial dress, battle tactics, the role of women in the war, and demonstrations of the Pennsylvania rifle. Stops during the day often include firing a commemorative salute at sites such as the grave of a Kings Mountain militiaman.

The reenactors are also invited to talk to school classes and assemblies. From time to time one or two marchers will break away from the day's journey to appear in their eighteenth-century garb to give local students a sense of the significance of the commemorative march that is passing through their community that day. The association has written and printed a teacher's guide that is used by elementary school teachers to prepare their students for the day the Overmountain Victory marchers come to town. In a further educational effort, the association sponsors a contest for schools along the route in which students submit a poster, essay, poem, or painting on the theme of the historic march; winners receive a cash prize and a certificate.

The educational efforts seem to have paid dividends. One boy in Rutherford County, North Carolina, listened to a talk by one of the marchers when he was six years old. Now a teenager, he appears each year when the marchers come through, brings along a couple of friends, and hikes with them for several days.

History rubs off on the younger generation. One sixth-grader was heard to remark: "I don't see how they could walk all the way from Virginia. My legs would be worn out—and they only got one set of clothes!"

North Carolina

By the time they marched out from Sycamore Shoals and Fort Watauga in 1780, the rapidly mobilized Revolutionary War strike force of frontiersmen was eleven hundred strong. Following in their footsteps today's marchers now tackle the hardest part of the trek as they push ahead into mountain gaps and thread their way up the steep slopes of the Blue Ridge Range of the Appalachians, the same mountain range that at the time of the Revolution effectively separated the overmountain settlements of the western valley from the settlements on the eastern piedmont.

The route leads through Roan Mountain State Park and on to Roan Mountain (6,285 feet), a bald mountaintop where few trees grow, but which displays one of the largest natural rhododendron stands in the world. In the spring this mountaintop brightens with masses of pink blooms; but when the original overmountain men gained the summit they found instead snow that was shoetop-deep.

The reenactors pass through part of the Pisgah National Forest, part of Cherokee National Forest, and through Yellow Mountain Gap (5,000 feet), where they cross the Appalachian National Scenic Trail, which follows the crest of the Blue Ridge and delineates the border between Tennessee and North Carolina. A trailside exhibit here tells the A.T. hikers the story of the Overmountain Victory Trail. For much of the way across the ridge the hikers follow U.S. Highway 19E, which closely approximates the Old Yellow Mountain Trail, the earliest connecting link between the eastern piedmont and the Watauga settlement. The highway then picks up the route of Bright's Trace, a footpath that the original contingent followed across the mountains. When the trail reaches the village of Spruce Pine, the marchers find a marker along the highway that points out where they can still see some of the original road ruts of the Old Yellow Mountain Trail.

Leaving the wagon road, the marchers strike off cross-country through woods and around rhododendron thickets as they follow the North Toe and Nolichucky Rivers, finally crossing the river on a swinging bridge. They pause to fire a rifle salute at the grave of Robert Sevier, who was severely wounded at Kings Mountain. Robert's brother John was one of the leaders of the overmountain campaign. Although warned by a doctor to remain behind to recuperate after the battle, Robert Sevier insisted that his men carry him home, but he died of his wounds during the trip back.

At Gillespie Gap the marchers cross the Blue Ridge Parkway, the scenic parkway that runs along the crest of the Blue Ridge Mountains for 355 miles from Great Smoky Mountains National Park in North Carolina northward to Shenandoah National Park in Virginia. A visitor center located where North Carolina 226 crosses the Blue Ridge Parkway contains the Museum of North Carolina Minerals, where specimens of all the state's minerals are exhibited.

The trail descends the eastern flank of the mountain range along North Carolina 126 and leads to the town of Morganton, North Carolina. Two centuries ago, before the present small city grew up, this was Quaker Meadows, the site of the farm and home of Colonel Charles McDowell and his brother Joseph, also a militiaman. Earlier in the rebellion, Charles McDowell had led his North Carolina militiamen on several hit-and-run guerrilla attacks on Ferguson's forces.

At the McDowell plantation the 1,000 men who had hiked over the mountains were augmented by 350 more under the command of Colonel Benjamin Cleveland and Colonel Joseph Winston, swelling the patriot force to its full 1,400 men. Diaries of the time relate that the militiamen were given permission to burn some of McDowell's fence rails to stoke up their fires against the mountain chill. The two-story brick home that replaced the one existing when the overmountain men camped there has been restored by the Historic Burke Foundation and is open to the public. A roadside marker tells the history of Quaker Meadows, a site included on the National Register of Historic Places.

South Carolina

The Overmountain Victory Trail now follows a zigzag route past piedmont farmlands and towns to its destination at Kings Mountain, which lies just over the border in South Carolina. From Morganton, the trail goes southwest, then swings back toward the east. This direction reversal reflects the historical fact that the overmountain men themselves changed their direction of march after they received reports from scouts on horseback that their foe was about to head northward toward Charlotte, where Cornwallis was camped with his main force. The patriots stepped up the pace, determined to engage Ferguson before he could move away. "Our forces have the Britisher Ferguson on the run," wrote a captain of the militiamen at the time. "We are on his trail and ... the Tories will remember our faces."

At Green River, near the present-day North Carolina–South Carolina border, the overmountain men prepared to do battle, choosing 910 of their best fighters and healthiest horses for the final push. Making only a brief stop at Cowpens (now a national battlefield that commemorates a later Revolutionary War victory over the British) the patriot force covered the final fifty miles in scarcely thirty-five hours, riding through the rain all night. The next afternoon at 3 P.M., October 7, 1780, they reached the foot of the elevated ridge called Kings Mountain.

The frontiersmen encircled the ridge and climbed its sides in the face of enemy fire, taking cover behind rocks and trees as they fired back at the loyalists. They repelled several attacks by the loyalist soldiers, picking off their attackers one by one. Tightening their circle they fought on up the wooded slopes. Hard-pressed,

Ferguson blew a high piercing note on his silver whistle and then astride his horse led a desperate charge to try to break out of the deadly circle. A rifle bullet struck him and seven more pierced his body as he fell from his mount. Not a loyalist soldier escaped being killed, wounded, or captured as the militiamen gained a complete victory at a cost of only twenty-eight killed and sixty-two wounded. The hard-fought engagement was over in an hour.

Today two monuments stand on the ridgetop where the climax of the battle took place. The grave of Patrick Ferguson is nearby, close to a great poplar that may date to the battle. When the reenactors reach the battle site they conduct a ceremony in the amphitheater of Kings Mountain National Military Park, which now preserves the ridgeline site. The ceremony normally includes a welcome from the national park superintendent, several speeches, and the awarding of certificates to all who have completed the 14-day march. Then everyone walks uphill for a short memorial service atop the ridge among the battle monuments.

For the marchers the two weeks of arduous walking and the experience at Kings Mountain have a strong impact. "It is important to stay connected to the past and our roots." said Sweeny, who has made the march twelve times. "It should be equally important to all Americans."

During a recent year's commemorative march the reenactors told the story of the historic trek to 2,500 students in schools along the route and attracted 500 people to ten community

Firing commemorative salute at Pemberton Oak.

presentations. "It brings us close to people," one of the participants said. "It's as simple as a homeowner offering us a drink or
as involved as a local group providing us with a hot meal or a
place to sleep."

After its two-week epic march each year, the latter-day militiamen disband and head home—just as their predecessors did
200 years ago. No sooner had the Battle of Kings Mountain been
won on that October day in 1780 than the overmountain men
disbanded as an organized fighting force. Back over the Appalachians they marched, back to their farms and shops and families
and the freedom to live the life they had fought for. Today the
route markers and interpretive signs of the Overmountain Victory National Historic Trail enable others to relive the success
earned by this instant army and to gain an appreciation of the
legacy left by the courage and determination of our forefathers.

Overmountain Victory Trail Association

The association grew from a group of history-minded individuals who
banded together in 1976 to reenact the march of the overmountain men to
Kings Mountain as part of the celebration of the bicentennial of the American
Revolution. Following the event the group played an active role in advocating
the establishment of the route as a national historic trail.

Its membership is composed of local people who live along the route,
descendants of the overmountain men, and Americans all over the country
who share an interest in history, colonial life, and American heritage. Each year
the association organizes the Overmountain Victory Trail reenactment, which
starts each September in Abingdon, Virginia, and concludes at Kings Mountain
National Military Park near Gaffney, South Carolina. It keeps its membership
informed through its quarterly newsletter.

In addition to the annual reenactment the association promotes public
education through hikes, tours, presentations, scholarship programs, trail
guides, and research on the historical significance of the patriots who took part
in the battle in 1780. It cooperates with local, state, and national groups to
identify and mark the route and to preserve the trail environment.

For more information write the Overmountain Victory Trail Association,
1651 West Elk Avenue, Elizabethton, TN 37643.

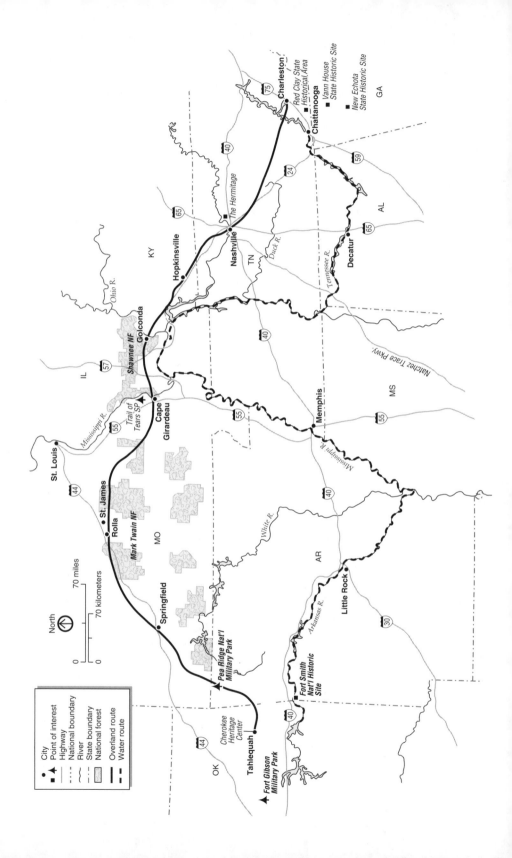

Chapter 10

TRAIL OF TEARS NATIONAL HISTORIC TRAIL

T HE YEAR WAS 1838, A FATEFUL YEAR FOR THE CHEROKEES. A KNOCK
could come at any time at the door of a Cherokee log or frame
home in North Carolina, South Carolina, or Georgia. The uni-
formed men who stood at the doorway were some of the seven
thousand U.S. soldiers who had been ordered into the Cherokee
domain to forcibly evict these Native Americans from the lands
they had farmed and fished and hunted on for generations.

"Men working in the fields were arrested and driven to the
stockades," wrote Private John G. Burnett of the Second Regi-
ment, Second Brigade of the Mounted Infantry, one of the soldiers
who carried out the forced removal. "Women were dragged from
their homes by soldiers whose language they could not understand. Children were often separated from their parents and driven
into the stockades with the sky for a blanket and the earth for a
pillow. And often the old and infirm were prodded with bayonets
to hasten them to the stockades."

This cruel transplanting of a whole nation was the last step in a
series of developments that dated back two centuries to the time
when immigrating Europeans first arrived in America. Tradition-
ally the Cherokees had lived in villages in the southern Appalachians—present-day Virginia, West Virginia, Kentucky, Tennessee,
western North Carolina and South Carolina, northern Georgia, and
northeastern Alabama. Here, in a land of valleys, ridges, mountains,
and streams, they had their own highly developed culture.

As more and more white settlers came the Cherokees responded by modifying their lifestyle, adopting many of the European ways, even bringing about a deterioration of their own culture. During the colonial period the Cherokees as well as other Indian tribes became embroiled in the European colonial wars. As a result the Cherokees, who aided the British during the American Revolution, were forced by treaties to give up parts of their homeland.

Nevertheless the Cherokees prospered as farmers and small businessmen. Some even owned large plantations and kept black slaves. Other Cherokees built European-style homes and farmsteads, laid out European-style fields and farms, developed their own written language, established a newspaper, and wrote a constitution. They learned English, went to school, operated stores and ferries, used metal tableware, ran sawmills and gristmills, and improved their roads. A series of treaties with the U.S. government recognized the tribe as a nation with its own land, laws, and customs.

But the developing United States was uncomfortable with this autonomous Indian nation in its midst. National policy to move all the eastern Indians to areas west of the Mississippi had begun to develop after the Louisiana Territory had been purchased from the French in 1803. When gold was discovered on Cherokee land in 1828 in northern Georgia, pressure from the whites, particularly in Georgia, redoubled. In 1830 Congress, at the urging of President Andrew Jackson, passed the Indian Removal Act, which gave the president the authority to use some of the new territory acquired west of the Mississippi to provide alternative homelands for all the eastern Indian tribes, including the Cherokees. The law specified that the president could act only with the Indians' consent, that the Indians would be compensated for their eastern lands, and that they would be given a new territory in the West to which they would hold perpetual title.

Tens of thousands of Indians, many of whom had intermarried with whites and owned homes, livestock, and farms, were caught up in the removal and were forced to leave with their families. The Choctaws, Chickasaws, Creeks, Cherokees, and Seminoles, known as "the five civilized tribes," were torn into factions as their leaders tried to determine the best policy for their people, whether to resist or to accept removal peaceably and build new lives elsewhere. Some Indians became so desperate they turned to violence; others petitioned the courts, addressing cries of injustice and appeals to the conscience of the white American population.

The first to leave for the West were the Choctaws, who emigrated amid great hardship in November 1831. The Creeks delayed for four years, but when anguished violence began to spread among them, the Army moved in, and in 1836 the entire membership of what was left of the once-mighty Creek confederacy was marched west, some of the Indians in handcuffs. In 1837 the Chickasaws were removed.

The Georgia legislature had passed laws taking possession of Cherokee lands and suspending the tribe's legislature and courts. The Cherokees, under their principal chief, John Ross, fought this discrimination in the courts and thought they had won a victory when the Supreme Court, in a decision written by Chief Justice John Marshall, sustained their right to their southeastern lands and declared the acts of the State of Georgia unconstitutional and in violation of solemn treaty rights. But President Jackson refused to enforce the court decision and in a final crushing blow to Cherokee hopes ordered the U.S. Army to remove them forcibly.

In 1835 a small minority group of Cherokees, led by Major Ridge, John Ridge, and Elias Boudinot, signed an agreement with the federal government agreeing to move west to Indian Territory in return for a payment of five million dollars. But John Ross and the majority of the tribe did not accept this treaty. Nevertheless, the Senate ratified it even though it knew that only a minority of Cherokees had accepted it.

Thus the stage was set for the "Trail of Tears," the movement of an estimated 13,000 to 17,000 Cherokees with only the barest of their belongings from their comfortable homes in the East more than eight hundred miles to the undeveloped and unprepared lands in the West, to the Indian Territory that would later become the state of Oklahoma, which means "Red People."

About a thousand Cherokees managed to escape the forced removal by fleeing as fugitives in their own land into the Great Smoky Mountains, far from the flatland farms that the whites had commandeered. When it became apparent that there was no easy way to round up these "renegades," the U.S. Army struck a deal with the Indians. This group would be allowed to remain if the Indians handed over for punishment one of their tribesmen, a Cherokee named Tsali, and his family. Some reports say that Tsali's wife had been mistreated by the soldiers during the removal. In retribution Tsali had killed two soldiers before escaping into the mountains. Tsali, his brother, and his two older sons were captured and shot to death by a detachment of Cherokees who were forced by the Army, against their wishes, to perform the execution. As a result of Tsali's martyrdom, the eastern band of the Cherokee Indians was granted formal title in 1876 to what is now the Qualla Reservation in North Carolina.

New Echota, Georgia

To understand what happened to the Cherokee people the logical place to start is New Echota in northwestern Georgia. Near Calhoun, 70 miles north of Atlanta and 40 miles south of Chattanooga just off I-75 on Georgia 225, is New Echota State Historic Site, where the village stood that served as the capital of the Cherokee Nation from 1825 to 1838. The town covered 100 acres, had thirty to forty buildings, and was home to sixty to seventy people.

New Echota is historically important for another reason as well—in a house in New Echota the minority group of Cherokees signed the treaty that resulted in the expulsion of their fellow tribesmen, an agreement that was disowned by the majority, and later cost the minority leaders their lives.

A group of white Georgia citizens living in nearby Calhoun in the 1950s purchased two hundred acres of the capital site and deeded it to the State of Georgia for the restoration of the Cherokee capital.

Visitors see the results of this impressive historic preservation effort when they walk the streets of the restored village today. A self-guided tour leads to a 14-by-16-foot, reconstructed hewn-log cabin typical of the homes of the Cherokee farmers of the early 1800s, who dressed much like other settlers in buckskins or breeches and white homespun shirts, but wore the traditional Cherokee turban. Other buildings include a tavern, built nearby around 1800 and moved to the site, and the reconstructed two-story courthouse where the Cherokee Supreme Court met. The Cherokees developed their own judicial system and had law enforcement officers to carry out the laws.

Another small log building calls attention to the fact that the Cherokee was the first Indian tribe to print its own newspaper. Established in 1825, the *Cherokee Phoenix* was printed in both English and Cherokee. Their language, which made use of symbols for syllables and sounds, had been developed only a few years earlier by Sequoyah, a Cherokee artist and visionary. The newspaper was distributed throughout the Cherokee Nation and even in Europe where some Cherokees had trading partners.

One of the most imposing structures in New Echota is a two-story, wood-sided house built by a New England missionary who settled among the Cherokees and later migrated with them to Oklahoma. The Reverend Samuel Worcester used the building as a church, school, home, and post office—he was for a time New Echota's postmaster. The Reverend Worcester was forced to leave New Echota because of his sympathy for the Cherokees—a white man won his house in a land lottery. Worcester made the long trek to Indian Territory and continued his close relationship with the Cherokees.

A contemporary park visitor center offers an audiovisual introduction to Cherokee history and culture, provides guided tours for groups, and exhibits documents, memorabilia, and artifacts that have been unearthed in archeological excavations of the old Cherokee capital.

Vann House

Seventeen miles north of New Echota, on Georgia 225 where it crosses Georgia 52, stands the Vann House, testimony to the fact that some Cherokees prospered as businessmen. James Vann, son of a Scotch father and a Cherokee mother, grew to be an enterprising adult who built and operated a sawmill, a gristmill, and a ferry, as well as Vann's Tavern, a structure that now stands among the buildings at the New Echota Historic Site.

With the fortune he amassed Vann constructed this two-story brick mansion in 1804, a residence that became "the showplace of the Cherokees," the first brick building in the Cherokee Nation. Its walls are crowned front and rear with a classic cornice. Each facade has two-story, whitewashed plaster pilasters and two fanlight doorways, one above the other, framed by large painted wood paneling and opening off wide hallways onto covered porches. An elaborately carved stairway, the oldest example of cantilevered construction in Georgia, leads upward from the first floor. The brightly colored interior walls are symbolic—bright blue for sky, green for grass and trees, yellow for harvest fields, and dark red for Georgia clay. Bricks were made on the property, and handwrought nails and hinges were produced in Vann's own black-smith shop.

After James Vann died a violent death his son, Joseph "Rich Joe" Vann, made improvements in the house and on the plantation lands and even entertained President James Monroe there in 1819. He and his family occupied the large brick house until 1835, when the State of Georgia, using one of the laws it had enacted to persecute the Cherokees, confiscated both house and property and evicted the wealthy Cherokee who migrated with his family to Oklahoma.

Red Clay, Tennessee

About twenty miles north of the Vann House, just over the Georgia-Tennessee border near Cleveland, Tennessee, is Red Clay State Historical Park, which commemorates the Cherokees' "capital-in-exile," the place they fled to after Georgia forbade them to hold council meetings at New Echota.

The words still seem to reverberate in Red Clay's replica council house as they did in 1837 when the Cherokees, pushed to desperation by the insatiable demands of officials of Georgia and unrelenting hostility from President Andrew Jackson, sorrowfully agreed to abandon their homeland and move to Indian Territory.

By the spring of 1838 approximately two thousand of the seventeen thousand Cherokees had moved west, going by boat down the Tennessee, Ohio, and Mississippi Rivers, then westward up the Arkansas River as far as Fort Smith. Increasing the pressure on the rest of the Cherokees to leave, the U.S. Army built stockades and forcibly herded the remaining Cherokee families into them.

The beginning point of this tragic forced migration comes alive when you visit Red Clay. Eleven decisive council meetings were held here between 1832 and 1838. It was at Red Clay in 1837 that the Cherokee people were given the final word that they must abandon their homeland and move to Oklahoma—the start of the Trail of Tears.

At the state park you will find the open-sided frame council house, built to look like the original. Inside are log benches arranged in groups for members of the seven clans. In front of each set of benches is a board smoothed off for writing. Narration from hidden sound speakers relates the story of the critical conferences held in the council house.

Near the council house are three log sleeping huts, which accommodated some of the thousands of overnight visitors who had to travel for miles to attend the council sessions. The huts are built of logs with space between them to allow for ventilation during the hot summer days.

A short walk along one of the park paths brings the visitor to a large, clear spring. The deep spring, which disgorges more than five hundred thousand gallons of water a day, was an important reason that the Cherokees picked Red Clay for their Tennessee council grounds. The pure water that comes from the underlying limestone maintains an annual temperature of about 56°F. The spring, called the Blue Hole, was sacred to the Cherokees, providing drinking water for the village. Tradition says that before some of the Cherokees embarked on the Trail of Tears they threw some of their most prized possessions—the ones they could not take with them—into the sacred spring.

To give visitors an idea of what Cherokee life was like in the early nineteenth century the park maintains a re-created farmstead—a two-story log house, barn, and corn crib. The chinked log house has sleeping quarters upstairs and living quarters below. Some nineteenth-century Cherokee farmers raised cattle while others had pigs or chickens. They grew corn, cotton, beans, potatoes, squash, and fruit trees.

On a nearby rise within the park is the Eternal Flame of the Cherokees. On the 1838 trek to Oklahoma the Indians carried hot coals from their council fire at Red Clay. Years later, in 1958, coals from the fire were transported from Oklahoma back to Cherokee, North Carolina, to signify the reuniting of the western and eastern branches of the tribe. Then, in April 1984, ten Cherokee runners from North Carolina carrying torches brought the fire back again to Red Clay, lighting the Eternal Flame Monument.

A contemporary interpretive center holds exhibits—artifacts, a video presentation, and well-executed displays that describe Cherokee life. The park staff welcome visitors to browse through the center's library and genealogy collection. On the first weekend of August each year the state park stages a two-day event when Cherokees gather to demonstrate native dances, music, storytelling, and crafts such as basket weaving, pottery, and corn grinding.

Cherokee, North Carolina

Although not a part of the Trail of Tears, Cherokee, North Carolina, is the result of the resettlement of those Cherokees the Army was unable to capture in 1838. Here, a hundred miles northeast of Red Clay in the foothills of the Great Smoky Mountains where their forebears hid from the troops, live the members of the eastern band of the Cherokees. In the years following the expulsion of their fellow Cherokees and other tribes, these Cherokees stayed deep in the hills and hollows. Only later did they reacquire about fifty-six thousand of the seven million acres seized from them, land that today forms the reservation of the Eastern Band of the Cherokees.

The town of Cherokee, located at the eastern side of the Great Smoky Mountain National Park, offers excellent exhibits, a drama, and living history presentations that portray the history and culture of the Cherokees. The Museum of the Cherokee Indian, just off U.S. Highway 441 which transects the national park, displays Cherokee history including crafts, clothing, and weapons. Nearby the Oconoluftee Indian Village represents a Cherokee community of the seventeenth century. Indians demonstrate the making of baskets, pottery, canoes, arrows, and blowguns. An amphitheater built into a mountain hollow provides the setting for the well-known drama, *Unto These Hills,* which has been presented every summer for many years. The play covers the period from the arrival of the first European discoverers to the tragedy of the Trail of Tears. Descendants of some of the Cherokees who survived the removal play roles in the drama.

Trail of Tears Routes

In carrying out the roundup of the Cherokees in Georgia, Tennessee, and Alabama in 1838, the Army moved the dispossessed Indians into thirty-one temporary stockades located close to Cherokee towns—thirteen in Georgia, five in North Carolina, eight in Tennessee, and five in Alabama. As soon as practical the

Indians were transferred from these removal stockades to eleven more centrally located internment camps—ten in Tennessee and one in Alabama.

During the roundup intimidation and acts of cruelty at the hands of the troops, along with the theft and destruction of Indian property by local residents, further alienated the Cherokees. Finally, Chief Ross appealed to then-president Martin Van Buren to permit the Cherokees to oversee their own removal. Van Buren consented, and John Ross and his brother Lewis administered the effort.

The Cherokees were divided into sixteen detachments of about a thousand each. Thirteen detachments used a northern land route that extended 826 miles from Tennessee through Kentucky, Illinois, Missouri, and Arkansas to reach the designated Indian lands in Oklahoma. Two other lesser-used overland routes were also followed. John Bell guided between 600 and 700 "Treaty Cherokees" to Indian Territory over a southerly route that led through Memphis; these Cherokees were the minority Ridge group that had consented to the Treaty of New Echota, which sold off the traditional eastern Cherokee lands. Another conductor, John Benge, led his detachment along a middle route between the northern route and Bell's route. Neither Bell's route nor Benge's route have been officially designated as part of the Trail of Tears National Historic Trail.

Chattanooga, Tennessee

A fourth route led west by water. This was the path followed by the first of the removal detachments, a group that left in June 1838 by steamboat and barge from present-day Chattanooga. The water route took the Cherokees along the Tennessee, Ohio, and Mississippi Rivers, then up the Arkansas to Indian Territory. The Indians subsisted, one account says, on "bacon, pork, flour and meal and a small quantity of fresh beef" during the three-and-a-half-week trip. Disembarking from the boats, they then traveled by wagon to their final destination in eastern Oklahoma.

Today the place where these Cherokees departed by water is commemorated by a riverfront plaza in downtown Chattanooga. At the time of the expulsion the spot was known as Ross's Landing. Here John Ross had built a store, wharves, and a warehouse, thus becoming the first settler in what later became the city of Chattanooga.

Today the historic site is on Riverfront Parkway, where it is part of Ross's Landing Park and Plaza, a civic development along the banks of the Tennessee River, which flows through the city. Included is the Tennessee Aquarium, a visitor center, shops, restaurants, and a pier where a sightseeing riverboat is tied up.

The historical significance of the site is not forgotten. A marker at the water's edge tells the story of John Ross, the longtime principal chief of the Cherokees who did his best to forestall the federal expulsion and finally led his people to Oklahoma. A bronze statue of a Cherokee Indian stands nearby, gazing out over the river.

In the sidewalk of the plaza that surrounds the popular aquarium, history lies beneath your feet. Quotations from people who played significant roles in Chattanooga's history are carved into the plaza's paving blocks. By walking along a "time band" visitors get an insight into the culture, tribulations, and removal of the Cherokees through the words of those who were closest to the events. Quotations representing broken promises are inscribed in a block with a crack running through it. Also etched in the stone paving blocks are the symbols of the Cherokee syllabary created by Sequoyah.

The overland treks, undertaken by thirteen thousand Cherokees, were a constant battle against exposure to the weather, lack of proper food and supplies, and the threat of disease and illness. The first detachment left in late August; the last did not start until September and had to endure the entire winter before the group reached Indian Territory the following spring. Before these brutal overland wagon caravans reached their destination, one-fourth of all the Cherokees forced from their homeland, an estimated eight thousand, would die, a terrible toll.

A wagon was provided for every eighteen to twenty persons. Each was pulled by a double span of oxen or by mules or horses. Each wagon carried a family's supplies, the few precious belongings family members could salvage from their homes, and the few clothes they could bring.

"The old and infirm were carried in the wagons or on horseback," one observer wrote after witnessing the sad procession. "The able-bodied, with their slaves, of whom there were many hundreds, were on foot. Each detachment was controlled by one or more chiefs. Stations were established about fifteen miles apart along the road, where provisions were supplied by contractors, and detachments passed about every forty-eight hours."

In an account of the tragic migration published in the *New York Observer,* another eyewitness wrote that "a great many ride on horseback and multitudes go on foot—even aged females, apparently nearly ready to drop into the grave, were traveling with heavy burdens attached to the back—on the sometimes frozen ground, and sometimes muddy streets, with no covering for the feet except what nature had given them ... . We learned from the inhabitants on the road where the Indians passed that they buried fourteen or fifteen at every stopping place, and they make a journey of ten miles a day on an average."

Following the Trail Today

Today only a few scattered landmarks and structures remain as tangible evidence of this cruel forced march. Paved roads have been built over the nineteenth-century roads taken by the wagon trains, roads that still run through large expanses of open countryside and a few major urban areas such as Nashville, Tennessee, and Springfield, Missouri. The trail route is not yet marked with a distinctive route symbol, and the National Park Service has yet to produce a folder that includes a map of the overland route or the water route, or an auto route map to guide those who want to trace the wagon journey. Interpretive signs, however, identify some of the historic sites along the way.

The overland trail route begins at Charleston, Tennessee, 25 miles northeast of Chattanooga just off I-75. Fort Cass, a stockade near the Hiwassee River that served as a primary emigration depot for the removal, is no longer evident, but the home of Lewis Ross exists as a landmark. Lewis Ross, the brother of Chief John Ross, administered the migration after the federal government allowed the Cherokees themselves to take charge of the removal. The two-story, white clapboard house stands on Market Street and is privately owned.

About twenty miles west of Charleston the Trail of Tears detachments crossed the Tennessee River at Blythe's Ferry. Until recently, a ferry continued to carry vehicles; later a bridge was built and now carries Tennessee 60 across the river.

The trail goes diagonally across central Tennessee to Nashville. Ironically, the migrants here passed close to The Hermitage, the home of their nemesis, President Andrew Jackson, who had given the order that forced them from their ancestral homeland.

The bridge the Cherokees used to cross the Cumberland River still stands in downtown Nashville.

From Nashville the trail winds northwestward, crosses into Kentucky, and continues to Hopkinsville. The Trail of Tears Commemorative Park, built by the town's citizens, is situated near the center of Hopkinsville at the site where a number of the Cherokee detachments camped during the migration. A wagon-wheel-shaped courtyard welcomes you to the park. Two bronze statues portray Cherokees who died on the trail and were buried here: Whitepath, a venerable leader and strong supporter of Cherokee tradition who, even when his own health deteriorated, insisted on mounting his pony instead of riding in a wagon so as to set an example for other Cherokees; and Fly Smith, a member of the Cherokee Council. The Cherokee flag flies over the visitor center, a log cabin, built in the 1830s, that was moved to the park. Another part of the park holds the Trail of Tears Indian Pow Wow, an annual event that includes dances, crafts, demonstrations, and ceremonials and raises money that maintains the park.

Continuing across the western tip of Kentucky, the trail crosses the Ohio River into Illinois at another river ferry, Berry Ferry. On the west side of the river, in Golconda, Illinois, is the Buel House. Built in 1836 or 1837, just before the migration, the house is mentioned in diaries of the journey. Two hungry Cherokees, it is said, were provided warm, cooked pumpkin by the hospitable Mrs. Buel. The historic house has been restored by the Pope County Historical Society and is open to visitors.

The trail cuts across the tip of Illinois, then spans the Mississippi River at Green's Ferry to reach Trail of Tears State Park in Missouri. Here the historic trail route is clearly identified as it makes its way through the 3,000-acre park. Along the route, one of the main roads in the park, a visitor center houses a display that tells the story of the removal. Along this park road you can also observe the marked grave of one of the estimated 4,000 Cherokees who died during the forced march: Otahki Hildebrand, wife of Lewis Hildebrand and daughter of Jesse Bushyhead, a prominent Cherokee and an ordained Baptist minister.

Near St. James, on Missouri Highway 8, one can still see the stone structures of the Massey Ironworks, the oldest ironworks in the state, a landmark noted by the Cherokees. The old ironworks have been incorporated into a park by the James Foundation along with a campground and picnic area. Nearby the Snelson-Brinker

Cabin, a landmark on the trail, has been restored by local preservationists and is open free to the public.

The trail parallels I-44 to Springfield, then turns southwest through Cassville to cross the northwestern tip of Arkansas. At Pea Ridge National Military Park, just over the Arkansas border, the trail is marked as it follows what is now Telegraph Road through the park. The visitor center explains the Trail of Tears although it devotes most of its attention to the later Civil War battle when two Cherokee regiments fought for the Confederates.

The trail route traces U.S. Highway 71 south through Rogers, Springdale, and Fayetteville, then turns westward to enter Oklahoma (Indian Territory in 1838) at Westville. This was the place where most of the detachments disbanded and the migrants set out to look for homesites. Although the government was supposed to give the exhausted Cherokees food and supplies for one year, records show that the new arrivals often got short shrift on both.

Most of those who took the Trail of Tears by water came to Fort Smith, Arkansas. Here, near the end of their journey, they received food and supplies. The frontier fort provided the U.S. Army a base to control the flow of Indians from the East into Indian Territory. Today you can tour Fort Smith National Historic Site, an installation preserved by the National Park Service in downtown Fort Smith. The fort later functioned as a supply base during the settlement of the West and during the Mexican and Civil Wars.

Upriver 80 miles past Fort Smith, the waterborne Cherokees disembarked at Fort Gibson, the end of the 1,220-mile water route. The Army built this log stockade on a tributary of the Arkansas River as part of a network of fortifications to suppress the Osage Indians, who wanted to use for their own hunting ground the land that the federal government had allotted to the Cherokees for resettlement. During the last half of the 1830s and into the 1840s, thousands of Creeks, Cherokees, and Seminoles stopped at Fort Gibson on the last leg of their journey to their new lands. Visitors are invited to walk around the old stockade of Fort Gibson Military Park, which has been restored by the State of Oklahoma and is administered by the Oklahoma Historical Society.

Tahlequah, Oklahoma

Midway between Fort Gibson, the end of the water route, and Westville, the end of the overland route, the Cherokees in

Cherokees demonstrate how blowguns were used to shoot poison darts to kill small game, Tahlequah, Oklahoma.

1839 established their new capital at Tahlequah. Those who survived the Trail of Tears settled and tried to build the new Cherokee Nation. The original Cherokee government buildings that remain today are the 1844 Supreme Court Building, the 1867 Cherokee Capitol Building, and the 1844 Cherokee National Prison.

The traveler can easily spend a day at the Cherokee Heritage Center, set amid the trees on the site where the Cherokees established a female seminary in 1851 in keeping with their strong emphasis on education. It was the first institution of higher learning for any women west of the Mississippi. A modern museum tells through exhibits and audiovisual displays the history of the tribe from the white man's arrival in North America to the present.

After getting an understanding of Cherokee history at the museum, walk down a short path to see a re-created village of the sixteenth century, called Tsa-La-Gi. A youthful Indian guide leads the visitor past several rectangular mud structures the early Indians used as dwellings. In front of each a Cherokee dressed in deerskin demonstrates skills such as flint knapping (fashioning a piece of flint into an arrowhead or spear point), basket-weaving, pottery making, bow making, canoe making, cooking, and using a blowgun to hunt game. Visitors end their tour by watching the Indian villagers perform a circular dance in the village square.

A musical drama, *Trail of Tears,* is presented Tuesday through Saturday evenings during the summer at an amphitheater in the woods. A cast of fifty Cherokee actors and dancers dramatizes the bittersweet story of the removal and heartbreaking trek and relates the troubles and triumphs of the tribe in the century-and-a-half since.

For many Cherokees today the Trail of Tears remains fresh in their tribal memory. "I have a plate that I treasure that my ancestors brought with them over the trail," said Troy Poteete, a Cherokee who heads the center.

"The significance of the Trail of Tears is not only that we suffered; anyone can suffer," Poteete said. "It is significant because, despite the tragedy of being brutally uprooted and exiled, the Cherokee people overcame. They triumphed over tragedy, reestablishing a thriving nation in the wilderness. The Cherokee people flourished by building schools, churches, homes, farms, and mills in a land others did not want."

Trail of Tears Association

The Trail of Tears Association, organized in 1993, promotes grassroots support for efforts to commemorate, interpret, and preserve the Trail of Tears in cooperation with the programs of the National Park Service.

When the association increases and its membership becomes self-governing and gains additional financial support, it will help to educate visitors about the trail, protect resources along the route, and monitor trail development. It plans to sponsor symposiums, contribute to public education about the trail, help preserve historic sites, and assist in marking the trail for the benefit of the traveler.

Membership is open not only to members of the Cherokee Nation of Oklahoma and the Eastern Band of the Cherokee Indians but to anyone interested in the Trail of Tears. For more information write the Trail of Tears Association, P.O. Box 2069, Cherokee, NC 28719.

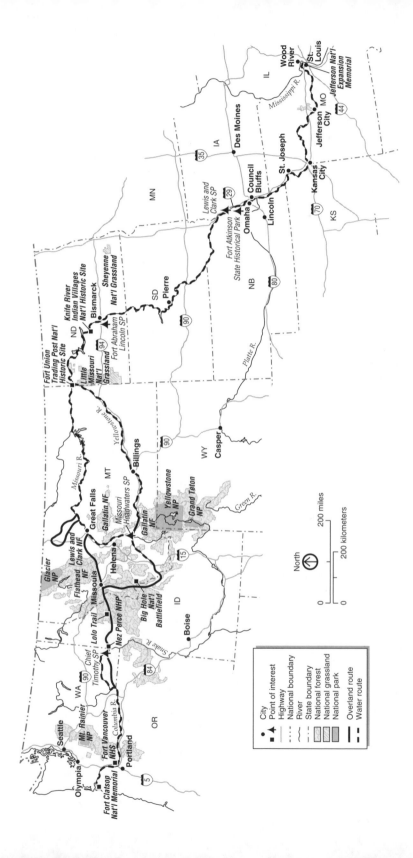

Chapter 11

LEWIS AND CLARK NATIONAL HISTORIC TRAIL

I N 1803 MERIWETHER LEWIS, 29 YEARS OLD, WAS AN EXPERIENCED frontier Army captain who had recently been appointed as secretary-aide to President Thomas Jefferson. William Clark, a Virginian like Lewis, was 33 and had been Lewis's commanding officer during an earlier frontier campaign against the British and their Indian allies.

When President Jefferson selected Lewis to be the leader of a trailblazing expedition to explore the newly acquired Louisiana Territory, Lewis requested that his former colleague Clark be designated as the expedition's co-commander. Both men were intelligent, adventurous, experienced frontiersmen and woodsmen as well as born leaders. Both were cool in a crisis and quick to make decisions, although they differed in temperament. Lewis, more literate and better educated, was introverted and enjoyed solitude. Clark, hearty and outgoing, related easily to the expedition members and possessed a good understanding of the Indians.

It was scarcely two decades since the signing of the peace treaty with England that had ended the American Revolution. The young United States consisted of the thirteen original states of the Eastern seaboard as well as Kentucky, Tennessee, Indiana, and Ohio, plus other unorganized territories that extended to the Mississippi River.

In 1803, as part of a strategy to place his enemy England at a disadvantage, Napoleon Bonaparte of France unexpectedly sold the entire Louisiana Territory to the United States. Its 830,000 square miles virtually doubled the size of the new nation.

This sudden expansion of the nation impelled President Jefferson and Congress to assess this new territory, and it was this challenge that Jefferson laid before the co-commanders. A primary objective of the expedition was to find a practical transportation link between the Louisiana Territory and the "Oregon Country," territory claimed by the United States following the discovery of the mouth of the Columbia River by Captain Robert Gray in 1792, but a territory also claimed by Great Britain. The exploration of the Pacific Northwest, it was felt, would also strengthen American claims against those of Britain and Russia.

The expedition, however, was to accomplish more than simply exploring this western geography. Jefferson, with his inquiring mind, wanted information on the resources and inhabitants of the new territory. The party was to scientifically observe and, if practicable, collect specimens of animals, plants, and minerals; record weather data; study native cultures; conduct diplomatic councils with Indian tribes; map geographic features; and record these observations and events in daily journal entries.

Lewis and Clark fully lived up to these high expectations. Despite the physical hardships, sickness, and danger that the expedition faced daily, only one man died during the 28 months, and he died early in the journey from a ruptured appendix. Fulfilling a requirement they had been given, the adventurers meticulously recorded observations about the characteristics, inhabitants, and resources of the country through which they passed. Few explorers in the history of the world have provided such exhaustive and accurate information on the regions they surveyed.

Prior to Lewis and Clark the region west of the Mississippi was largely unexplored, unmapped land. The members of this plucky expedition made their way through this vast territory, living off its resources and adapting themselves to its harsh conditions. They encountered primitive tribes and menacing animals. By boat, on horseback, and on foot they pushed over forbidding mountain ranges, across seemingly endless plains, through dense forests, and against powerful river currents to successfully accomplish their assigned mission—and safely return home.

Travelers today can follow in the wake of this epic trans-continental expedition by auto, by boat, and even on foot in a few locations. Those who wish to trace the trail will probably want to obtain a copy of the trail folder, "Lewis and Clark Trail," published by the National Park Service, the agency that administers the historic trail. It outlines the explorers' route, depicting the portions of the Missouri, Clearwater, and Columbia Rivers where they proceeded by boat and the portions where they went overland by foot and on horseback. To obtain a free copy of the folder, write to the National Park Service, Lewis and Clark National Historic Trail, 700 Rayovac Drive, Suite 100, Madison, WI 53711.

Although the explorers used a keelboat, two pirogues (flat-bottomed canoes), and dugout canoes as they traveled by water for four-fifths of their journey, tourists today can follow by boat only on certain segments. Long stretches of the Missouri and Columbia Rivers they followed are now interrupted by a series of dams and impounded lakes. Commercial sightseeing boats are available, however, on the Upper Missouri Wild and Scenic River segment and on the "Gates of the Mountains" segment, both in Montana.

A more popular way to trace the Lewis and Clark route is by car or recreational vehicle on roads that parallel or cross the actual river route and are closely aligned to the segments where the explorers struck out overland. Many of the designated roadways are marked with either a rectangular or triangular brown-and-white sign whose design portrays Lewis and Clark and identifies the road or highway as part of the Lewis and Clark route. Highway route numbers for the overland segments of the trail are also shown on the National Park Service trail folder. Some states like North Dakota have their own Lewis and Clark historic route markers, provide interpretive sites, and publish their own state trail guide. Using the trail folder and a state highway map, travelers can closely duplicate the historic route and find their way to the numerous historic sites associated with this remarkable expedition.

Several segments of the trail are open to those who wish to hike, ride horseback, or use four-wheel-drive vehicles. West of St. Louis a hiking and biking trail that closely follows the Missouri River has been developed on a former railroad bed; 125 miles of the 200-mile-long Katy Trail State Park traces Lewis and Clark's route. Other pathways are a 17-mile hiking, horse-back, and snowmobiling trail that parallels the Missouri River in North Dakota and a 7-mile hiking trail in Ecola State Park in Oregon.

But perhaps the most notable segment is in Idaho, where an 80-mile national forest road follows the Lochsa and Clearwater Rivers through the Bitterroot Mountains—traversing the rugged terrain that proved to be one of the severest tests for the exploring party. Here hikers and horseback riders may retrace part of the actual track that Lewis and Clark took.

St. Louis Vicinity

The Lewis and Clark National Historic Trail begins at Wood River, Illinois, 20 miles upriver from St. Louis where the Mississippi River meets the Missouri. Although the changing pattern of the river's flow has obliterated "Camp Wood," where Lewis and Clark carefully trained the members of their exploring party, a monument stands near the river in Lewis and Clark State Park near Alton, Illinois. Here the explorers gathered their supplies, scientific instruments, weapons, and trade items for the Indians. They made frequent trips to nearby St. Louis as they fitted out the keelboat and the pirogues they would use on the first leg of their journey.

At the Jefferson National Expansion Memorial at St. Louis, exhibits at the Museum of Westward Expansion beneath the famous Gateway Arch summarize the Lewis and Clark expedition and its significance.

On May 15, 1804, the small flotilla of three craft and forty-seven men set off up the Missouri. Daily journal entries by Lewis and Clark as well as other members of the crew have left a vivid record as this troop of men began their journey. They pulled the keelboat by ropes upriver against the strong springtime current. Dodging treacherous sandbars and pushing off snags, they inched their way upstream. As spring turned to summer, the days turned muggy and hot, only to be relieved from time to time by sudden storms that drenched both men and cargo. A couple of crewmen who had been designated as the expedition's hunters roamed the woods ashore while the boats moved upriver, bringing back deer, rabbits, and other game that provided plenty of fresh meat.

Fort Atkinson, Nebraska

By August the expedition had made its way some six hundred miles up the Missouri, reaching a location just north of present-day Omaha. The commanders chose this spot, where high bluffs bordered the river, to meet with the chiefs of two neighboring Indian tribes to try to cement the friendly relations that President Jefferson had directed them to pursue. Lewis explained to the assembled chiefs that a new "Great Father" would be their new chief in Washington. After they shared a peace pipe and accepted gifts from the explorers, the chiefs concurred and seemed pleased. The explorers called the site of this first meeting with a group of Indians "Councile Bluffs," a name perpetuated by the Iowa city of the same name.

Fifteen years later the U.S. Army built a fort on the site that the explorers had recommended as a good place to protect river traffic. Today Fort Atkinson, a state historical park 10 miles north of Omaha on U.S. Highway 75, welcomes visitors as a restored frontier fort. Exhibits describe the Lewis and Clark expedition while living history interpreters during the summer months portray life at the fort.

Lewis and Clark State Park, Iowa

For most travelers tracing the Lewis and Clark Trail means touring on roads that closely follow the explorers' route, noting historical markers erected along the way that identify campsites, council meeting places, and noteworthy events. Since the expedition traveled the length of the Missouri River by boat, the history buff yearns to see a reminder of the explorers' life on the river.

This is what he gets at Lewis and Clark State Park, just off I-29 near Onawa, Iowa. On an oxbow lake that once formed part of the river floats a replica of the 55-foot keelboat that did yeoman service on the early part of the journey. It carried a cannon in the bow, a superstructure at the stern, and lockers with lids that could be raised to form a protecting breastwork along the gunwales amidships.

Local volunteers, under the guiding hands of a volunteer boatbuilder, constructed the keelboat as well as replicas of the two pirogues, all by using the design plans that Clark sketched in his journal.

At a festival at the park on the second weekend of each June, "buckskinners" man the three boats. Sailing them onto the lake, they demonstrate how the versatile keelboat could be rowed with its twenty-two oars, poled by men standing on deck, pulled upriver with cordelle ropes hauled by men ashore, or—if a southerly wind prevailed—sailed by the power of the wind.

North Dakota Indian Villages

The expedition toiled upstream against the current, making its way through the gently rolling prairie landscape. The keen-eyed explorers sighted and reported "new" animals: prairie dog, coyote, white-tailed jackrabbit, and western gray wolf. They discovered a new species of deer and called it a mule deer because of its large ears. They identified the antelope we now know as the pronghorn and described the prickly pear cactus.

Autumn was advancing into winter, and they had to push on toward winter quarters. As they reached what is now North Dakota ice began to cling to the river's edge. It was time to establish their camp, wait out the cold north plains winter, then prepare to continue westward in the spring.

In their log for October 22 the explorers mentioned that they had seen nine deserted Mandan Indian villages along the river within the last 20 miles. Today's visitor may still see the remains of a seventeenth-century Mandan village that is preserved within the boundaries of Fort Abraham Lincoln State Park four miles south of Mandan on North Dakota 1806. Portions of the On-a-Slant Indian Village have been reconstructed on the original site, including five earth lodges.

At the time of the expedition the numerous villages of the Mandan, Hidatsa, and Arikara people along the Missouri River were compact settlements of earth lodge houses that together held some five thousand Indian dwellers. For hundreds of years before they came in contact with European explorers these Indians had developed a well-organized and productive way of life based on agriculture and the hunting of animals such as bison. Women in this matrilineal society harvested much of the food for each village from rich floodplain gardens—mainly corn, beans, squash, and sunflowers. These proficient farmers traded their surplus produce to nomadic tribes for buffalo hides, deerskins, dried meat, and other items in short supply.

Some of the guides at the On-a-Slant Indian Village are descendants of the Mandans. They show visitors through the dimly lit earth lodges and describe the sweat lodge, which played such an important role in Mandan life. Water was thrown on hot rocks to create steam within the small lodge. Those in the lodge breathed through sprigs of sage that created a pungent aroma, adding to the steam's curative effects. The Fort Abraham Lincoln park also preserves the site of a 1780 fur-trading post as well as part of the frontier fort from which General George Custer rode to his death in the Battle of Little Bighorn in 1876.

For their winter quarters Lewis and Clark selected a spot with good wood for fires and abundant game, a site two miles from one of the friendly Mandan villages. Although later shifts of the Missouri River have inundated the original site, the McLean County Historical Society has erected a replica nearby of the triangular fort, which had log rooms at either end and a lookout tower in the middle. Its third side, which faced toward the river, was a palisade. Fort Mandan is located just west of U.S. Highway 83, 30 miles north of the capital at Bismarck.

Nearby, a few miles farther west at Stanton, North Dakota, is the Knife River Indian Village National Historic Site. Here a visitor center, museum exhibits, a full-scale earth lodge, and ranger-led and self-guided walks reveal the culture of the Hidatsa and Mandan Indian people. During spring, summer, and fall these farmers lived in earth lodges on the river terraces, while in the winter they moved into less permanent earth lodges in the forested river bottom.

Archeological investigations at this important site have uncovered the remains of earth lodges and thousands of pottery shards and stone tools that represent an unbroken record of 500 years of human habitation. Earlier people used this area as long as eleven thousand years ago.

It was over the winter at the Hidatsa villages that the expedition gained two new members and lost six others. Lewis and Clark took on Toussaint Charbonneau, a French-Canadian fur trapper who lived among the Indians, and his teenage wife Sacagawea ("bird woman"), who had just had a baby. Charbonneau, they felt, would be helpful since he spoke several Indian languages. Sacagawea, a Shoshoni who had been kidnapped from her tribe four years before, could aid the expedition when it came time to negotiate with her tribesmen for the horses they knew they would need to cross the mountains. Her presence helped in another way as well: The fact that the expedition included a woman and her baby signaled to other Indians that the explorers came with only peaceful intentions.

According to a prearranged plan Lewis and Clark sent six men back to St. Louis with the keelboat, which was too large for the narrowing river. Along with the keelboat and crew they sent their growing collection of priceless scientific specimens and their journals to date.

Great Falls, Montana

With the arrival of spring, the expedition continued upriver. It now consisted of thirty-three people, with two large pirogues and six dugout canoes the men had built over the winter. They passed the spot where the Missouri was joined by the Yellowstone River, a tributary Clark would explore on his return trip, and continued westward. Today a 149-mile segment of the river in this vicinity, from Kipp State Park to Fort Benton, has been preserved as the Upper Missouri Wild and Scenic River. The natural setting provides the visitor with an opportunity to see the river as Lewis and Clark saw it and to retrace this part of the expedition's route. Those who take a float or boat trip on the scenic river see the same sandstone rock formations and treeless desert riverbanks that fascinated the explorers almost two centuries ago.

The Upper Missouri Wild and Scenic River visitor center at Fort Benton offers a slide presentation that depicts the expedition and displays the area's natural and cultural resources. On the riverfront levee in the historic town is a heroic-sized statue of Lewis and Clark, with Sacagawea and her son. The explorers spent an exasperating nine days near here in June 1805 making sure that a tributary, the Marias River, was in fact not the main stem of the Missouri. The crew unanimously believed the Marias to be the main fork but the captains thought otherwise—and proved to be right.

So it was with relief, which later turned to misery, that they heard and then saw the thundering of Great Falls, "one of the most beautifull objects in nature, a cascade of about fifty feet perpendicular stretching at right angles across the river from side to side to the distance of at least a quarter of a mile." Today little of this glory that Lewis wrote about remains; hydroelectric projects near the city of Great Falls have smothered the five waterfalls. An audio-tour tape that recounts Lewis and Clark's experiences at Great Falls is available at the Cascade County Historical Museum in the city.

The misery came later when they had to portage around the majestic falls. It took them two weeks to cover the rugged 18 miles, hauling their boats atop a makeshift wagon up steep slopes, around gullies, over rocks and prickly pear cactus, as they pushed and pulled and dragged and heaved their heavy log canoes.

Back on the river again, they guided their canoes between towering cliffs of limestone that soar to 1,200-foot heights on both sides of the Missouri as it passes through the Gates of the Mountains. Bighorn sheep and mountain goats still haunt the heights, and osprey, eagles, and falcons soar aloft. Travelers can sample the river canyon today aboard tour boats that leave daily from the Gates of the Mountain Recreation Area marina 20 miles north of Helena on a side road off I-15.

Three Forks, Lemhi Pass

At this point in their journey Lewis and Clark, as expedition leaders, knew they were nearing the time when they would have to leave the river and surmount the treacherous Rocky Mountains. To do this they badly needed to find the Shoshoni Indians and barter with them for horses to carry their gear across the steep mountain ranges they now saw to their west.

In late July the expedition reached the spot in western Montana where three tributaries merge to form the Missouri. The commanders named the tributaries the Jefferson, Madison, and Gallatin in honor of the president and two of his cabinet members. It was here that Sacagawea had been kidnapped by other Indians and here that she thought they would find her tribesmen, the Shoshonis. Missouri Headwaters State Park, 35 miles west of Bozeman just off I-90, commemorates the site with an interpretive shelter, hiking trails, and a picnic area.

The voyagers struggled up the Jefferson and Beaverhead Rivers, hauling their boats through the rapids. The river frayed into shallow channels choked by brush and beaver dams. The dugouts grated across the stony-bottomed riffles. They were discouraged at not finding the Indians. "If we do not find them or some other nation who have horses," Lewis wrote, "I fear the successfull issue of our voyage will be very doubtfull."

Desperate, Lewis and three men set out overland, eventually cresting the Continental Divide at Lemhi Pass on the present-day Montana-Idaho border, and found a spring whose runoff flowed westward! Soon they came across the Shoshoni, whose chief, Cameahwait, agreed to go back over the Divide to aid the remainder of the hard-pressed expedition.

Then occurred a dramatic high point of this remarkable expedition—Sacagawea recognized Cameahwait as her long-lost brother. The diary entries relate how she ran to him, threw her blanket round him, and wept.

Lolo Trail

After scouting possible rivers leading westward—and deciding they were too treacherous for their boats—Lewis and Clark transferred their gear to the horses they had bought from the Shoshoni and moved up the Bitterroot Valley along the route today followed by U.S. Highway 93.

History buffs who want to follow the expedition trail have a great opportunity as it heads westward across the narrow northern panhandle of Idaho. The Lolo Trail, once a well-used Indian trade and hunting route, crosses the Clearwater and Lolo National Forests and has been designated as a national historic landmark.

This section was one of the most critical parts of the journey for Lewis and Clark; it was during the difficult trek through the Bitterroot Range of the Rockies that early winter snows caught the explorers. The desperate, half-starved men killed several of their horses for meat, melted snow to drink, and even ate candles. Pack animals fell over cliffs. In "those tremendious mountains," Clark later wrote to his brother, "we suffered everything which hunger, cold and fatigue could impose." The men, already exhausted by their ordeal on the Upper Missouri, were close to collapse. Finally they staggered into a friendly Nez Perce Indian village.

By driving along U.S. Highway 12, a winding mountain road that runs westward from Missoula, Montana, 167 miles to Orofino, Idaho, the traveler can catch the spirit of the disheartened expedition. Lewis and Clark's route took them along the ridgelines atop these rugged mountains; U.S.12, on the other hand, hugs the deep valleys cut by the Lochsa and Clearwater Rivers. Tree-covered mountains slope sharply upward. The sightseer can take advantage of numerous turnouts along the river to stop for scenic views and interpretive historical signs relating to the Lewis and Clark story, signs placed there by the Idaho Historical Society. The Forest Service operates a visitor center atop the 5,233-foot Lolo Pass during the summer. Nowadays river rafting and kayaking are popular pastimes on these whitewater rivers.

For those who want to hike, ride, or drive a four-wheel-drive vehicle to trace the actual historic ridgeline route of the Lolo Trail, the U.S. Forest Service maintains a one-lane dirt road that closely follows the original trail for 100 miles. More than thirty interpretive signs relating events of the Lewis and Clark expedition have been erected along this backcountry roadway. Because of the deep snows that still blanket these mountains, as they did when the explorers battled their way through, the forest road is usually open only from July through October. Those who desire to follow in the footsteps of the trailblazers may get a folder, "Lewis and Clark Across the Lolo Trail," by writing to Clearwater National Forest, 12730 Highway 12, Orofino, ID 83544.

By River to the Pacific

After the eleven-day ordeal of the Bitterroots, the expedition rested several days with the Nez Perce. In fact, historians say, were it not for friendly Indians like the Nez Perce who were willing to help them, Lewis and Clark and their expedition would never have reached their goal.

Jubilant at having "tryumphed over the rockey Mountains," the party was ready to get back on the navigable rivers that would carry them westward. Leaving their horses with the Nez Perce to hold for them until they returned, they spent the next two weeks cutting down trees and hewing and burning out five new canoes that would carry them down the swift-flowing Clearwater.

Travelers will discover the site of this canoe camp five miles west of Orofino as they continue along U.S. 12 on the Clearwater Canyon Scenic Byway. An interpretive sign describes how the explorers adopted the Indian technique of setting a fire and burning away the insides of a log to save themselves some work as they hollowed it out to make a dugout canoe.

Marker on U.S. 12 along the Clearwater.

In their newly made boats the party drifted down the Clearwater. Reaching the Snake, the expedition rode for six days through currents one of the men termed "swifter than any horse could run." Although the Pacific lay not far ahead, they had to keep moving for the weather was steadily growing colder.

The Snake fed into the Columbia, one of the major rivers of North America, and swirling rapids and rocks now became "large and too noumerous to notice." At one place the Columbia split into narrow channels and a foaming cataract. Baggage had to be portaged and the empty boats carried and floated over the barrier. In the rapids below the falls one of the boats broke loose, but a group of helpful Indians retrieved it. At The Dalles—nine miles of wildwater rushing through a narrow cut—Lewis and Clark amazed a group of Indians who watched them as they successfully knifed through the foaming rapids.

By following a scenic highway—I-84—along the Columbia River, travelers today may trace the Lewis and Clark route along much of the river. From the highway they get panoramic views, particularly in the Columbia River Gorge National Scenic Area, where they peer up at cliffs 2,000 feet high, unusual rock formations, and eleven waterfalls including 620-foot Multnomah Falls. But the raging rapids and foaming falls that Lewis and Clark knew are gone; a whole complex of dams to provide hydroelectric power has turned the formerly turbulent river into a chain of placid ponds.

For another 180 miles the explorers would paddle their canoes toward the Pacific Ocean. To reach this point today the traveler needs to drive 100 miles west of Portland, Oregon, cross over the bridge at Astoria, and drive 15 miles west on North Highway 101 to Fort Canby State Park in Washington. Here, on a high promontory on November 18, 1805, Clark and eleven of the men gazed out at their hard-won objective, the Pacific Ocean. The view they saw is just as spectacular today. Inside the Lewis and Clark Interpretive Center, exhibits lead the visitor through a portrayal of the expedition's adventures captioned with entries from the journals. Displays point out the important contributions made by many of the Indian tribes the explorers encountered.

Several days later, their spirits dampened by continual rainy weather, the captains decided to move the site for their winter quarters to the south side of the river, where elk promised to be more plentiful and where they would be less exposed to the weather. It took them three weeks to construct Fort Clatsop, a sturdy log structure set in the midst of a spruce and hemlock forest. Designed by Clark, it was only 50 feet square and consisted of two rows of cabins separated by the typical Army "parade ground."

As part of the Lewis and Clark sesquicentennial in 1955, local volunteers accurately rebuilt the fort. Three years later they donated both site and fort to the National Park Service. Now, each summer, park rangers in buckskins demonstrate for the visitors some of the tasks performed by the Lewis and Clark party, including canoe building, woodworking, candle making, rendering, tanning, music and dance, sewing buckskin, and firing a flintlock muzzle loader.

During its brief existence Fort Clatsop bustled with activity. The men worked on their journals and collected and cataloged botanical and wildlife specimens. They served on wood and guard details, in hunting parties, and at a coastal salt-making camp nearby. It took three weeks to boil 1,400 gallons of seawater into three and a half bushels of salt, which they would use to preserve their meat for the return trip.

But almost constant rain and the monotonous diet of elk meat lowered morale. It rained all but 12 of their 106 days at the fort. It was cold, it was crowded, and it was wet—but they survived.

Without regret, on March 23, 1806, the explorers abandoned the outpost for the eastward journey that in six months would bring them back to St. Louis to conclude their epic 8,000-mile journey. Fort Clatsop had served its primary purpose of sheltering the expedition. But in addition, as the first Army post on the Pacific coast, it had also helped establish American claims to the Oregon country.

Volunteer John Adams shows how men poled the keelboat, a replica of the one used by Lewis and Clark.

By carrying the flag of the young nation westward from the Mississippi across thousands of miles of mostly unknown land, the Lewis and Clark expedition had fired the imaginations of the American people and brought home to them for the first time the full sweep of the continent on which they lived. Equally important, the political and economic ramifications of the trek vitally affected the subsequent course and growth of the nation.

Before Lewis and Clark the land beyond the Mississippi was largely unexplored. Aside from a tiny fringe of French-American settlements in the St. Louis area and along the Mississippi, and small Spanish colonies in the Rio Grande Valley of New Mexico and in California, the region was inhabited only by Native American peoples. These western lands were almost as strange to the Americans of those days as the surface of the moon would be to a later generation.

The hardy explorers made their way through this vast land, living off its resources and adapting themselves to the conditions it imposed. They encountered dangerous animals and Native Americans with strange customs. On foot, on horseback, and by boat they pushed over mountain ranges, across seemingly endless plains, through tangled forests, against powerful currents and raging waters. In doing so they fulfilled all of the basic objectives of their complex mission and wrote one of the most dramatic and significant episodes in the history of the United States.

Lewis and Clark Trail Heritage Foundation, Inc.

The Lewis and Clark Trail Heritage Foundation, Inc. was organized in 1969 to promote interest and scholarship in the epic expedition and the historic trail that commemorates it.

The nonprofit organization has 1,500 members in fifty states and seven other countries, including federal, state, and local government officials, historians, scholars, and those with an avid interest in the Lewis and Clark expedition. The foundation cooperates with and coordinates festivals, educational seminars, and celebrations arranged by individuals, firms, corporations, and government organizations that seek to commemorate the trail. Its members work with the National Park Service, coordinator of the national trail, to identify and document trail sites, mark them for travelers, and plan exhibits and visitor centers.

The foundation publishes and distributes to its members a quarterly magazine, *We Proceeded On,* which features news of developments along the trail and includes scholarly articles on aspects of the 1804–1806 expedition. To inquire about membership write the Lewis and Clark Trail Heritage Foundation, Inc., P.O. Box 3434, Great Falls, MT 59403.

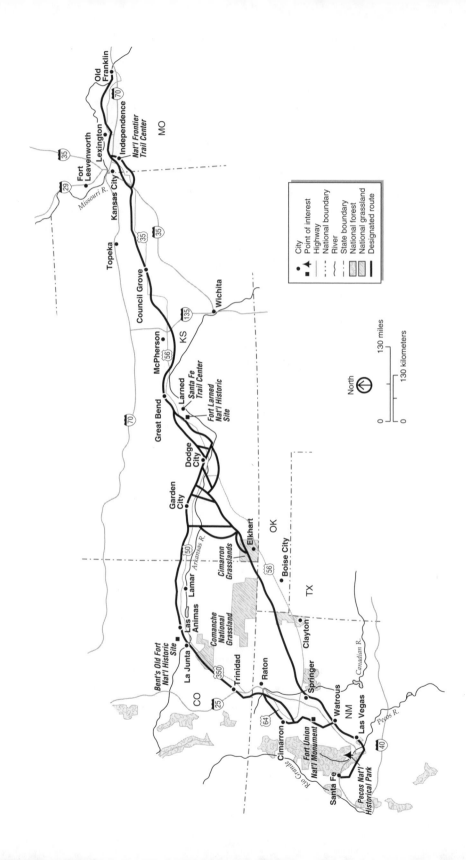

Chapter 12

SANTA FE NATIONAL HISTORIC TRAIL

T HE SANTA FE TRAIL WAS AN IMPORTANT TWO-WAY AVENUE FOR commerce, a sort of early "interstate truck route" for the exchange of goods between the eastern United States and the newly independent Mexico.

It became a popular trading route practically overnight when military units in Spanish-controlled Mexico revolted in 1821 and Mexico shook off three centuries of Spanish colonial rule. Once freed from Spain, Mexico opened trade doors that had previously been closed to the growing United States. Immediately merchants and tradesmen of Franklin and other early settlements along the Missouri River, then the western boundary of the United States, saw an opportunity to develop new markets for their manufactured goods in the former Spanish colony.

For those desiring to trace all or part of this old wagon trail the best way to do it is by auto following a motorist's tour map that identifies the major historic sites and natural landmarks that are open to the public along the route. It denotes the roads and highways that most closely parallel the Santa Fe Trail, noting several sites such as Boone's Lick State Historical Site and Arrow Rock State Historic Site, which served as earlier starting points for the trail. By using the motorist's tour map together with a detailed state highway map, the traveler can effectively trace the old trail. To obtain a copy of the auto tour route folder write to the Branch of Long Distance Trails, National Park

Service, Southwest Field Office, P.O. Box 728, Santa Fe, NM 87504-0728.

The auto route described in the folder is reinforced on the ground at many places with the triangular symbol of the Santa Fe National Historic Trail, which shows a covered wagon and team of oxen. Interpretive signs at pulloffs along the roadways add to visitor understanding as the route crosses Missouri, Kansas, Oklahoma, Colorado, and New Mexico. At several locations the spirit of the old Santa Fe Trail comes alive through interpretive displays and living history demonstrations provided by National Park Service rangers and volunteers—at Fort Larned in Kansas, the reconstructed Bent's Old Fort trading post in Colorado, and the ruins of Fort Union and the Pecos pueblo site in New Mexico. Other historic structures along the route are preserved and interpreted by state, county, and private organizations.

Most remarkable of all, the traveler can make a visual connection to these events of a century-and-a-half ago. The sightseer can still see actual evidence of the old wagon trail: Wagon ruts are engraved in the earth or stone at thirty or more locations along the trail. These historic impressions rarely take the form of a narrow track or wheel tread; rather they vary from a shallow depression in the earth to a gentle swale to a deep trough worn through sandstone by the iron wheels of hundreds of wagons. Visitors can sometimes recognize a trail tread by a difference in the color of the vegetation, the result of rainwater collecting in the tracks and different grasses growing in the wet areas.

It was the fall of 1821 when William Becknell, a farmer-turned-merchant from Franklin, outfitted an expedition of six men; loaded up with a cargo of cloth, hardware, and cutlery; and led a pack train to Santa Fe. Following the Arkansas River through western Kansas, he and his team then left the river and struck out overland. Becknell's caravan made it across many dry miles to Santa Fe, where the entrepreneurs turned a handsome profit on their pioneering venture.

The route they took evolved into the "desert route," or Cimarron Route. During a later period when skirmishes with the Indians made the desert route perilous, the Santa Fe traders switched to a longer but safer "mountain route" that swung northward, continued along the Arkansas River to Bent's Old Fort in Colorado, then made its way through the mountains and Raton

Pass into New Mexico, where it met up with the desert route near the juncture of the Mora and Sapello Rivers known as La Junta (present-day Watrous, New Mexico).

Becknell's pack train was soon superseded by wagon caravans that could carry a bigger load. By the spring of 1822, other American entrepreneurs were making their way over the plains, deserts, and mountains to get their share of the trade. Within a few years wagons began their journey from Independence, a town that soon grew to be the major debarkation on the Missouri River and the major starting point for caravans. Piled high with merchandise from eastern factories, the wagoneers protected their valuable cargo from prairie storms by fitting their wagons with a canvas cover stretched over a wooden frame. From a distance these slow-moving wagons with their white canvas tops looked like ships on the plains, an appearance that earned them the nickname of "prairie schooner." The term later became a symbol for the entire western pioneer movement.

As soon as a wagon train arrived in Santa Fe its owners would pull out their wares and start trading in the streets. Mexicans were eager to replace their old clothes with colorful American calicos; they exchanged their rugs, furs, blankets, and gold and silver coins for American hardware, foods, spices, medicines, wines, tobacco, tableware, toiletries, oil lamps, inks, and paints. In 1824 one group of twenty-five wagons left Missouri carrying $35,000 worth of merchandise; in Santa Fe the goods were sold or bartered for $190,000 in gold, silver, raw wool, and furs.

When the Mexicans saw the profits being made they decided that such lucrative trade should run in both directions. Soon Mexican traders were putting together pack and wagon trains of their own and heading east to compete with the merchants of Independence and St. Louis. One of the most desirable things the Mexicans had to sell was a large mule. Faster than an ox, tougher and more sure-footed than a horse, the New Mexico mule journeyed to the United States by so many thousands that eventually it changed its nationality and became the symbol of the state of Missouri.

National Frontier Trails Center

The best place to start an auto tour along the historic Santa Fe Trail is the National Frontier Trails Center at Independence,

Missouri. Although Becknell and others first set out for Santa Fe from Franklin, a town on the Missouri River 110 miles east of Independence, it was only a few years until traders were equipping their caravans to leave from Independence. The debarkation point for steamboats from St. Louis gradually moved upriver, shifting westward as the wagoneers sought to shorten their overland journey. Franklin, a booming town in the 1820s, was later obliterated when the Missouri River changed course and swept it away.

The Trails Center is testimony to the fact that Independence was the jumping-off place not only for the Santa Fe Trail but for the emigrants of the later Oregon Trail and California Trail as well. The center is housed in a renovated red brick flour mill located at a site where the Santa Fe wagonmasters once came to fill their barrels with springwater. Within walking distance are a number of historic sites associated with all three of the trails, including a swale that remains where the wagons crossed a creek at Santa Fe Trail Park.

The exhibits and a 17-minute film at the center underline the differences between the Santa Fe Trail and the emigrant trails. The Santa Fe Trail was nine hundred miles long; the Oregon and California Trails were more than two thousand miles long. The size of the wagons differed too. Big Conestoga wagons were popular on the Santa Fe Trail because they could carry a lot of cargo; smaller wagons were required on the Oregon and California trails, wagons that could be pulled more easily over the mountains.

Visitors enter the exhibits through a "main street," with its saddlery, dry goods, and blacksmith shops, shops that made Independence between 1830 and 1850 one of the busiest provisioning towns on the frontier. The center also houses an important collection of books, diaries, and letters of the pioneers in the Merrill J. Mattes Research Library. If they wish visitors may delve further into America's great westward movement or trace a pioneer ancestor who traveled on one of the trails.

Council Grove, Kansas

The auto tour folder guides travelers through Independence and metropolitan Kansas City toward Council Grove, Kansas, along highways that closely follow the original Santa Fe Trail. At

State Line Road near 85th Street in Kansas City stands the home of Alexander Majors, one of the leading freighters on the Santa Fe Trail and later a partner with William Russell and William Waddell in the Pony Express venture. At Olathe, 20 miles southwest of Kansas City just off I-35 (Exit 220), is the Mahaffie Farmstead and Stagecoach Stop, the only known Santa Fe Trail stage station open to the public.

Owned and operated by the city of Olathe, the two-story lime-stone homestead in the 1860s did double duty as living quarters for the large Mahaffie family and as a food stop and a place to change horse teams on the stagecoaches that in later years shared the Santa Fe Trail with the larger freight wagons. Of particular interest are the dining room and kitchen in the cellar. When each stagecoach arrived at this first "eating station" west of the Missouri River, its six to fifteen passengers entered the cellar door and had their meal at a large table. The kitchen was at the opposite end. A well-preserved stone ice house and a wood peg barn are also part of the farmstead. An annual event, "Bullwhacker Days," is held each June to commemorate the days of the trail with wagon and carriage rides, a craft show, and demonstrations of cooking, butter churning, and candle making.

Council Grove, a place on the trail where the wagoneers could purchase supplies for the long trek, owes its name to a meeting that took place in 1825 between Osage Indian chiefs and a U.S. commissioner. The meeting resulted in a treaty whereby the tribes-men allowed a survey to be made of the Santa Fe Trail and guar-anteed safe passage for all traders through their lands in return for $800 in merchandise. A physical reminder of that event—the stump of the Council Oak under which the treaty was signed—still stands on Main Street, now protected by a shelter.

Travelers may have lunch if they choose at the Hays House, a restored building and restaurant constructed right on the Santa Fe Trail in 1857 by Seth Hays, founder of the town and great-grandson of Daniel Boone. He was licensed by the federal govern-ment to trade with the local Kaw Indians. From the mid- to late 1800s, the building served as a mail distribution point, courthouse, government offices, church, theater, and printing site for the town's first newspaper.

Council Grove was a common rendezvous point for the west-bound wagons. When all the wagons had arrived a captain was chosen by vote of all the men, whether independent traders or hired hands. The captain in turn appointed a wagon boss, a pack train boss, a chief scout, lieutenants for the various divisions, and a wrangler for the loose stock, animals that were driven along as replacements. Rules were laid down, the position of each division in the caravan was set, and each man was assigned his hours for night guard duty.

At Council Grove the caravans found ample water, grass, and wood in the region's extensive groves of hardwoods. Blacksmith and supply shops sprang up to support the wagon trains coming through. A number of businesses developed, one of which was the Last Chance Store; the building still stands, as do several other historic structures. For three days in the second week in June, Council Grove honors its early history with a parade, powwow, carnival, pioneer crafts, trail rides, and tractor pulls.

Larned, Kansas

The auto route continues along U.S. Highway 56, a highway that closely follows the original Santa Fe Trail's desert route all the way from Kansas City to the vicinity of Fort Union in New Mexico. One of the finest examples of trail ruts anywhere along the trail can be found near U.S. 56, 110 miles west of Council Grove. Four miles west of Chase, Kansas, then one mile north on a side road, brings the traveler to "Ralph's Ruts," so called because they lie on Ralph Hathaway's farm. A DAR marker, one of the many stone markers that the Daughters of the American Revolution erected as a public service between 1906 and 1912 to identify the Santa Fe Trail, indicates where to find these grassy swales. Up to seven swales appear side by side at some places.

The Santa Fe Trail wagons, after rolling across the Kansas prairie for several weeks, and 250 miles from Independence, reached the Arkansas River near the present-day town of Great Bend, Kansas. Those who chose the desert route followed the Arkansas for another 100 miles before striking out across the water-poor prairie in Becknell's footsteps; those who would lead their wagon trains over the mountain route continued up the river another 200 miles.

Another trail landmark along U.S. 56 is Pawnee Rock, six miles northeast of Larned. One of the best-known natural features along the trail, it is noted in many of the diaries as a potential

Indian ambush spot. Hundreds of those who passed by carved their names in the soft red Dakota sandstone, reputedly including Kit Carson, Robert E. Lee, and Susan Shelby Magoffin, a young wife who kept a diary of her journey that has been a great help to historians. It is difficult if not impossible to discover many of these names today because settlers and railroad crews stripped nearly twenty feet of stone from the top of the 100-foot rise to use in building their homes and the roadbed of the Santa Fe Railroad. Nevertheless Pawnee Rock still offers a panoramic view of the surrounding Kansas prairie from the park's observation point atop the hill.

As the result of the vast new southwestern territories won in the Mexican War and the gold strikes in California in 1849, traffic increased over the trail. Some eighteen hundred wagons crossed the Santa Fe Trail in 1858 alone. Inevitably this influx of settlers, merchants, gold-seekers, and adventurers disrupted the Indians' way of life. Believing their very existence to be in jeopardy, the Indians began to strike back, attacking the commerce, mail shipments, and emigrants on the trail. To counter these attacks the Army established five posts along the route.

One, Fort Larned, was constructed in 1859 near the Arkansas River, seven miles upstream on a tributary. Like the other military outposts, Fort Larned offered not only protection and refuge for the travelers, but also respite from the rigors of the journey and a chance to replace broken axles and dwindling supplies. With increasing Indian resistance Fort Larned by 1859 was providing armed escorts for mail coaches and by 1864 armed escorts for freight caravans as well. Later the fort served as a distribution point for annuities paid by the U.S. government in food, clothing, and other necessities to the Cheyennes, Arapahoes, Kiowas, and Comanches; in return for the annuities the Indians promised to settle on the reservations assigned to them.

Visitors to Fort Larned walk into a classic U.S. Army frontier fort—sandstone and timber buildings surrounding a parade ground with a flagpole in the center. A barracks, a hospital, a commissary, an arsenal, a quartermaster storehouse, a building that contains a bakery and a blacksmith shop, a schoolhouse, and officers' quarters—all are open to the public. A visitor center and museum offer a slide program and exhibits of the clothing, weapons, and equipment used by the soldiers and the Plains Indians. An original Conestoga wagon is on display in the Quartermaster Storehouse. National Park Service interpreters and volunteers play the roles of some of the soldiers, craftsmen, and wives who lived at the fort.

Fort Larned.

Three miles west of Larned is the Santa Fe Trail Center, a regional museum. Exhibits describe the prehistory of the area, the commerce over the trail, and the resulting settlement of the region. A reconstruction of a freight wagon and other exhibits attract the attention of the numerous school groups that visit. The center also collects artifacts, maintains an extensive research library, and every other year conducts an annual Rendezvous Seminar for scholars of the trail. It also serves as the headquarters of the Santa Fe Trail Association.

Cimarron (Desert) Route

Leaving Fort Larned, the Santa Fe wagon trains continued along the Arkansas River to what is now Dodge City. A vivid reminder of the old trail days greets today's traveler nine miles west of Dodge City. Wagons, often traveling four abreast, have left parallel tracks that still crease the flat plain for almost a mile. These ruts follow a low ridge and have been preserved by the Boot Hill Museum of Dodge City.

At this point in the journey wagon captains after 1846 had to make a decision—whether to take the mountain or the desert route. Each had its advantages and disadvantages. The mountain route was not only 100 miles longer, it was more rugged. Wagons, which found use after 1846, had bumpy going over the ravines and steep slopes, especially at Raton Pass. Here rain often turned the loose soil into sticky mud that could bog down a wagon. On the other hand mountain creeks and springs provided the wagon trains with adequate water, and the route skirted much of the trouble with the Indians.

The Cimarron Route led from the Arkansas River in southwestern Kansas across the barren plains to the Cimarron River and thence into New Mexico. Here it rejoined the mountain route near Fort Union. It was shorter but also drier and hotter. By 1847 this route was vulnerable to raids by Cheyenne, Arapaho, Kiowa, or Comanche Indians, and its use had resulted in the deaths of more than forty traders, destruction of many wagons, and the loss of thousands of head of livestock.

It was the Cimarron that Becknell had pioneered on his second trip to Santa Fe. He and his men struggled across the so-called *jornada,* a 60-mile stretch of waterless flatland where little grew but shortgrass, sagebrush, and prickly pear. From that hard-won experience Becknell learned the location of the few springs and other water sources that exist along this otherwise waterless route.

Even when they reached the Cimarron River, they found it to be a dry riverbed that fills only rarely during a summer storm. But by digging down 6 to 18 inches into the sand they were able to find water. Today, although not in those times, the traveler can find the location of a river in this desert by noting the cottonwood and tamarack trees that often line its bank.

It is difficult for the modern traveler to imagine these hazards of the *jornada* because today this part of southwestern Kansas and Oklahoma is covered with knee-high prairie grass punctuated with grain storage towers. Cattle feedlots dot the landscape. Once a part of the Dust Bowl of the 1930s, the region has been revegetated.

To view a segment of the trail as it actually might have appeared to the early wagon drivers visit the Cimarron National Grassland near Elkhart at the southwesternmost tip of Kansas. The U.S. Forest Service has laid out a 50-mile tour road, 23 miles of which retraces the historic trail across fenceless prairie that stretches to the horizon. The grassland was established in 1938 when the federal government bought many acres of land from drought-stricken farmers and used a variety of reseeding techniques to restore the prairie grasses.

Sandstone markers have been erected within the swales that show the outline of the trail as it runs alongside the grassland's tour road and the nearby Cimarron River. This is one of the few places along the entire Santa Fe route where the tourist can walk along the historic trail in a setting similar to what the trail freighters experienced.

Here the traveler can also see one of the few springs that were vital to wagoneers' survival. Springs along the Cimarron Route were generally about a day's travel apart. Today at Middle Spring the visitor finds cottonwood trees ringing a small lake, a surprising oasis in this barren prairie. The Forest Service has developed a picnic area beneath the trees; an interpretive sign points out, however, that during the trail days the grass here would have been trampled and the water muddied by the thirsty livestock that crowded in to drink. By the time the trail party arrived at the spring, one of the traders wrote, all you could do was "close your eyes, hold your nose and drink it [the water] anyway."

There are several other interest points along the tour road. A distinctive landmark, Point of Rocks, rises 108 feet above the Cimarron riverbed and was used by the Indians as a lookout to watch for buffalo. A short side road leads to an active prairie dog town. Another stop describes one of the few remaining prairie chicken booming grounds in the country. Each spring the male prairie chicken performs its fascinating ritual in the morning and evening, a ritual mating dance (see page 70) that visitors may watch from a nearby observation blind.

Mountain Route

When the United States declared war on Mexico in 1846, the Army of the West under Colonel Stephen Watts Kearny made use of the well-trod Santa Fe Trail to move against the Mexicans. To avoid the Indians who menaced the Cimarron Route Kearny's men improved the mountain route that led over Raton Pass.

To retrace the mountain route today follow U.S. Highway 50 and Colorado 191 from Dodge City to Bent's Fort near La Junta, Colorado. Wagon travelers needed at least three weeks to cover this distance; today's traveler can drive it in six hours.

The fort was the most important port of call and trading hub along the way after the mountain route was opened. A fortified trading post, it was constructed in 1833. The sturdily constructed adobe structure was built by three partners, Charles and William Bent and Ceran St. Vrain, all enterprising trappers and traders. They chose a spot far up the Arkansas River where U.S. territory met Mexico. The fort's location on the frontier made it a perfect meeting place for trappers to barter their furs, for Plains Indians to barter buffalo robes, and for traders on the Santa Fe Trail to buy or barter for food, wagon and gun repairs, and horses.

The old trading post has been painstakingly reconstructed by the National Park Service as Bent's Old Fort National Historic Site. It was called the "Castle of the Plains" by diary writers on the trail, a reference to its two-foot-thick adobe walls, armed bastions at the corners, and reinforced front gate.

Rangers guide visitors across the large courtyard to see the trade and council room; dining room and kitchen; William Bent's quarters; shops for blacksmiths, carpenters, wheelwrights, coopers, and gunsmiths; trappers' quarters; warehouses; and quarters used by soldiers who came with Colonel Kearny on the way to fight the war with Mexico but who fell ill with dysentery and scurvy. The colorful Indian trade room has shelves stacked high with blankets, sugar, food, rifles, and barrels of flour. The proprietors' dining room boasted a white tablecloth, china, fine wine, and food prepared by a black slave. The fort even had a billiards room with a table brought from St. Louis. Interpreters portray trappers and American Indians as they bring to life this historic fort, which added a touch of civilization to the frontier.

From La Junta motorists follow U.S. Highway 350 to Trinidad, Colorado, then I-25 southward over Raton Pass to Santa Fe. At first this part of the Santa Fe Trail was suitable only for pack trains, not wagons. The bottleneck was the Raton Pass, a rugged, twisting, 20-mile gap through the mountains. The uncorking of this bottleneck came in the 1840s, when a roadway was cleared and roughly graded into a usable wagon road. In 1846 the U.S. Army engineers improved the roadway through the mountains so the Army could pull one thousand wagons and supplies to Santa Fe. Twenty years later a private rancher, "Uncle Dick" Wootten, further improved and shortened it, charging a 25-cent toll for each wagon and 10 cents for each head of livestock that made its way through the pass.

Fort Union National Monument

The road to Santa Fe took on new importance after the U.S. victory in the Mexican War (1846–1848). Wagon trains laden with military supplies joined the commerce of the prairies. Mail and passenger coaches hurried back and forth between Missouri and Santa Fe. The war, which drew Texas, New Mexico, and California within the national boundaries, made the United States a continental nation. Henceforth the Santa Fe Trail would serve as a vital corridor to the new southwestern possessions.

To protect this lifeline between the states and New Mexico, the Army in 1851 established Fort Union near the junction of the Cimarron and mountain routes. It served not only as a base of operations but as the principal quartermaster depot for the Southwest. During its first few years Fort Union's mounted troops also provided armed escorts for mail stages, the troops often riding in wagons behind the stage drivers. Until the Civil War period the Santa Fe caravans for the most part had provided for their own defense.

The visitor to Fort Union finds only the skeletal remains of many of the adobe buildings that once made it the largest U.S. military installation on the nineteenth-century frontier. To help bring the ruins to life the visitor is given a folder that contains an illustration depicting the fort as it formerly existed and is then directed on a self-guided tour of the extensive ruins. At many of the building sites an audiotape gives a fictional conversation that could have occurred at this location. A wagon teamster, for example, expresses his relief as he nears the end of the trail and describes for the Army quartermaster the cargo he is carrying.

The park staff also provide visitors with a self-guiding tour map of nearby Santa Fe Trail sites. The map identifies the location of some of the most dramatic ruts to be seen anywhere on the trail. Most of the ruts are shallow depressions in the landscape, but others have been deepened by erosion from rainstorms. Another significant nearby site is the town of Watrous, where Mexican wagons gathered before heading east along the trail.

History comes to life at Fort Union.

Santa Fe

For its final 80 miles to Santa Fe the historic trail is closely paralleled by I-25. The highway is marked with the familiar brown-and-white historic trail logo. Travelers can identify some of the historic ruts alongside the highway from time to time.

One of the last campsites for those who trekked the Santa Fe Trail was at Pecos, a deserted Indian pueblo, a site often mentioned in the diaries of the early trail travelers. The writers probably little appreciated the antiquity of the site. Today archeologists at Pecos have unearthed one of the largest ancient Indian pueblos in the country as well as two mission churches built under the direction of Franciscan priests in the seventeenth and eighteenth centuries. Pecos Pueblo, originally settled in prehistoric times, is preserved as a National Park Service historic park. Visitors tour the ruins of the adobe and masonry pueblo and its church and view the exhibits at the park visitor center.

Finally Santa Fe! In the glory days of the trail, the long wagon trains would come rumbling into Santa Fe, once the capital of the Mexican province of New Mexico, later the capital under U.S. rule of the New Mexico Territory. Oxen would snort and mules bray as the bullwhackers snapped their whips and guided the wagons down the narrow streets packed with shouting Mexicans. The drivers shouted exaggerated "Hoo-haw-w-ws" as they circled the city plaza and rolled up to the warehouses. Soon the wagoneers would barter their farm tools, cotton goods, and linens for silver and gold, mules and furs.

Visitors to Santa Fe can still capture the feeling of the old days as they walk under the shaded portico of the Palace of the Governors, constructed in 1610 by New Mexico's second governor. American Indians sit on blankets under the portico selling jewelry, baskets, and clothing to the passing tourists. The Palace is home to the Museum of New Mexico with its collection of early artifacts. The boisterous days of the trail are relived each August when the Palace Rendezvous and Buffalo Roast celebrates the trail's importance with a costumed 1850s trade fair in the plaza.

As Santa Fe became saturated with goods traders shifted their attention to the interior of Mexico. In the 1840s and 1850s they began carrying more supplies to meet the increasing needs of western military forts. Following the Mexican War in 1848, emigrants began to join the tradesmen on the Santa Fe Trail toward the Southwest although the trail remained primarily a route of commerce.

The clash of cultures along the trail brought increased American pressures on the Indian population in the Southwest, leading to disruption of tribal life and the loss of traditional lands. Negotiated treaties between the United States and Native Americans were violated or not fulfilled. During and after the Civil War Indian tribes increasingly threatened and attacked the traffic on the trail.

But it was the iron horse that finally brought an end to the oxen and mule—and indeed to the Santa Fe Trail itself. Railroad construction toward the Southwest started from the Missouri River near the end of the Civil War. As the railroads laid their track westward the wagon trail grew progressively shorter. On February

9, 1880, the first steam engine passed near Santa Fe, ending nearly sixty years of heavy overland use of the Santa Fe Trail.

The era of wagons, oxen, and mules hauling loads of manufactured goods to exchange for Mexican goods faded into history. No longer would the creaking wagons and the snorting oxen need to rumble across the rutted plains as the Santa Fe Trail faded from active use.

Santa Fe Trail Association

The Santa Fe Trail Association, organized in 1986, promotes the appreciation of the significance of the Santa Fe Trail. The association counts thirteen hundred members, people who live throughout the United States and several foreign countries. It aids the National Park Service in defining the trail, encourages landowners along the trail route to preserve historic buildings, assists in marking the route so people can follow it, preserves graves, and undertakes research on the trail. It publishes and mails to its members an informative quarterly newsletter and sponsors a biennial symposium at which members present papers on historical aspects of the trail.

The association has its headquarters at the Santa Fe Trail Center. For more information write the Santa Fe Trail Association, Santa Fe Trail Center, R.R. #3, Larned, KS 67550.

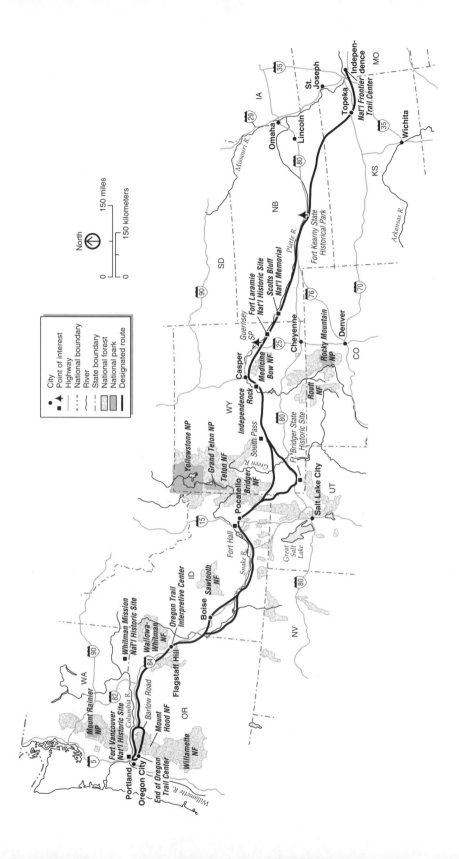

Chapter 13

OREGON NATIONAL HISTORIC TRAIL

T HE WAGON TRAIN WAS STRUNG OUT ACROSS THE PRAIRIE A MILE IN length, each wagoneer avoiding the plume of dust from the wagon ahead by keeping slightly to the right or to the left. The thud of oxen hooves and the occasional snap of a whip provided a counterpoint to the rattle of tinware and cooking utensils inside the wagons as the caravan jostled slowly along at a rate of 10 to 15 miles a day.

Each of the canvas-covered wagons was piled high with flour, pilot bread, and beans; bacon, dried fruit, and coffee; sugar, salt, and vinegar; plows, axes, and bucksaws; rocking chairs and chamber pots; cast-iron skillets and Dutch ovens; linsey-woolsey shifts and buckskin shirts; feather beds and patchwork quilts; water kegs and butter churns; violins and books.

A few of the emigrants—the nineteenth-century name for the pioneers who crossed the continent, leaving the United States behind—rode saddle horses but most of them trudged along on foot. Only the sick, some of the women, and the smallest children rode inside the wagons; there was no room for the others in the packed interior of a wagon 12 feet long, 10 feet high, and 4 feet wide. Both the riders and the walkers prodded along the loose herd of milk cows and the extra oxen and mules that brought up the end of the wagon train. Relatively few of the oxen and cows, it should be noted, would make it to the end of the trail; a number would be slaughtered as other sources of food ran out.

The oxen strained heads-down against the rattling chains and hickory yokes. Above the shouts of the teamsters, a wagon axle squealed for an application of grease. Inside a wagon, something tipped and fell with a crash, causing a napping infant to awake with a wail.

These were the sights and sounds of the four- to six-month, 2,000-mile journey over the Oregon Trail. It had been four decades since the Lewis and Clark expedition had pointed the way to the Pacific Northwest, and the mountain men and trappers had broken the first trails across the mountains. Now, in the 1840s, settlers were following their lead.

The trek of 1843 was the first to take entire families—some 260 men, 130 women, and 610 children—by wagon all the way to today's Oregon. During the next 25 years as many as 350,000 people in an estimated 75,000 covered wagons would complete the trek, leaving behind a vivid record of their journeys in the pages of hundreds of journals. Excerpts from these journals form a graphic part of the exhibit at the Museum of Westward Expansion at the Jefferson National Expansion Memorial at St. Louis.

Their destination, Oregon country, was a region of some five hundred thousand square miles that encompassed what is today Oregon, Washington, Idaho, British Columbia, and parts of Montana and Wyoming. As a result of the War of 1812, the United States and Great Britain had agreed to a unique proposition—that the people of either nation could settle in this unpeopled territory.

The families of the 1843 expedition gathered at Independence, Missouri. The United States was in the midst of a severe depression, and farmers in the East and Midwest faced low market prices for their produce and forbidding mortgage payments on their farms. Seeking a way out of their troubles, many hitched up their wagons, loaded their families and belongings, and headed for the free land that beckoned on the new frontier in the West.

Even so, costs for procuring a wagon, animals, and supplies for the migration could cost $1,000 or more. The confidence of prospective settlers was boosted, however, by new maps and the journals of those who had preceded them. John C. Frémont of the U.S. Army map making corps had only recently traveled through the West and had written precise details of the best route through the Rockies. Frémont's maps were submitted to Congress in 1843 and immediately published. They helped convince thousands of would-be settlers that travel on the Oregon Trail could be safe and practical.

From the main jumping-off point at Independence, Missouri, the Oregon Trail angled west across the Kansas grasslands and into Nebraska. From there it followed the broad and shallow Platte River, rising gradually through the Nebraska prairies into the dry, desolate high plains. Past Fort Laramie, in what would later become Wyoming, the trail climbed through an undulating landscape covered with sagebrush and bunchgrass toward the snow-covered Rocky Mountains. It crossed the Continental Divide at a low saddle called South Pass (seven thousand feet in elevation), the only known wagon route through the Rockies north of New Mexico.

After crossing at South Pass the trail entered the arid eastern regions of the Oregon country, an area too harsh and intemperate to attract settlers. It followed the winding, well-named Snake River through a succession of difficult mountain ranges before reaching the surging waters of the Columbia River. The last hundred miles down the Columbia was the hardest part of the entire journey; the emigrants had to build rafts to float their wagon bodies downriver through treacherous falls to reach the promised land—the fertile Willamette Valley. Only later, in 1846, would Samuel Barlow complete a wagon road over the mountains that skirted the river and proved to be a safer, easier route to western Oregon.

Starting Out

All the hopes and dreams for a new life in the West came together at Independence, Missouri, where the settlers got off the steamboat that had brought them upstream from St. Louis. Present-day visitors who view the exhibits at the National Frontier Trails Center at Independence (see page 179) will sense the mingled feelings of anticipation and sadness felt by many of the pioneers—anticipation of a better life for them and for their children; sadness at leaving behind loved ones they would likely never see again.

At the Trails Center today's visitors walk along "Main Street," which represents the rough-hewn Independence of the 1840s. The original log huts of the town by this time had given way to a collection of clapboard structures holding dry goods stores, barbershops, grog houses, and emporiums that housed wheelwrights, blacksmiths, saddlers, harness makers, and every other sort of craftsman needed to prepare an expedition for the cross-country journey. Traders, trappers, and emigrants thronged the streets. The noise of cracking whips mingled with the braying of mules as men broke in their oxen and mule teams and waited for the grass out on the prairie to grow green.

The Trails Center makes as good a jumping-off point for today's motorist as it did for the original pioneers. Travelers should pick up a free foldout National Park Service folder, "Oregon Trail" (GPO 1993-342-398/80012), a comprehensive and informative map that highlights the historic sites along the trail and identifies the highways that most closely follow the original trail. The Trails Center also offers an excellent research library where visitors may uncover information about their forebears who went west on the Oregon Trail. A few city blocks from the Trails Center is the historic Brady Cabin, the site of a free-flowing spring where the settlers filled up their water barrels.

Kansas

Before setting out across Kansas, each group of emigrants elected officers for the trek. Then, one April morning, they headed west. Usually it was an ex–mountain man who was selected to lead the train with its cargo of dreams, inexperience, and determination.

The first weeks were shakedown. The men learned how to keep a team moving and the proper techniques for fording or ferrying across a stream. Women learned to cook unfamiliar foods over a buffalo-chip fire. And kids, on the greatest adventure of their young lives, saw their first lizard and stepped on their first cactus. The family wagon would be "home" for the next four months or more. These were not the heavy freight-carrying Conestoga wagons used on the Santa Fe Trail; these were smaller and lighter-weight wagons that could be more easily pulled by oxen or mules and could be hauled up or lowered down a steep slope.

Some thirty miles west of Independence, the Oregon Trail crossed the Santa Fe Trail, the trail of commerce that by then had been in use for 20 years. The wagon trains traversed the northeastern corner of what is now Kansas, crossing the Kansas River near present-day Topeka.

Nebraska

Angling across what became the states of Kansas and Nebraska they reached the Platte River, the river that would serve as both a trail guide and a source of drinking water for many miles westward. *Nebraska* is an Indian word meaning "flat and shallow"; *platte* is a French word meaning the same; both apply to the Platte River, a broad, muddy band of water that flows in lazy curves from the Rocky Mountains to the Missouri. One disenchanted traveler wrote that the river is "bad to ford, destitute of fish, too dirty to bathe and too thick to drink."

Maybe so, but it provided much-needed water for the oxen, cattle, horses, and mules. The plains on either side were covered with short-grass but bare of trees. Emigrants marveled at the animals that roamed these plains—antelope, coyotes, grizzly and black bears, prairie dogs, and buffalo. One journal reported a herd of buffalo that took two days to pass by. The pioneers discovered that the buffalo were invaluable as a source of fuel as well as meat. Buffalo chips—dried dung—that littered the ground were essential to the pioneers to cook their meals and warm their bodies on these timberless plains. The chips could be brought to a blaze only in a well-drafted fire pit rather than an iron stove so wagon train women had to learn new techniques of cooking over an open fire.

Where the trail meets the Platte River, a spot called the "Gateway to the Great Plains," the U.S. Army in 1848 built the first of a chain of military forts that would stretch to the Rockies and protect the overland migration routes. Today's traveler will find the reconstructed Fort Kearny along I-80, just south of the river from the city of Kearney. Visitors may wander around the fort's stockaded grounds and peer into a log-and-sod powder magazine and a well-equipped blacksmith and carpenter shop. A visitor center, museum, and slide show tell the fort's story.

To continue to trace the Oregon Trail follow I-80 and the Platte River 150 miles west to the village of Brule. Near here the wagon trains had to cross from the south bank of the river in order to connect with a tributary, the North Platte, which continued westward. In May or early June, when the settlers usually arrived, the river was swollen from melting mountain snows, and the crossing was hazardous. Men, teams, and wagons simply plunged in and by swimming or floating wrestled the heavily laden wagons across the flowing river with its sandy bottom. At times of high water wagon wheels would be removed and the wagon box turned into a flat-bottomed boat and floated across.

Once across they had to climb a steep grade, California Hill, then descend into the valley of the North Platte on a slope so steep they had to lock wagon wheels and lower the wagons by ropes. Their reward was Ash Hollow, a veritable oasis that many settlers fondly remembered in their diaries. This verdant campsite offered wood for cutting into firewood, water from a spring, and shade that contrasted with the hot sun of the open prairie. Wagon ruts are still visible a century-and-a-half later where the wagons slid down Windlass Hill, now part of a Nebraska state park. Walking paths lead the traveler to the historic spring, an early schoolhouse, a 1850s trading post site, and a visitor center.

To continue take U.S. Highway 26 west, which runs parallel to both the North Platte and the old Oregon Trail. Thirty miles before reaching Scotts Bluff, today's traveler gets the same view that yesterday's settler did when he sees on the horizon the striking landmark called Chimney Rock, a rocky shaft that rises from a conical base 500 feet above the surrounding prairie. To the settlers this stone dagger pointing into the sky was more than a wonder of nature. To them it signaled that the second phase of their long journey west—the difficult mountain passage—was about to begin.

Another monument on the trail, Scotts Bluff is a massive sandstone and clay formation that soars 400 feet skyward from the flat tableland. "Hill that is hard to go around," the Indians called it, and it was. Early wagon trains detoured eight miles in order to bypass it. After 1850 the corrugated land at the foot of the bluff was smoothed out enough to allow the wagons to take this shorter route and avoid the detour.

Now visitors walk where the pioneer wagons rattled through. A footpath leads along trail ruts that have eroded deeper than the length of a person's head. From the trail sightseers look up at the tan flank of Scotts Bluff, called by the pioneers the "Nebraska Gibraltar." Visitors can reach the top of the bluff either by hiking a 1.6-mile trail or driving a curving two-lane roadway to the crest. A self-guiding trail at the summit leads to two overlooks and a spectacular view of the countryside. The visitor center of this national monument contains the nation's best collections of photographs, sketches, and paintings by the well-known western photographer William Henry Jackson.

Scotts Bluff National Monument.

Wyoming

Soon after entering Wyoming, the trail follower comes to Fort Laramie, the second in the series of frontier forts. Originally a fur-trading post, it was purchased by the Army in 1849. For the next forty years it offered Indians, trappers, traders, missionaries, overland pioneers, gold-seekers, and miners an outpost of civilization where the prairie met the Rocky Mountains.

Much of the feeling of the old fort has been preserved by the National Park Service at Fort Laramie National Historic Site. Visitors tour the typical quadrangle-shaped military fort with a "Historic Buildings Guide," a pamphlet that tells the story behind each structure. At some buildings they meet a "cavalryman," a "trader," or an "officer's wife"—a living history personality who helps the visitor step back in time and get the feeling of what life was like at the fort in the 1800s. A visitor center in the commissary storehouse presents a film, displays artifacts, and contains a bookstore that offers a wide selection of historical publications.

Fifteen miles west of Fort Laramie, near Guernsey, Wyoming, are probably the most dramatic trail ruts remaining from the Oregon Trail. Here rugged terrain forced the wagons to go single file to surmount a narrow ridge of sandstone. The continual crunching, grinding, and scraping of thousands of hoofs and wagon wheels gradually wore deep ruts in the stone, eventually shaping a trough that cuts five feet deep into the stone surface.

Close to the "Guernsey Ruts" is Register Cliff, another trail landmark. Both are preserved as part of Wyoming's Guernsey State Park. Today's traveler looks through a protective chain-link fence to read the names of those on the Oregon Trail who scratched their names and hometowns into the chalky surface of the cliff. Other names of more recent vintage have also been etched in the cliff, so it is difficult to tell the historic graffiti from the more recent.

Several more days' travel brought the pioneers to present-day Casper, where the North Platte swings due south, and the caravans had to cross the river to continue westward. Travelers might want to pay a visit to Fort Casper, another in the string of military posts. Adventurous tourists may want to sign up with a local outfitter here to ride in Conestoga wagons on a one- or two-day adventure that retraces a portion of the Oregon Trail.

To the settlers the land here seemed mostly barren. From a distance the mountainsides looked like green meadows, but up close they turned out to be dry sand and rock, dotted by stunted clumps of sage and greasewood. Water and good grazing were scarce until the pioneers connected with the Sweetwater River, a river that probably got its name from the relief it brought the wagon trains.

A favorite campsite along the Sweetwater lay beside a granite monolith known as Independence Rock. This feature is as eye-catching to the motorist on Wyoming 220 today as it must have been to the emigrants, a great rounded shape that rises from the flatland like a giant beached whale.

To get a closer look stop at the contemporary exhibit shelter the Wyoming Highway Department has built near the foot of the rock. Then, as now, people could climb up the sloping surface. But no longer can visitors etch their names into the rock of this "Great Register of the Desert." In 1860 an English traveler estimated he could count some forty thousand to fifty thousand signatures. Although most have been erased by wind and weather, some of the older names are still visible. Some emigrants, it is reported, charged up to five dollars to write on Independence Rock the name of one of their party who was illiterate—an act that would assure a measure of immortality in the event that person did not live to reach the end of the trail.

The trail now heads for South Pass, a critical spot where the Oregon Trail surmounts the Rocky Mountains and the Continental Divide. Only when the wagoneers learned of the existence of South Pass did they decide that a wagon route to the Oregon Territory was feasible. Fremont's survey had brought to the attention of the trail bosses in Independence the existence of the high pass, a route that had long been known to the Indians and to early mountain men, but had since been forgotten.

Historical marker at South Pass along the Oregon, California, and Mormon Pioneer Trails.

Surprisingly South Pass is not a pass at all but a high table-land, unvegetated, featureless, and smooth enough for wagon travel. It is the only practical passage through the Rockies for hundreds of miles. "Had we not been told," one pioneer wrote in his journal, "we should have passed over the dividing ridge through the grand pass of the Rocky Mountains without knowing it." Today an overlook along Wyoming 28 that runs through the pass gives travelers a view of the trail route where it crosses the Divide at 7,550 feet. With a little extra effort, it is possible to see the actual trail ruts and commemorative markers along a pristine section of the trail by leaving the paved road and following directional signs on dirt roads for several miles. One marker at the true pass identifies the Oregon Trail; the other honors Narcissa Whitman and Eliza Spalding, the first two white women to cross South Pass and go west on the Oregon Trail.

Beyond South Pass the overlanders arrived at "the Parting of the Ways," where some wagons broke away from the main trail to take the Sublette Cutoff; it was shorter but lacked water and good grass. Most, however, took the longer but safer route to Fort Bridger, another "pit stop" on the long trek where they could get needed supplies or make repairs.

The trading post had been established at an oasis on a branch of the Green River in 1842 by Jim Bridger and Luis Vasquez. Already a legend in the West, Bridger had been a hunter, trapper, fur trader, and guide in the early days of opening the western mountains and carried the map of half a continent in his head. He had discovered Great Salt Lake and scouted South Pass, which proved to be the western gateway.

"I have established a small fort with a blacksmith shop and a supply of iron in the road of the emigrants," Bridger wrote in advertising his new venture. "They [the emigrants], in coming out, are generally well-supplied with money, but by the time they get here are in want of all kinds of supplies ... horses, provisions, smith work, etc."

A reconstruction of Bridger's log-and-mud trading post lies today just off I-80 in the southwesternmost corner of Wyoming, preserved within Fort Bridger State Historic Site. Visitors who walk into the stockade turn the clock back in time as they meet a "trader" and his wife, both in period frontier dress, who show them through a dim interior stocked with staples and tins of food, black powder, lead, coats, pants, and moccasins. Blankets and furs hang on pegs at the front of the cabin. A recipe for hardtack, a staple of the trail, is free for the taking. The blacksmith shop stands next door. A milk house, wash house, icehouse, and carriage house complete the picture. Cattle graze in a nearby field; emigrants reported that Bridger would even sell them an ox to replace an animal they had lost on the trail.

Each Labor Day weekend all this comes to life when the annual Fort Bridger Rendezvous draws thousands of buckskinners, history buffs, and visitors to the restored trading post. Black powder shoots, archery competitions, Indian dances, blanket judging, and storytelling fill the days with a colorful parade of events.

Idaho

By the time the emigrants reached what is now Idaho, their caravans had been diminished by a number of wagons cutting off to head for the Great Salt Lake and California, leaving the Oregon Trail to the Oregon-bound emigrants only. These emigrants, in turn, had seen their ranks thinned by death as the trek continued. The few evidences of civilization—way stations, forts, and supply points—that had grown up along the eastern half of the trail were not available in Idaho and the emigrants found themselves on their own.

One rest stop did await them, however—Fort Hall, near present-day Pocatello. Fort Hall was a fur-trading post originally established by an American, Nathaniel Wyeth. By the time of the overland migration it had become a post of the British Hudson's Bay Company. This was during the time of U.S. and British joint occupation of the territory. For this reason those on the Oregon Trail who reached Fort Hall were welcomed to Oregon Territory, 1,200 miles from Independence, by Britons rather than Americans. An authentic replica of Fort Hall stands in a city park in Pocatello, just off I-15. Visitors to the museum walk through displays of Indian life, the fur-trading era, and life on the Oregon Trail. Bison, elk, deer, and pronghorn antelope graze in a field outside.

From Fort Hall the emigrants followed the Snake River westward across the state for 300 miles. Western rivers like the Snake, the pioneers found, flowed much more swiftly than the lazy Platte. The Snake at places rushes in torrents through jagged walls of lava canyons. Several rapids and falls interrupt the river's flow as

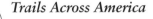

the Oregon Trail parallels the river and I-84 parallels the trail. At Three Island Crossing State Park, just off the interstate, displays at the visitor center describe how the emigrants had to use ropes to wrestle their wagons and teams across the river and how the three islands provided stepping-stones for the crossing. A reenactment of this difficult crossing by the pioneers is staged at the park each August.

Oregon

Entering the Oregon country the landscape gradually changes from treeless desert to a rolling landscape dotted with wooded areas and pastureland. The verdant vistas the pioneers saw confirmed the Oregon they had been told about. Even with weeks to go in their journey, they could anticipate the end of their hardships on the trail.

Ahead, to be sure, lay the Blue Mountains, a forested range that had to be crossed before the early snows. But even as they pushed and shoved the wagons over the rough spots they marveled at the trees they were seeing. They pulled their battered, fixed-up wagons around the brow of a hill—Flagstaff Hill—and caught a glimpse of this promising landscape.

Flagstaff Hill today—just off I-84 near Baker City—is the site of the National Historic Oregon Trail Interpretive Center completed in 1993 by the Bureau of Land Management as part of the 150th anniversary celebration of the Oregon Trail. From an expansive glass window in the contemporary center, the visitor sees the same view of the landscape the emigrants saw—plus eight miles of unbroken trail ruts left from those days. Inside a life-size tableau of plodding, exhausted pioneers is dramatically re-created—voices and all. A film follows a typical trail family that leaves its home in Ohio, endures the rigors of the journey, and finds a new home in Oregon. Outside in a wagon train encampment living history interpreters portray what it was like to live on the trail. Walking trails lead visitors out to see the historic ruts themselves.

Whitman Mission National Historic Site is 31 miles north of the Oregon Trail just over the Washington border, but its history is indelibly tied to the early years of western migration. The mission was established in 1836 by Dr. Marcus Whitman, a Methodist missionary determined to bring religion and civilization to the

Indians of the Pacific Northwest. Whitman and his wife, Narcissa, along with the Reverend Henry and Eliza Spalding, made the long overland journey to Oregon in 1836, helping to blaze what would become the Oregon Trail. Following a route first used by fur traders and trappers, their journey helped establish the possibility of using the trail as a major migration route. The marker back at South Pass commemorates Narcissa Whitman and Eliza Spalding.

The Whitmans' mission became an important way station on the Oregon Trail in 1843 when Marcus Whitman, returning from a trip to the East, guided the first wagon train to the mission. For the next two years the Oregon Trail came through the settlement; later a shorter route bypassed it, thus saving several weeks' travel. Even then the mission continued to serve as an emergency station for those who fell ill or wagons that needed repairs.

Visitors to this National Park Service site see outlines of the buildings of the mission; it was at the mission that Whitman and his wife were later killed in an Indian attack. A film telling the Whitman story is shown at the visitor center. A one-mile, self-guiding trail leads to the former building sites, a restored millpond, apple orchard, a portion of the Oregon Trail and the graves of the Whitmans.

Footsore, exhausted, and low on provisions, the settlers finally reached the mighty Columbia River at The Dalles, a French word meaning "trough," an apt description for the Columbia River Gorge, which carries the river through the Cascade Range. Here the pioneers had to make a decision: either raft the wagons down the treacherous Columbia or take the rough but serviceable Barlow Road that skirted 11,239-foot Mount Hood. The Barlow Road was cheaper and an easier route for livestock, but it was longer and strewn with tree stumps and ravines through a dense forest.

Those who chose to dare the raft trip downriver had to unload their wagons, take off the wheels, and heave the wagons onto rafts that with luck would float them through the gorge. The price to rent a raft from the riverbank entrepreneurs could be steep: $50 to $100, an exorbitant amount for emigrants who had been on the road for months. Many had to trade some of their oxen to pay for it. Once past The Dalles they had to portage around another place where a landslide had clogged the Columbia.

Today's traveler can only imagine these last backbreaking obstacles faced by the Oregon emigrants. The rapids, cascades, and rocks that once made the river so dangerous have been replaced by the still water that backs up behind modern hydroelectric dams; the jouncy wagon trail has been replaced by the concrete lanes of I-84. Thus transformed, the remaining natural beauty of the river valley from The Dalles to Portland is preserved as the Columbia River Gorge National Scenic Area, with its wide river, sheer palisades, and tumbling waterfalls. An interpretive kiosk and a small museum at The Dalles tell the story of the trail.

With the rapids of the Columbia River behind them, the emigrants floated downstream to Fort Vancouver, a prosperous fur-trading post of the British Hudson's Bay Company. They could hardly believe the good fortune that awaited them here in the person of the chief factor, the man in charge, Dr. John McLoughlin. The Canadian took it upon himself to help the new arrivals. As the rafts and boatloads of exhausted pioneers arrived at Fort Vancouver, McLoughlin gave them food, clothing, medicine, agricultural implements, and seeds, sometimes for cash, sometimes on credit. He loaned them boats to take them up the Willamette River to their land grants and even transported some of their livestock. This guardian of the emigrants did whatever he could to make sure the hard-pressed settlers could survive the winter and get off to a good start in the spring. Were it not for his benevolent policies, many of those who made it to the threshold of their destination might have perished.

Travelers will find at Fort Vancouver today an authentic reconstruction of this center of the Hudson's Bay Company's fur-trading empire. Five reconstructed buildings are within the stockade, which lies just across the river from Portland. They include the factor's comfortable house with its furnishings imported from England. The blacksmith shop and the Indian trade shop look as they did a century-and-a-half ago. A visitor center contains an imaginative museum that displays artifacts dug up by archeologists at the site.

Meanwhile those who chose the Barlow Road had to overcome a different set of obstacles. In 1845 two pioneer leaders, Samuel Barlow and Joel Palmer, decided they could find a wagon route around the southern slope of Mt. Hood and bypass the treacherous and expensive Columbia River raft trip. Barlow, Palmer, and a few other men pushed into the Cascades to seek a pass. The conifer forest grew thick and dark, many trees reaching one hundred feet or more in height on the steeply pitched slopes. Rushing streams cut through ravines and snow blanketed the forest for half the year. But Palmer climbed high up Mount Hood and spotted a pass that a road could go through as well as a meadow within the forest where livestock could graze.

After hacking a wagon road partway around the mountain, the Barlow party had to leave their wagons and goods cached for the winter and use their livestock as a pack train to make their way to their destination at the Willamette Valley before winter snows closed in. The following spring they returned to complete cutting the road through the formidable forest. They opened the route as a toll road in the fall of 1846, and it quickly became the most popular choice for the Oregon Trail.

Trail followers can still trace much of the Barlow Trail by car or by foot. At its eastern end hikers, mountain bikers, or four-wheel-drive vehicles can negotiate 23 miles of the primitive trail that lies within Mount Hood National Forest. The trail looks much the way it did originally. Deep troughs indicate where the wagons rolled although in some places trees have grown up within the depressions.

Motorists driving U.S. Highway 26 across the flank of Mount Hood toward Portland closely follow the Barlow route. Several interpretive pullouts along the highway guide the traveler to historic trail sites. One of these is the Pioneer Woman's Grave, a rock-covered mound, the final resting place of an unknown woman who lost her life within days of reaching her destination. Nearby is the grave of the Barclay baby, an infant who was born while her mother was on the trail, but did not survive to journey's end.

But perhaps the most compelling spot a visitor sees along the Barlow Road is Laurel Hill, a steep talus slope where wagons had to be lowered almost vertically by rope down over loose rocks. "Oh, what a hill!" wrote Charles A. Brandt in his diary in 1851. "We looked in dismay and the cattle seemed to moan in distress. But others have descended; so must we."

Determination like this brought tens of thousands of emigrants over the Oregon Trail to settle the green valleys of Oregon and begin a new life. Whether they completed their last lap on the Columbia River or over the Barlow Road, they had traveled some two thousand miles on a journey that had taken about five months.

The last camp for those who came over the Barlow Road was in a meadow near a village that served as the capital of the Oregon Territory. It was grandly called Oregon City. Soon thereafter the new arrivals would appear at the territorial office in Oregon City to stake their claim for the land grant the federal government had promised them.

At the site of their last day's camp, called Abernethy Green—a site now located along I-205 at the outskirts of the city—stands an interpretive center that marks the end of the Oregon Trail. Built to resemble three covered wagons the center portrays the ordeal of the trail from beginning to end. Inside the first wagon-shaped structure visitors view a typical store where emigrants might have bought their supplies at the trail's beginning in Missouri. An audiovisual presentation in the second "wagon" shows images of the long trek across prairie, river, desert, and mountain. In the third "wagon" the emigrants receive their grant of land, begin farming, and settle the Willamette Valley. A Heritage Garden, planted by volunteers, contains plants such as flax, which the pioneers introduced to the Northwest.

The message is clear. For most of those who came over the Oregon Trail the journey was the great passage of their lives. Although it meant leaving friends and family, it opened for them new vistas and a brand-new life. But death and tragedy were common on the trail, too. Rarely, though, was death or injury caused by Indian attack. From 1841 until 1865 on all the historic trails, 362 pioneers died as the result of Indian attack while the wagoneers themselves caused the death of 426 Indians. Instead tragedy usually came as the result of accidents involving firearms, animals, or disease, often an ordinary disease made worse by trail weariness and unsanitary conditions—or most dreaded of all—cholera. About 10 percent of those who started never made it.

A few were disappointed when they arrived—newspapers back East had been full of exaggerated reports. But it truly was a rich land—worthy of the financial and physical risks they had taken. Many of the pioneers founded successful farms and communities. And it was largely because of settlement by these new arrivals that Oregon and Washington became part of the United States as a result of an agreement with England in 1846.

Oregon-California Trail Association

The National Frontier Trails Center at Independence, Missouri, also serves as headquarters for the Oregon-California Trail Association, an organization dedicated to the preservation, appreciation, and enjoyment of all the trans-Mississippi migration trails to the West—"the trails that made the U.S. an ocean-to-ocean nation."

The association has some two thousand three hundred members who belong to ten chapters located in states along the trails. It has members as far away as Japan and played an important role in the commemoration of the 150th anniversary of the Oregon Trail in 1993. Local chapters arrange field trips to trail sites and present programs that throw new light on the historic trails.

OCTA members watch over the historic routes to prevent destruction of trail remnants, graves, and other trail-related sites. Members place markers along the trail and maintain existing signs.

The association encourages scholarly research, publishes articles, and presents educational programs in schools. Its members collect historical data from trail diaries, old newspapers, maps, and other documents that reflect the "Great Migration." A quarterly publication, *The Overland Journal,* carries articles and book reviews. A newsletter brings news of national and chapter activities to the members. An annual convention is held at a trail site each year during the second week in August.

OCTA welcomes new members who have an interest in either the Oregon or California Trail. For more information write the Oregon-California Trail Association, 524 South Osage Street, Box 1019, Independence, MO 64051-0519, or telephone (816) 252-2276.

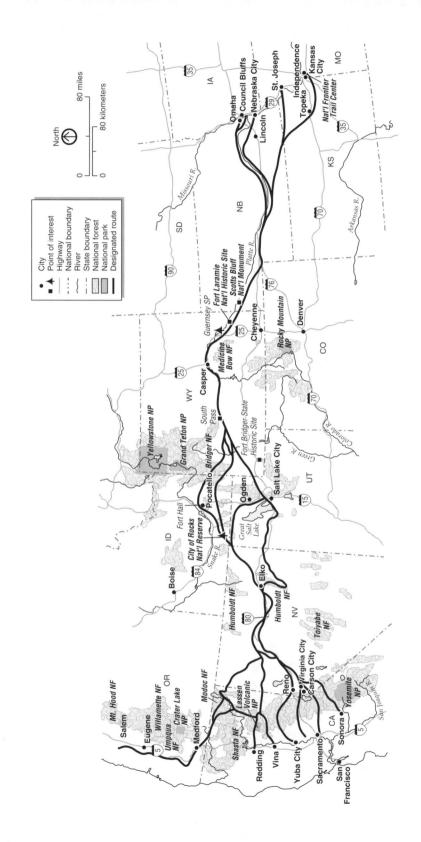

Chapter 14

California National Historic Trail

THE JANUARY DAY THAT IGNITED THE CALIFORNIA GOLD RUSH OF 1849 began routinely enough for James Marshall, the skilled carpenter who was busy building a sawmill for his boss, John Sutter. The mill structure itself, located in the foothills of the Sierra Nevada in California, had been completed. All that remained was to deepen the tailrace so more water would flow through it to power the mill's waterwheel.

On the morning of January 24, 1848, Marshall walked alongside the millrace to see how much his workmen had deepened it. Looking down he spotted some flecks shining at the water's edge. He scooped them up and pressed his fingernail into the yellowish pieces. Then he laid them on a flat rock and pounded them with another rock. Marshall knew that gold was the only yellow metal that would not break into pieces when vigorously pounded; bits of gold tend to meld together into a single piece under pressure. Another difference: Minerals such as iron pyrite (fool's gold) and mica "wink" as light strikes their various facets; pure gold reflects light the same way from any angle.

Placing the fragments inside the crown of his hat he hurried back to announce to his workmen: "Boys, by God, I believe I have found a gold mine!" To make sure, he tried other tests—pounding, boiling in lye, and heating. The shiny fragments passed all the tests.

So Marshall saddled up and rode the forty miles to Sutter's Fort, carrying the gold flecks in a handkerchief, to report his discovery to John Sutter. Today visitors at the well-preserved Sutter's Fort in Sacramento can read the notation Sutter made in his diary that day, stating simply, "Mr. Marshall arrived from the mountains on very important business." It was important, all right. It was gold, Sutter and Marshall agreed.

Although the two tried to keep the discovery a secret—after all, earlier gold strikes in California had soon petered out—the news soon reached beyond the Sierra foothills. A San Francisco newspaper broke the word of the find in March. By June San Francisco was reported to be "half empty" as able-bodied males departed for the mines. The scene was repeated up and down the California coast as people reacted spontaneously to the irresistible cry of "Gold!"

Newspapers in New York City reported the incipient gold rush in August. President James K. Polk confirmed the rumors in his annual message to Congress after an Army officer brought a teapot filled with gold nuggets to Washington. By early 1849 booklets were being printed describing how to mine for gold and how to get to California. Picks and shovels and sluicing pans sold as fast as they reached the stores. Gold fever had struck the nation and the forty-niners were on their way.

There were several routes to California. The safest and most convenient was to take a sailing ship around Cape Horn. Aside from the monotony and the poor food, the chief disadvantage of going by water was that it took so long—six boring months—and cost so much—about $300 per person. A shorter way was to go by sea to Panama, cross the isthmus, and take another ship to California. The port cities of Colon and Panama, however, were filthy and the jungle threatened travelers with cholera and fever. So while it was quicker than sailing around the Horn, it was more inconvenient and dangerous. An advantage of going by water, however, was that the gold-seeker could start his voyage in the winter while those crossing by land had to wait for spring.

Many more of the forty-niners found their way to the goldfields on overland routes. Here the travelers faced all the hardships experienced by the early trail pioneers. In their frantic haste to get to the goldfields to get rich quick, the forty-niners were often poorly equipped and physically soft. Unlike their predecessors, many of whom were farmers with calloused hands and strong backs, many of the gold-rushers were city people unaccustomed to the rigors of outdoor living. Sadly their inexperience sometimes cost them their lives.

By 1849 22,500 gold-seekers had joined the wagon trains already following the route west. In 1850 the figure doubled as 44,000 gold-rushers hit the overland trail.

The Overland Route

Those caught up in the gold fever began their trek by following the same trail west that had been pioneered by both the settlers headed for good farmlands in Oregon and the Mormons headed for their Zion near the Great Salt Lake. Only after going through South Pass in the Rocky Mountains did the California Trail diverge from the Oregon and Mormon Trails as it stretched toward California like the frayed end of a rope.

Thus today's traveler who follows the California Trail sees the same landmarks along the first half of the journey. By this time new overland jumping-off places had been added to Independence, Missouri; Omaha, Nebraska; Westport, Kansas; and St. Joseph, Missouri. And by now many of the gold-seekers were forced to use horses or mules to pull their wagons because the demand for oxen by trail bosses on the other trails had reduced the supply of the favorite draft animal.

Crucial river fords along the Platte River grew to be mud holes from the sheer mass of eager emigrants. Their 60,000 animals clogged the campgrounds and competed with each other for the limited grass of the plains. To compound the problem the city-bred travelers making their way to the goldfields were unfamiliar with animals, axes, and shovels, but made up for it with their youthfulness and enthusiasm.

Greenhorns often tried to carry too much in their wagons. Diary writers noted that the rest areas at Fort Kearny and Fort Laramie, littered with discarded goods, looked like junkyards.

Beyond South Pass those headed for California had to make a big decision. Some of the forty-niners accompanied the Oregon Trail settlers northward as far as Fort Hall, a resupply point on the Snake River in Idaho. They then turned southwestward to reach the Humboldt River in Nevada, a lifesaver of a stream that flowed like a ribbon of hope through the surrounding desert, leading westward toward the Sierra. Others turned southward after South Pass, following the Mormon Trail with its resupply point at

Fort Bridger. At the Great Salt Lake most of them turned north-ward up the valley of the Salt Lake, finally joining up with the others on the Humboldt River route.

Still remaining, however, was the most difficult section of the trail—the 250 miles from the place where the Humboldt comes to its end in a marshy "sink" in western Nevada, across a parched expanse of desert, then over the formidable Sierra to finally reach California. When they reached the Sierra gold-rushers had to make another decision—where to cross the mountains. Should they try the route up the wheel-wrenching Truckee Canyon? Or take the route that led across the Forty Mile Desert to the Carson River, around the southern end of Lake Tahoe, and ended in a hard climb over the Sierra? Or should they take one of several cutoffs developed in the gold rush years to attract miners or settlers to other localities in California?

Fort Hall Route

To trace the Fort Hall route, which swings to the north from South Pass in Wyoming, follow U.S. Highway 191 northwest to its junction with U.S. Highway 26 near Jackson. The traveler then continues on U.S. 26 along the Snake River, just as the gold-rushers did, to reach Fort Hall, located near present-day Pocatello, Idaho.

Following the Snake downstream for 40 miles the emigrants turned southward along the Raft River and soon passed a major landmark on the trail, the City of Rocks. Located near today's Almo, Idaho, only a few miles from the Utah border, these towering formations of granite resemble a silent city.

Many of the overlanders left their names inscribed with axle grease on these rocks, and their journals provide vivid accounts of their impressions. Visitors can still see the trail ruts left by the passing wagons and stock. The City of Rocks served as a junction landmark for other cutoffs as well, including the Salt Lake Valley Cutoff.

City of Rocks National Reserve is now jointly managed by the National Park Service and the Idaho Department of Parks and Recreation. Its granite pinnacles are internationally known as a challenge to technical rock climbers who eagerly come to scale promontories such as Morning Glory Spire, Animal Cracker Dome, and the Boxtop.

Entering Nevada at its northeastern corner, the Fort Hall route reached the Humboldt River at the town of Wells. Appropriately named, the site provided the emigrants with welcome springs in addition to the river itself. The Humboldt offered a lifeline that guided the gold-seekers for three hundred miles across Nevada to a point where the river dwindles into its marshy sink.

Today's traveler drives I-80 along the Humboldt, sharing the same scenery—if not the discomfort—of the pioneer experience. "It is indeed a dreary prospect to look upon," wrote Bennett Clark in July 1849. "Nothing but the hot sterile lands and dusts immediately around us and naught in the distance … . The eye tires and the mind wearies of this tasteless monotony of scenery. The deserts of Arabia could not be more sterile nor more unpleasing to the sight than the country bordering this river. And we have no compensation in the … surly, deep, turbid and narrow water course, bordered with willow and banks abrupt and steep and loose, reminding one continually of the banks of the Missouri."

Other emigrants were wryly amused at the names of rivers and creeks. "Several streams on our route seem to have been named for negative qualities," wrote Henry Allyn. "Raft River because there is nothing within thirty miles that a raft could be made of … Wood Creek with nothing but a little shrubbery on it; Sugar Creek which runs through the soda springs and is so sour man or beast cannot drink it … ."

Towns such as Elko, Winnemucca, and Lovelock grew up where the emigrants found springs and meadows. At places such as this the caravan leaders often decreed a day or two for resting, washing clothes, and cutting hay to prepare for the barren and mountainous stretches ahead.

Although many parties traveled by night through the barren stretches to escape the day's sledgehammer heat, the half-starved animals still frequently collapsed from overwork. More and more possessions had to be abandoned as wagons fell apart. In final desperation many of the wayfarers loaded a few bare essentials on their backs and set out to finish the journey on foot.

Into the Sierras

The California Trail further divided as the overlanders reached the Sierra Nevada. One of the early routes, the one followed by the swiftly flowing Truckee River into the mountains, quickly fell out of favor after the disaster that befell the Donner party in 1846.

To get the full impact of this gripping tragedy drive 35 miles west of Reno on I-80 and visit Donner Memorial State Park high up in the mountains. Here are several sites where members of the ill-fated party built cabins as they tried to survive the early winter weather that eventually brought tragedy to the group. A 22-foot Pioneer Monument and a visitor center and museum mark the summit location where forty-two of the Donner party died of starvation and exposure in the high Sierra.

Fate was against the Donner brothers, George and Jacob, from the beginning. Although they started from Missouri in May, when prairie grass had greened for the cattle to eat and winter's chill had faded, the Donner party soon fell behind schedule. Taking the advice of an unreliable trail promoter, Lansford Hastings, the Donners lost thirty-six oxen, four wagons, and three weeks of valuable time when they took the Hastings Cutoff across an 80-mile stretch of broiling salt desert west of the Great Salt Lake. Other caravans with wiser leaders swung to the north, following the longer but safer Fort Hall route.

The group also suffered internal troubles. James Reed, one of the leaders, was banished after he killed a man in self-defense in a knife fight. Miraculously Reed managed to make it the rest of the way to California on his own.

Even with all this adversity the Donner members might have succeeded in getting up the steep-flanked eastern slope of the Sierra—hauling their wagons laboriously by rope—had they not taken an added week to rest and then been enveloped in a late October snowfall. As it turned out the winter of 1846 was one of the worst ever recorded in the Sierra, with snows accumulating up to 22 feet in drifts, the height of the stone base of the Pioneer Monument, which visitors see at the state park that commemorates the location of the Donners' final camp.

They could go no farther in the heavy snow. Hurriedly they built log cabins and brush tepees for shelter, hoping a thaw might permit them to push on. Three times members of the party tried to move onward but were turned back. Over the next few months weather and lack of food took its toll as a number of members died. In a last desperate effort to break out, ten men and five women set out on foot to get help. Seven of them finally made it to a settlement, having survived on the bodies of their dead companions.

Not until the following February did a relief party succeed in struggling through the deep snows to rescue some of the survivors. A second relief party was led by the once-banished James Reed. Finally, in April, a fourth party of rescuers reached the camp and brought out the lone remaining survivor. Only forty-eight of the ninety members, including most of the women and children of the party, survived the terrible ordeal.

Johnson Route

The Johnson Route, one of the "frayed ends" that leads south of Lake Tahoe and across the Sierra Nevada, soon became the main gateway to California. U.S. Highway 50 traces this route today as it follows the Carson River (now channelized as an irrigation canal). After skirting Carson City and huge Lake Tahoe, it crosses the summit of the Sierra at Echo Summit (7,382 feet), a considerably easier way than two alternate routes, the Truckee and the Carson-Mormon routes.

Ironically one of the gold rush campsites along the Carson River lies only a few miles from what only ten years later would become known as the famous Comstock Lode. This later rush to the Comstock Lode would produce nearly a billion dollars in gold and silver and almost as much excitement as the earlier California gold discovery.

At Genoa, just off U.S. Highway 15 near Lake Tahoe, is Mormon Station State Historic Park. Pioneering Mormons built a simple trading post here in 1850 to sell or barter goods with emigrants on the Carson route. Exhausted travelers would often trade their weary animals for a meal; the traders would then fatten up the animals and resell them to the next customer coming down the trail. A small museum at the park displays relics of this last supply point before reaching the Sierra.

By the time they encountered the mountains about two-thirds of the emigrants were on foot or were packing their gear on animals they had salvaged from their teams. The few who retained their wagons struggled to get them over this last cruel mountain barrier. Although the gold-seekers knew little and probably cared less about the geology they were crossing, they might have been interested to know that the Sierra Nevada, are the result of an upthrusting of the earth's surface that occurred some 15 million years ago, leaving this range with a steep eastern flank and a western slope that declines more gradually toward California's central valley.

The road, rough and rocky, was heavy going for those riding horseback and for foot travelers; for wagoneers it was downright dangerous and frustrating. The wagons had to be lowered down the steep slopes by rope, then hauled and wrestled back up even steeper slopes, leaving every ox or horse and man gasping for breath.

One gold rush veteran, writing in his diary in 1850 after one such torturous day in the mountains, concluded: "This was as much as the horse was able to climb although she had little to carry. They do get wagons up, but how I do not know."

The few who reached the California "diggings" with their wagons intact, however, were well rewarded for their efforts. Wheeled vehicles of any kind and well-trained draft animals were at a premium at the mines. The forty-niner who arrived at the goldfields with a healthy horse and a usable wagon often found he could make more money at the hauling business than he could panning for gold in the rivers.

Today U.S. 50 follows the western slope of the Sierras toward the historic prospecting sites that still remain to remind us of the gold rush. The highway crosses the Eldorado National Forest to Placerville, the heart of the Mother Lode country, and continues to Sacramento. This early wagon route, called the Placerville Road, was suitable for stagecoaches and freight wagons; later it was improved as part of the Lincoln Highway and more recently evolved into U.S. 50—an example of how the old pioneer trails often were the precursors of our modern highways. California 49, which bisects U.S. 50 at Placerville, now links many of the gold rush communities of the Sierra foothills. Along this road through the Mother Lode region travelers will see mines and the remains of several boomtowns that are preserved in a variety of state parks.

Other "frayed ends" of the California Trail unraveled from the Humboldt River during the 1850s as thousands more overland emigrants made their way to the goldfields. These alternate cut-offs led to a variety of destinations. Most were opened as commercial ventures by either towns or private businessmen eager to attract new settlers, laborers, and consumers. Use of these alternate routes varied from year to year according to the destinations of the gold-rushers and emigrants and the salesmanship of various promoters who went east to intercept the approaching wagon trains.

The Applegate Trail, developed by Oregon pioneers as a "backdoor" to Oregon, became yet another route to the goldfields. When news of the California Gold Rush reached Oregon a small rush southward ensued as eager gold-seekers poured down the Applegate Trail into northern California and the diggings.

The other cutoffs ended at various destinations in California. The Lassen Trail, a difficult journey over rugged terrain, was no shorter, and thus never became popular. The Beckwourth Trail, laid out to attract new miners, was also little used. The Nobles Road, which led directly into northern California, attracted gold-rushers to the Shasta City–area mines; it later became a great favorite for livestock drivers bringing herds of sheep and cattle into California. The Sonora Trail was cut through in 1852 in order to bring relief supplies to a group of stranded and starving forty-niners.

Sutter's Fort State Historic Park

The goal of many of the forty-niners on the Johnson Route was the prosperous trading post of Sutter's Fort, today preserved as a state historic park within the city limits of Sacramento. More than a trading post it was actually a self-sufficient community where the trappers, traders, and emigrants could get supplies, buy a fresh horse, and repair their equipment.

John Sutter, a Swiss adventurer and entrepreneur, had built the adobe fort and other buildings of "New Helvetia" (New Switzerland) in 1841. He greatly enjoyed the role of host, graciously welcoming all who came to his fort to help him harvest what he considered the real wealth of California: grapes, wheat, and other crops. Herds of cattle grazed his pastures, and schools of salmon flashed in the undisturbed and unpolluted freshwater streams. The adobe fort was 320 feet long and 150 feet wide. Inside the two-and-a-half-foot-thick walls Sutter employed 350 Native Americans in a blacksmith's shop, carpenter's shop, bakery, distillery, shoemaker's shop, dining hall, and hat and blanket factory. Nearby he had a tannery and a flour mill. To the trail travelers the place must have seemed a veritable shopping center after their days of deprivation on the trail.

Early on John Sutter had foreseen the wave of emigration that "no force will be able to stop." He generously provided food, lodging, and supplies to all who entered his fort in the hope that some of the skilled workmen on the caravans might stay and become part of his workforce. Ironically, when many of Sutter's workmen deserted him to search for gold themselves, his enterprises languished, and eventually he went bankrupt.

When the Donner party came to grief in 1846 it was Sutter who organized the four relief parties that tried to rescue the snowbound emigrants. The starving and half-frozen survivors, when they were found, were brought by their rescuers to Sutter's Fort to recuperate.

Present-day visitors enjoy a varied experience at the reconstructed Sutter's Fort. Using self-guiding audio wands they wander through the re-created fort, observing the activities in its craft shops and admiring the relics of pioneer life and gold rush days on exhibit. Colorful living history volunteers in period dress each summer play the roles of craftsman, soldier, trader, fisherman, and farmer, bringing the old fort to life as they saw, hammer, spin, weave, dip candles, fire muskets, and share with the visitors their knowledge of everyday life in the frontier settlement. Area elementary school students spend a day and a night at the fort with selected teachers and parents under an innovative Environmental Living Program, learning firsthand the skills required of the early settlers of their state. Each summer interpreters in period dress share with visitors their knowledge of these skills of the 1840s.

Marshall Gold Discovery State Park

It was ironic that the sudden influx of the gold rush emigrants that he so openhandedly welcomed brought about the downfall of John Sutter's commercial empire. After all it had been his employee, James Marshall, who had discovered the gold deposits at the nearby American River as he supervised the building of the sawmill, a mill that would add yet another dimension to Sutter's productive enterprises.

But the river, instead of becoming the scene of a frontier sawmill methodically turning out lumber, became the scene of a horde of get-rich-quick gold-seekers panning frantically along its banks. The quiet crossroads village of Coloma soon boomed to a population of 10,000. In the wake of the ever-hopeful miners came storekeepers, doctors, women, lawyers, gamblers, and ministers, all offering services to the miners in return for some of the gold dust the prospectors found. From the American River waves of miners soon fanned out to look for gold in other far-flung river canyons and up in the mountains.

The days of the forty-niners, when prospectors filled the river valley, are recalled at the Marshall Gold Discovery State Historic Park, which lies forty miles east of Sacramento on U.S. 50, then six miles north on California 49. Visitors who walk along the south fork of the American River see a remnant of the mill tailrace where Marshall made his momentous discovery. Nearby stands a replica of the sawmill itself. Trails that wind through the park lead past some of the mining machines the forty-niners used. Two small stone buildings housed Chinese shopkeepers who sold groceries to the numerous Chinese prospectors. A stone monument marks the grave of James Marshall atop a hill, Marshall's hand pointing toward the site of his discovery. Many of the trees that now shade the park—Tree-of-Heaven, black locust, catalpa, and persimmon—were planted by homesick miners to remind them of the homes they longed for.

The exhibits at the park's visitor center depict the three methods of gold mining: placer, hard rock, and hydraulic. Sightseers get a good look at the gold pan, the basic tool of the trade that prospectors used to separate flecks of gold from the gravel and sand that washes down a river from the slowly eroding rock found in a "mother lode." Such bits and flecks, called placer gold, collected in "holes" in the river bottom and sandbars along its edges.

When a prospector ventured into new country he looked first in the streambed placers, which he called "poor man's mines" because any gold that accumulated there could be collected without costly equipment. Having found a promising placer the prospector brought into play his gold pan. This was a three- or four-inch-deep basin made of tin plate or sheet iron with sloping sides. It measured about ten inches across its flat bottom and about fifteen inches across the top.

He shoveled some sand into the pan, submerged the pan in the stream, and spun it slowly with a flipping motion to wash the light sand and silt out over its rim. After five or ten minutes the pan would be washed clean of everything but a spoonful of heavy residue called the drag—probably a corruption of "dregs." Then, with a skillful flick, the prospector fanned out the drag across the bottom of the pan, revealing, if he was in luck, a little comet tail of gold flecks, called colors. He picked out each fleck of gold with a knife or his fingernail and stashed it in a bottle or can, transferring the gleanings to a leather pouch when he quit work in the evening.

In a long day spent squatting in a cold mountain stream, a miner could process about fifty panfuls of sand, and he could make ends meet at high boomtown prices if he averaged 10 cents' worth of gold per pan. In rich placers a miner could sometimes wash panfuls of sand worth $50 each, but such days were the exception.

Even by 1850 placer streams like the American River were becoming overloaded with gold-seekers. Here is what George Shepard, a would-be prospector from Illinois, found when he arrived at the South Fork in August 1850 after a four-and-a-half-month trek:

> We found quite a stream of water of swift current and a company of men every little ways making dams acrost the river and turning the water through ditches dug on one side to leave the bed of the river dry so they can dig there. We found five or six of these dams going down the river three or four miles … . It appears that every place that is thought worth digging is already taken up and still men are passing up and down almost continuously in search of a place where they can thrust their spade to through [throw] up the yellow dust.

Such temporary disappointments, however, were not enough to stop gold-rushers like Shepard and thousands of others from setting off in search of a new site where they might make their fortune. It was men like Shepard and thousands of other adventurers who produced the great thrust of people across the Sierra Nevada in 1849 and 1850 and gave a big impetus to the westward movement.

The success of these thousands of forty-niners, in overcoming the barren desert stretches and hacking their way through the rugged Sierras, removed any lingering doubts created by the Donner tragedy about the feasibility of the overland route. The California

Trail confirmed that the newly won western third of the United States could be, and would eventually be, populated by emigrants advancing in successive waves from the East to seek their fortunes and establish new lives in the growing West.

Oregon-California Trail Association

Enthusiasts of the California Trail belong to the same association as those interested primarily in the Oregon Trail. The Oregon-California Trail Association, headquartered at the National Frontier Trails Center at Independence, Missouri, has some two thousand three hundred members who belong to ten chapters located in states along the trails. Local chapters arrange field trips to trail sites and present programs that throw new light on both the Oregon and California Trails.

OCTA members watch over the historic routes to prevent destruction of trail remnants, graves, and other trail-related sites. Members place markers along the trail and maintain existing signs.

The association encourages scholarly research, publishes articles, and presents educational programs in schools. Its members collect historical data from trail diaries, old newspapers, maps, and other documents that reflect the "Great Migration." A quarterly publication, *The Overland Journal,* carries articles and book reviews. A newsletter brings news of national and chapter activities to its members. An annual convention is held at a trail site during the second week of August each year.

OCTA welcomes new members who have an interest in either the California or Oregon Trail. For more information write the Oregon-California Trail Association, 524 South Osage Street, Box 1019, Independence, MO 64501-0519, or telephone (816) 252-2276.

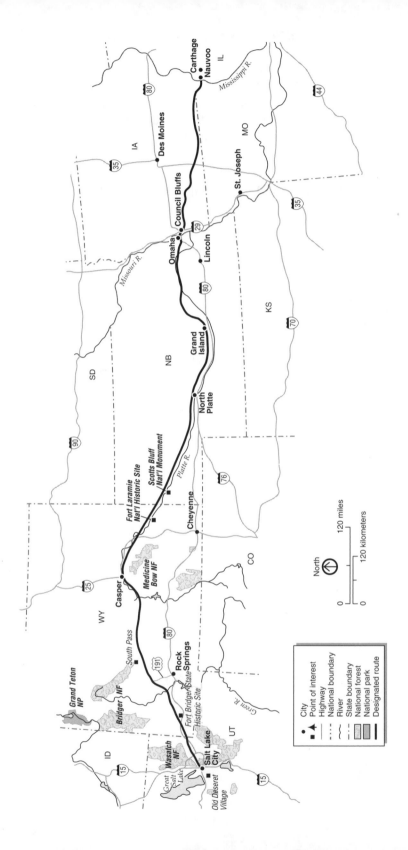

Chapter 15

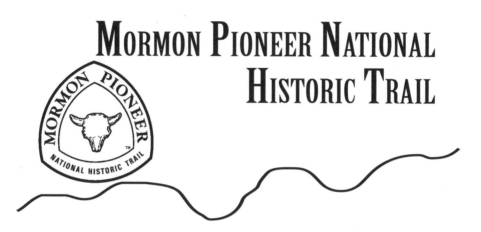

MORMON PIONEER NATIONAL HISTORIC TRAIL

I T WAS BOTH FEAR AND FAITH THAT IMPELLED MORE THAN SIXTY thousand Mormon pioneers to leave the settled eastern states and cross the prairies to the valley of the Great Salt Lake between 1846 and 1860—fear of violent persecution by people who would not tolerate a different religion, and faith that their leaders would find a way to get them to a promised land where they could live in peace.

These converts to a new form of Christianity had previously been driven out of Ohio, then out of Missouri when the state passed an "Extermination Act" that said any Mormon could be shot on sight. People were suspicious of the Mormons, fearful of their political power, and perhaps envious of their prosperity. The "Saints," as they called themselves, fled to Illinois, where they industriously turned a swamp on the banks of the Mississippi River into a model city called Nauvoo. Pious, hardworking, puritanical—and sometimes polygamous—these members of the Church of Jesus Christ of Latter-day Saints constructed a city that in its time ranked as the tenth largest in the United States, larger even than Chicago at that time.

But the discrimination and suspicion that had dogged them for so many years continued. Friction developed between the Nauvoo community and longtime residents of the area. Others feared the "Mormon Army," a force of 4,000 armed militiamen that had been formed to protect Nauvoo. Still others resented the Mormons' ability to influence political decisions with the large bloc of votes they controlled. In 1844 their leader, Joseph Smith, even ran for president of the United States. With feelings running high Smith was arrested in 1844 and thrown into the county jail in nearby Carthage. Despite being in the protective custody of the jailer Joseph, his brother, and two others were murdered by an armed mob that illegally burst into the jail.

With such vigilante violence threatening them the church leaders saw no alternative but to move again, abandon the city they had built, and head westward. They elected Brigham Young to replace the martyred Smith and lead them on what would be one of the largest mass migrations in U.S. history. The route they took is now commemorated as the Mormon Pioneer National Historic Trail.

After confusion and uncertainty at its beginning in 1846, the migration became probably the best organized of all the emigrant movements. Unlike other sometimes loosely disciplined wagon trains, the Mormon pioneer company was organized in semimilitary fashion into tens, fifties, and hundreds and led by Brigham Young as general. Others served as company captains, hunters, and scouts.

Forced by the State of Illinois to leave, the Mormons abandoned their comfortable homes, left behind most of their possessions, packed up, and departed from Nauvoo during the cold winter of 1846. Ferrying across the icy Mississippi the pioneers crossed Iowa by wagon and spent the remainder of the winter and the next year suffering from disease and hunger at sites near what is now Omaha and Council Bluffs on opposite sides of the Missouri River. Here at Winter Quarters 3,483 Saints tried to survive in caves, sod houses, and crude log cabins. More than six hundred died of fever and other afflictions. By spring more pioneers had arrived; now some ten thousand Mormons were encamped on both sides of the Missouri River.

Recognizing that it was impossible even for so well organized a people as the Saints to move such a large number all at once, Brigham Young and the ruling Council of Twelve Apostles determined that an advance company should be sent ahead to mark the trail, measure the hazards, and lay the groundwork for the new Zion. By now Young had decided that their destination would be the valley of the Great Salt Lake in what is now Utah. Brigham Young knew about the valley and had rough maps, but few people at that time had even glimpsed that empty desert.

On April 19, 1847, President Brigham Young and his advance company of 144 men, women, and children struck out on a four-month journey that would locate the new Mormon homeland and lay out a route for the main body to follow. All the others stayed behind at Winter Quarters.

The Mormon Pioneer Trail, like the Oregon and California Trails, parallels the Platte River. The Mormons, however, kept to the north bank, following old trappers' trails that avoided the "Gentiles" who were using the Oregon Trail route on the south side. Using the north side also gave them the advantage of better forage for their livestock. When they reached present-day Wyoming the Mormons followed the Sweetwater until they left the river to climb over South Pass, the "Cumberland Gap" of the far West, where the trail crosses the Continental Divide.

Unlike many other emigrant companies the Mormons improved their route for those who would come later. They measured distances and set up mileposts. They noted good locations for camping, wood, water, and forage and smoothed rough spots in the trail.

At Fort Bridger, one of the few settlements on this deserted frontier, the Mormon Trail diverged from the Oregonians who turned north. The Mormons turned southwest toward the rugged Wasatch Range.

The final 100 miles through these mountains were the most difficult of the journey. Work parties had to slash at tangles of willows, heave rocks out of the pathway, and sometimes even lay down a crude roadway. The wagons, mile by painful mile, pushed on. They passed places that now ring in Mormon Trail history— Echo Canyon, Big Mountain, Little Mountain, Emigration Canyon. On July 24, 1847, the advance party caught its first full view of the valley of the Great Salt Lake, a vast and forbidding area that stretched for more than two hundred thousand square miles. The valley was the first site suitable for building a new Zion that the pioneer leaders had seen since Nauvoo. In the months that followed a city was laid out, crops were planted, and homes, a fort, and a site for worship services were prepared.

Today travelers can retrace the Mormon route over more than thirteen hundred miles of national, state, and local roads that closely follow the original wagon train trek. The roadway is marked at numerous places with a distinctive marker for the Mormon Pioneer National Historic Trail, a brown-and-white, rounded triangle that depicts at its center the skull of a buffalo. Brigham Young sometimes left messages for those who followed him inscribed on the bleached skull of a buffalo. The States of Illinois, Iowa, Nebraska, Wyoming, and Utah, which the trail crosses, have erected interpretive historical signs to describe interest points along the route. The National Park Service publishes a folder that outlines both the historic trail and the auto-tour route. To obtain a copy write to the National Park Service, Long Distance Trails Office, 324 South State Street, Salt Lake City, UT 84145-0155.

Illinois

Nauvoo, the jumping-off place for the Mormon Trail, presents to the current traveler much the same scene the Mormons left behind when they departed hurriedly to find a new home in the West. The town is located at a bend in the Mississippi River, midway along the western boundary of Illinois. It is 24 miles north of U.S. Highway 136, which runs east-west and bisects the state.

Whereas other well-known jumping-off places for the West such as Independence, Westport, and St. Joseph, Missouri, have been overlaid with layers of later construction, Nauvoo looks much like it did in 1846 when the Mormons left the town they had spent the previous seven years building. Sorrowfully they locked the doors of their tidy homes, loaded a few possessions into their wagons, and set off to follow Brigham Young.

So well preserved is Nauvoo that it has been called the "Williamsburg of the Midwest." Fortunately for later preservationists, a number of its 2,500 homes were constructed of brick and held up well through the years. Only one or two of the many log homes, however, have survived. But the overall effect is that the stage is still set much as it was when the Saints left.

Today Mormon missionaries, some of whom are descendants of the Mormon pioneers, welcome visitors to the carefully restored Nauvoo, a name that denotes "beautiful place" in Hebrew. The best place to begin a tour is at the contemporary Information Center of Nauvoo Restoration, Inc., operated by the Church of Jesus Christ of Latter-day Saints. A scale model of the town of 1846 prepares the sightseer to take a walk or a horse-and-carriage ride or to drive through the 500-acre historic community. Laid out in a pattern of four-acre squares, the town at its peak was home to some twelve thousand people. Fifty college-age and "senior couple" missionaries show visitors through the two dozen homes, shops, and gardens that have been restored, complete with bustle ovens, quill pens, and chinaware common to the time. Onlookers watch as a tinsmith, cooper, brick maker, and printer demonstrate their crafts. At the blacksmith shop a smithy fashions a "prairie diamond" from a horseshoe nail and gives it to a lucky visitor.

The famous Browning rifle and gun collection is on display at the home of Jonathan Browning, a gunsmith who invented several types of repeating rifles. The Mansion House, home of Joseph Smith, has been restored as it was during the Smith family's residence from 1842 to 1869. The home of the colonizer, Brigham Young, contains the office where a meeting was held that produced the Mormons' heartbreaking decision to abandon their homes and take to the trail to try to outdistance their persecutors.

Brigham Young House, Nauvoo, Illinois.

The two-story Cultural and Masonic Hall, Nauvoo's community and cultural center, is the scene on summer evenings of a musical performance that depicts the settling of the town and the trek westward. Tours pass the site where the temple once stood, an imposing Greek Revival structure of gray limestone that was the largest building in Illinois at the time. The building had not been completed when the exodus occurred, but workmen stayed behind and finished it so it could be dedicated. It was destroyed by vandals a year later.

Nearby at Carthage, the county seat, the Mormons have pre-served the scene of one of the most devastating events of the church's history—the slaying of their founder and first leader, Jo-seph Smith, Jr.

The scene that greets visitors today—the brown brick walls of the restored jail, a tidy visitor center, and a garden—is in stark contrast to the event that took place at this small county jail on June 27, 1844. The charismatic leader of the church had obeyed a court order and come to Carthage to stand trial on a charge of "treason" for having forcefully prohibited the publishing of a newspaper in Nauvoo. He, his brother Hyrum, and two others were locked up in the protective custody of the jailer. But feelings against the Mormons were running high, and in the late after-noon an armed mob surrounded the jail. Bursting through a door, attackers shot and killed both Joseph and Hyrum and wounded one of the others.

The murder of the Mormon leader did not, however, lead to the disintegration of the church, as the anti-Mormon mob had hoped. Instead, after a spirited controversy over who would be their new leader, Brigham Young was selected, and he be-gan to make plans for the future. Members of a minority group of Mormons who did not want to go west moved to Wisconsin and to other parts of Illinois. Later, under Joseph Smith III, this group formed into the Reorganized Church of Jesus Christ of Latter-day Saints, which today has its headquarters at Inde-pendence, Missouri.

Iowa

Forced to sell their homes and shops at bargain prices, the Mormons began moving out of Nauvoo as early as February 1846, crossing the Mississippi on ferryboats loaded with families, ani-mals, and belongings. A handful of cabins were hastily constructed to shelter them on the Iowa bank. Slowly they made their way across the prairie, making use of the hundreds of wagons the wheelwrights of Nauvoo had made during the winter months. They moved in small, manageable segments, each detachment divided and subdivided in military fashion. Duties were clear-cut. The first groups plowed fields and planted crops. Later groups harvested the crops and left behind new plantings for those coming afterwards.

Those tracing the trail today can see how this worked by following Iowa 2 to the town of Garden Grove, where an advance party cleared three hundred acres of land for a way station, planted crops, built log houses, and cut 10,000 rails for fencing and enough logs to build an additional forty houses. A blacksmith shop began operations. A granite marker that stands on private land north of town marks the site and a burial ground containing graves of unknown Mormons who died there. Farther on, just off U.S. Highway 34 twenty miles west of Osceola, is the site of Mount Pisgah, another way station that at one time held 3,000 people. Markers and monuments and a two-acre cemetery commemorate the site.

The Mormon Trail reaches the Missouri River at Council Bluffs, a city that got its name from the meeting Lewis and Clark had with several Indian chiefs 40 years earlier; the Mormons, however, called it Kanesville. It was here and at Winter Quarters, across the river in Nebraska, that most of the Mormons would endure the harsh winter of 1846–1847, resuming their long march the following spring.

At Council Bluffs 549 young men were enlisted in the Mormon Battalion to take part in the Mexican War. From here they marched 1,850 miles to San Diego, following the Santa Fe Trail much of the way, in what has been called "the longest infantry march in U.S. Army history." By providing the battalion to help the United States fight the Mexican War, which had just broken out, Brigham Young proved that the Mormons would answer their country's call to arms despite the persecution they had endured. The Mormons themselves also stood to benefit: The conscripts would thus be transported at government expense to the West where the Mormons were destined to go, could keep the arms they were issued, and would draw military pay. The new soldiers turned over their pay and clothing allowances—a total of $50,000—to help the struggling church elders finance the mass movement to Utah. After a five-month march under the command of Colonel Stephen W. Kearny the battalion arrived in San Diego, but never fired a shot. Many of the men were finally reunited with their families after three years.

Nebraska

Leaving Iowa and crossing the Missouri River, the Mormons built Winter Quarters, laying out a town with street names that still reverberate in the Omaha suburb of Florence today. A school was opened almost immediately, followed by buildings for church meetings and square dances. A gristmill was erected and a stockade constructed for their protection. Wagon makers and blacksmiths set to work.

The names of hundreds who died here are inscribed on a monument in the Mormon Pioneer Cemetery in Florence, near the Nebraska side of the Mormon Bridge, which carries I-680 across the Missouri River. At a visitor center across the street from the cemetery, missionary guides show visitors a film of the Mormon trek and take them on tours of the cemetery. Part of the original gristmill, the oldest existing structure in Omaha, stands just down the street.

When they reached the Platte River the Mormons followed the same Great Platte River Road traced by the Oregon Trail and the later California Trail and Pony Express Trail, choosing the northern side of this busy river road. I-80 takes travelers along this route today.

Everything on the trail was carefully prescribed—when to go to bed, the exact length of the noon rest, when to take guard duty, even the rotation of places in the wagon train so that all would spend equal amounts of time breaking trail and choking on the dust.

With plenty of time to think as they walked, several pioneers invented a "roadometer," a device that was attached to a wagon wheel to measure the miles traveled. Prior to this someone had to keep track of the distance by tying a red cloth to a wagon wheel and counting the revolutions. The roadometer and a detailed journal later made it possible for one of the Saints, William Clayton, to publish his famous "Latter-day Saints' Emigrants' Guide."

After weeks of traveling the flatlands of Nebraska the Mormons were as relieved as any other emigrants were to see the dramatic outline of Chimney Rock on the horizon across the river. One traveler complained that he rode four days and never seemed to get any closer to the pinnacle! Other diaries reflected the same sentiment.

The visitor center at Scotts Bluff National Monument, a landmark on the Oregon Trail, tells the story of the Mormons as well.

Although they were still traveling on the north side of the river at this point, the Mormons could easily wade across the shallow North Platte to trade for food or obtain spare wagon parts. Nearby is the grave of Rebecca Winters, a Mormon woman who died on a later caravan. Hers is one of the few known graves of the more than six thousand Mormons who perished trying to reach their destination.

Wyoming

Crossing the North Platte River at Fort Laramie (then called Fort John) the Saints joined the other trail travelers who were making their way along the well-used Oregon Trail. Mormon names can be seen chiseled alongside those of the Oregon Trail emigrants at Register Cliff. Mormon wagon wheels helped deepen the trough through the remarkable sandstone ridge at Guernsey.

Family history echoes from Register Cliff.

At the place where Fort Casper was later built all the emigrants had to leave the North Platte to head out across the desert. The Mormons cut trees in the mountains nearby and constructed rafts to ferry people to the north side. They developed such an efficient system that Brigham Young ordered eight men and a blacksmith to stay behind and earn some badly needed dollars by operating the ferry for others crowding up behind on the Oregon,

California, and Mormon Trails. The entrepreneurs erected a sign back down the trail for all to see: "Ferry, good and safe; manned by experienced men; blacksmithing, horse and oxshoeing done; also a wheelwright."

The Mormon ferry cut down on the drownings, which had earlier been common at this crossing. But later it turned out to be a bottleneck. At the peak of later migrations along the trail emigrants encountered delays of up to a week before they could get their wagons across on the small rafts.

Visitors to the reconstruction of Fort Casper at Casper, Wyoming, see a replica of these rough-hewn rafts of the Mormon Ferry, rafts built to carry one wagon at a time. At the exhibit of artifacts in the museum they read Brigham Young's instructions to the ferry crew, including the fee schedule he set down: "For one family, you will charge $1.50 payment in flour and provisions at stated prices or $3.00 in cash.—June 18, 1847." It was the beginning of what would become an extensive system of ferries, most of them operated by Mormons for the benefit of their own people, but available at a stiff price to others as well.

To trace the route of the Mormons across the dry sandy stretch to the Sweetwater River, motorists should follow Wyoming 220, U.S. Highway 287, and Wyoming 28 to South Pass, stopping as the emigrants did to see the distinctive landmark of Independence Rock. At the Fort Casper Museum pick up a folder that describes the route.

A few miles east of South Pass, on private land, is a cemetery and monument to seventy-seven members of Captain James G. Willie's handcart company who died here in October 1856 when the group was caught in an early snowstorm while waiting for a relief party to reach them. Between 1856 and 1860 ten companies of Mormon converts from Europe took to the trail, pulling their children and all their worldly possessions in two-wheeled handcarts. Families divided the labor, with father and mother pulling and children pushing. The Mormons were the only ones of the western emigrants to attempt this type of grueling travel. Handcarts were less expensive and more maneuverable than wagons, but had to be pulled by the emigrants themselves rather than by animals. And of course they carried a lot less. Although they paid a heavy price in lives lost, the great majority of the handcart pioneers survived to reach the destination they so greatly desired.

Like those on the Oregon Trail the Mormons registered relief at the ease with which they surmounted the Continental Divide of the Rocky Mountains at South Pass. Once across this high table-land and over the Rockies, many of the Oregon Trail pioneers veered north on the Sublette Cutoff to head for Oregon. The Mormons continued southwest on the Oregon Trail's branch to Fort Bridger.

On June 28 Brigham Young and his advance party camped to the west of South Pass beside the Big Sandy River. By luck they met here the well-traveled mountain man and explorer Jim Bridger. Bridger gave the Mormon leader valuable advice about his destination, the valley of the Great Salt Lake. Creeks flowed into the valley, Bridger said, but he doubted the land would make good farmland. As a matter of fact, he joked, he would personally give Brigham Young $1,000 if he could raise a bushel of corn in the Valley. Undiscouraged Young is reported to have replied, "Wait a little, and we will show you!"

The party pushed on to the trading post of Fort Bridger itself, the point where the Oregon Trail turns northward, departing from the Mormon Trail. At Fort Bridger the Mormons purchased supplies and rested up for what lay ahead—the march through the Wasatch Mountains, the most difficult part of their journey. Eight years later they would buy this trading post from Jim Bridger and his partner Luis Vasquez and run it to provide provisions and repairs to later Mormon caravans and other emigrant parties.

The grounds at Fort Bridger State Historic Site bear the evidence of the various developments that changed the nature of this fort over the years. The reconstructed trading post, a replica of the rough-hewn fort Jim Bridger built, welcomes visitors. In addition archeologists have uncovered part of the cobblestone "Mormon Wall," a 100-by-100-foot protective wall the Saints built when they purchased the post in 1855. Exhibits at the museum tell the rest of the curious history of the site. Two years after the Mormons bought it the U.S. Army threatened to take over the trading post by force because the federal government said the Mormons were evading federal authority. Rather than allow the Army to seize it the Mormons burned it to the ground. Some years later the Army constructed a sizable frontier fort on the site, completely surrounding and enveloping the former small trading post.

Utah

Today's motorist, approaching Salt Lake City from the east on the well-engineered I-80, cannot help but be impressed by the ruggedness of the terrain the Mormons faced as they urged their wagons through the Wasatch Range of the Rocky Mountains to reach the "promised land." This was the same narrow, nearly impassable trail that had fatally delayed the Donner party the summer before.

For days the wagoneers had traversed the gently rolling high plains. Now, still 50 miles from the great valley, they found themselves in Echo Canyon, so named because the steep walls of the 16-mile-long gorge echoed with the impatient shouts of the wagon drivers. Today exhibits at a Utah welcome center along I-80 relate how the experience gained by the Indians, trappers, explorers, and wagon trains that preceded them helped the Mormons find their way through this forbidding canyon.

Emerging from the gorge near what is now the town of Henefer, the Mormons climbed to Hogsback Summit, where they got a disheartening view—more crumpled landscape directly ahead. Faint trail ruts from their wagons can still be seen. Sensing the difficulties that lay ahead, the well-organized Brigham Young advance party sent ahead two small groups, one to scout and mark the trail, the other to bushwhack its way into the valley and plant crops that could feed the new arrivals.

Now came Big Mountain Pass (7,420 feet), the third-highest point on the entire trail. It was undoubtedly at this point that Brigham Young and the emigrants caught their first view of their new home. And it was here, tradition says, that the Mormon leader, although ill with "mountain fever" and confined to a wagon, uttered his famous words: "This is the right place. Drive on."

The wagons still had to make the treacherous descent into the valley. Because brakes were crude or nonexistent chains had to be fed through the wagon wheels and logs pulled along behind to slow their descent. Once down, the last miles led through Emigration Canyon, another narrow defile. Today the brown-and-white Mormon Pioneer National Historic Trail signs show the way along Emigration Canyon Road. A historic marker denotes the last camp of the 1847 party. It had taken them nineteen days to prod their teams, wagons, and horses through the Wasatch Mountains to reach their goal.

At the mouth of Emigration Canyon sightseers find an appropriate conclusion to the Mormon Trail—the 500-acre Pioneer Trail State Park. Within it stands a massive memorial to the Mormon pioneers. Sixty feet high and 84 feet wide, the monument was designed by Mahroni M. Young, sculptor and grandson of Brigham Young, and erected in 1947. It features fifteen plaques and numerous bronze statues and bas-reliefs that honor the pioneers as well as the men who came before them and explored the Great Basin.

A visitor center looks out on the memorial. An eight-minute audiovisual presentation focuses on episodes on the Mormon trek, episodes that are depicted in mural form on three interior walls of the center. Some four hundred thousand people visit the park each year.

For those who want to feel even closer to the overland route, a four-mile hiking trail leads through Little Emigration Canyon from Big Mountain to Mormon Flat. Utah state park rangers lead a hike along the trail each year on National Trails Day.

The park has also brought together a number of original dwellings of the early settlers to form a mid-1800s pioneer community called Old Deseret Village. *Deseret* is a Mormon-coined word meaning "industrious community pulling together for the common good." The Mormon symbol, the beehive, is derived from the industriousness of bees and is still used today as the symbol for Utah.

The dwellings in Old Deseret range from a crude early dugout home to substantial adobe structures, a blacksmith shop, social hall, sheep shed, and bowery. It represents a Mormon village typical of the ones that sprang up in Utah between 1847 and 1869 as the Saints colonized the region. Its square blocks and wide roads are laid out on a north-south axis in the same fashion as Nauvoo and Salt Lake City, typical of the Mormon plan for the cities of Zion.

Horse-drawn wagons take tourists along Old Deseret's unpaved streets. During the summer the village is peopled with living history guides who demonstrate crafts such as blacksmithing, cabinetmaking, milling, shearing, and weaving.

As soon as they arrived at Great Salt Lake the Mormons set to work. Within days Brigham Young laid out a plan for what would later become Salt Lake City. Within a month a massive fort enclosing twenty-nine cabin homes, a smithy, a corral, and a communal storehouse had risen near the center of the city-to-be. The new arrivals plowed the harsh land, dug irrigation ditches, and built their homes.

From these modest beginnings has grown the city of today, a cultural and ecclesiastical center as well as the political capital of Utah. Visitors to Salt Lake City are greeted at a handsome visitor center at Temple Square and may join a tour to view prominent buildings such as the Mormon Temple and Tabernacle, and the Beehive House, Brigham Young's residence.

Five weeks after he arrived Brigham Young resolutely turned around and marched back overland with a company of 106 men, retracing hundreds of arduous miles over the trail that had so recently brought them west. Their mission: to report the founding of the settlement to those who waited in Iowa and Nebraska and point them toward the new Zion.

The next year the Mormon leader returned to Great Salt Lake with three thousand more emigrants. Even more recruits to Mormonism were gathered up by missionaries in England, Scandinavia, and Germany and sent on their way to America, then dispatched to Utah, many of them laboriously pulling the handcarts. By 1860 the nucleus of pioneers who entered the valley in 1847 had grown to thirty thousand, as they had founded a number of new communities up and down the valley. Not only farmers, but also skilled individuals such as shopkeepers, artisans, and mechanics, came over the trail with just the variety of skills needed to build up these new communities.

The Mormon Trail continued to be a two-way road, a continuous route used to pick up supplies and new converts, to meet faltering companies, and to help get them safely to Salt Lake City. The Mormons graded the steep approaches to some of the river fords and cleared boulders from the path to make the trail easier.

To assist the emigrants the Mormons established semipermanent communities and ferry crossings of major importance along the route. In southern Iowa, particularly, the Mormons established some of the first communities, roads, and bridges in the region. They made Winter Quarters (Omaha) and Kanesville (Council Bluffs) into outfitting points that rivaled the Missouri towns of Independence, Westport, and St. Louis.

The Mormon Pioneer National Historic Trail commemorates the epic march of a plucky people to find a homeland where they could carry on their lives without interference, live in peace, and build with their own hands a "City of Zion." Toughened by the rigors of the trail and strong in their faith, the Mormons succeeded where few would have given them a chance to survive.

Mormon Trails Association

The Mormon Trails Association, organized in 1991, supports the planning, marking, and preservation of the historic route through a variety of efforts. The association also serves as a repository of information about the trail.

Its volunteers, a number of whom are well qualified in mapping techniques, have assisted the National Park Service by surveying and mapping segments of the trail. Some of its other 800 members have worked, for example, with government agencies and citizens in Iowa, encouraging tourism in towns located along the Mormon Trail.

Through the efforts of the association Utah declared 1996–1998 to be the sesquicentennial of the pioneer trek across the Mormon Pioneer Trail, an occasion celebrated with a variety of events.

To learn more about the association write the Mormon Trails Association, 2011 East Bryan Avenue, Salt Lake City, UT 84108.

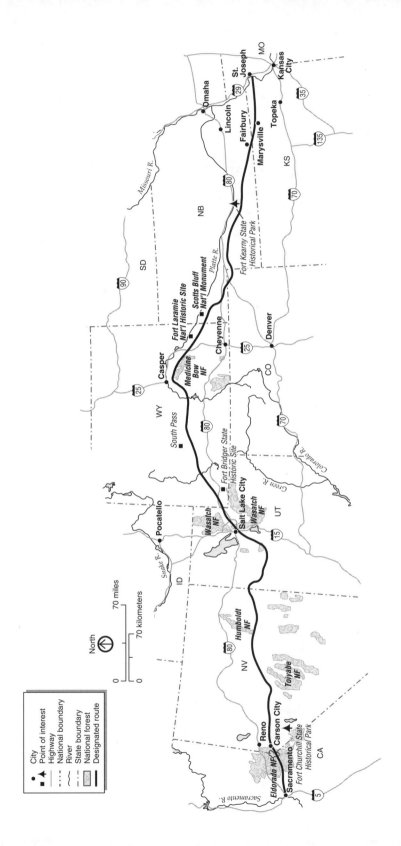

Chapter 16

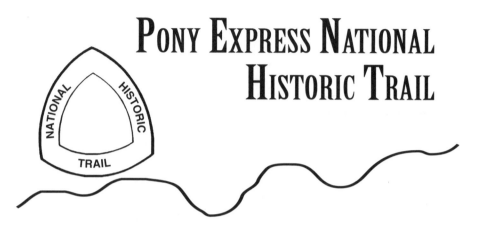

PONY EXPRESS NATIONAL HISTORIC TRAIL

IT WAS TWILIGHT ON APRIL 3, 1860, WHEN THE TRAIN REACHED the end of the line at St. Joseph, Missouri, and unloaded a small batch of letters and newspapers, urgent mail that would test the speed and courage of the newly organized Pony Express courier service.

The crowd that had come out to see the start of the inaugural run had already stood through several speeches, including remarks by William H. Russell, the founder of the Pony Express and a partner along with William B. Waddell and Alexander Majors in a freight and stagecoach company. These owners of the Central Overland, California, and Pikes Peak Express Company were gambling on the success of this new venture—a fast mail delivery system from the Midwest to California.

One of its fastest horses, a fleet bay mare, had been led out of the company stable. A lightweight saddle was cinched to its back, placed atop a unique rectangular leather apron called a *mochila* (mail pouch) with pockets at each of its four corners. Three pockets called *cantinas* were filled with the letters and papers from the train and stayed locked for the entire journey; the fourth pocket would be filled with letters the rider would pick up and deliver along the way. Johnny Fry, an ex-jockey and the first of many intrepid riders who would carry the mail west, was ready.

At 7:15 in the evening, to the boom of a brass cannon and a great shout from the crowd, Johnny Fry shook hands with William

Russell, bounded into the saddle, galloped down the streets to the banks of the Missouri River, and clattered aboard a waiting ferryboat. In about half an hour he landed on the far shore in Kansas Territory, in the hamlet of Elwood, and spurred his mount westward. He found the route easy to follow, even after darkness descended. Blazed by emigrants who knew it as both the Oregon and the California Trail, it had since been turned into a broad, grassless strip by the heavy traffic of forty-niners and the freight wagons that followed them across the rolling prairie.

About 45 minutes beyond Elwood Fry trotted into the first relay station at Troy, Kansas, and got a two-minute break while the station attendant threw the *mochila* and the saddle onto a fresh horse. Then Fry galloped off, reaching the little settlement of Granada at 11:30 P.M., where he turned the *mochila* over to the next rider. At 5:25 in the afternoon of April 13 the final westbound rider galloped into Sacramento, redeeming the Pony Express's promise to deliver the mail in the new record time of ten days.

Thus began the inaugural ride of the Pony Express, a short-lived but dramatic effort to create a fast mail service over a central overland route that would cut by half or more the time it took for messages to get from the East to California. The Pony Express operated from April 1860 to October 1861, when the completion of a telegraph line across the country provided a speedier way to send messages.

By 1860 almost half a million Americans were living west of the Rocky Mountains, most of them in California. The new settlers yearned for news from back home in those settled states east of the Missouri River. A standing joke of the time was that events had already been forgotten on the East Coast before they were known on the West Coast. Moreover, as civil war loomed, people yearned for news of the approaching conflict. Such isolation of the West fueled secessionist hopes of persuading California to join with the southern states in their confederacy.

Before the Pony Express mail to California could take as long as six weeks by packet boat from New York via the Panamanian isthmus. The Butterfield Stage could get it there in three weeks over the so-called Oxbow Route, which curved southward through Yuma, Arizona.

The prime objective of the Pony Express was to prove the feasibility of a year-round central route as an alternative to the secessionist-threatened southern route. Once it was proved feasible the new route would make it logical for the federal government to send its mail on the central route and thereby provide a handsome profit for the entrepreneurs.

In the short span of two months before the inaugural run Russell, Majors, and Waddell had already accomplished a minor miracle as the company put together a chain of more than 150 relay stations 10 to 15 miles apart, with four hundred horses, some eighty young riders, plus station keepers, stock tenders, route superintendents, and shuttling supply wagons.

Beyond Salt Lake City, where the route departed from existing stage and freight lines, new stations had to be constructed. Because of the lack of timber in parts of the Great Basin, particularly western Utah and Nevada, stations were made of adobe brick or stone. In some instances dugouts and tents served as temporary shelters.

On the eastern portion of the trail many of the stations had already been built and were operating as the company's overland stage stops. The distance between all the stations was based on how far a horse could travel at its fastest sustainable speed over the existing terrain before it would become fatigued. For the entire distance, the average rider speed was 250 miles in a 24-hour period, an average of 10.7 miles per hour. Individual riders would cover from 75 to 100 miles before reaching a home station to be relieved by another rider.

Initially eighty riders were recruited by division superintendents. "Young, skinny wiry fellows not over eighteen," one advertisement called for. "Must be expert riders willing to risk death daily. Orphans preferred. Wages—$25 per week." Some riders weighed only 100 pounds. Many were already skilled guides, scouts, and couriers. Each rider took an oath, was issued a small Bible, and was housed and fed at company expense.

The route the pony riders traveled is now commemorated as the Pony Express National Historic Trail, a nearly two thousand-mile track that runs through Missouri, Kansas, Nebraska, Colorado, Wyoming, Utah, Nevada, and California. Understandably there are few historic remains of the actual trail—a solitary rider leaves little physical trace of his presence. What's more, the riders changed their routes from time to time because of weather, swollen streams, snow, and the threat of Indian attack.

Approximately a dozen of the historic relay stations and home stations, however, have been preserved, restored, or reconstructed. Interpretive signs at waysides mark a number of significant points along the trail although an official auto-tour route has yet to be laid out.

Each June members of the National Pony Express Association who live in the seven states along the trail reenact the historic ride. As many as 600 reenactment riders don the typical brown western hat, red plaid shirt, brown vest, yellow scarf, blue jeans, and boots and maintain the same timetables as the actual express riders as they ride the distance in the customary ten days. People line town streets as the latter-day riders gallop through. Whereas the pony rider of 1860 rode a section of about 75 miles and changed horses every 12 to 15 miles, reenactment riders cover a shorter segment of 3 to 5 miles and use their own horses, turning the *mochila* over at the end of their ride to the next rider. The trail association has staged the rerun almost every year since 1960, the centennial of the Pony Express. Riders go eastbound one year and westbound the following year.

Just as in the old days each rider is given a special edition of the Bible, similar to the one given the original Pony Express horseman, and takes the traditional oath: "I do hereby swear before the great and living God that during my engagement with Russell, Majors and Waddell, I will under no circumstances use profane language, that I will drink no intoxicating liquors, that I will not quarrel or fight with other employees of the firm, and that in every respect I will conduct myself honestly, be faithful in my duties, and so direct all my acts as to win the confidence of my employers. So help me God."

The trail association prints a commemorative letter each year that interested persons may purchase by writing to the association. The letters are carried across the country by the reenactors, canceled at St. Joseph and Sacramento, then mailed to the recipient as a memento.

The original Pony Express riders followed the established overland trails wherever they could. As a result the Pony Express Trail follows the same track as the well-defined Oregon, California, and Mormon Pioneer Trails through Kansas, Nebraska, Colorado, and Wyoming, then traces the Mormon Pioneer Trail and Salt Lake cutoff of the California Trail from Fort Bridger to Salt Lake

City. At Salt Lake City the pony trail departs from the other overland trail routes as it cuts across central Utah, crosses the Great Basin through central Nevada, then follows the Carson River until it scales the Sierra Nevada on its way to Sacramento.

Missouri

St. Joseph, the starting point, captures the spirit of the trail at its Pony Express National Memorial, a museum housed in the same brick stable where Johnny Fry mounted his horse for the first ride. Visitors come face-to-face with that moment as they step into the darkened interior of the restored structure. Behind the stable doors a spotlighted, lifelike "stablehand" holds the reins of a full-sized "horse" as the "rider" prepares to burst out to begin his run. Another "stablehand" prepares to swing wide the big doors to allow the rider to be on his way.

In other parts of the museum a series of dioramas dramatize the changing scenes faced by the Pony Express rider: crossing the Missouri River bottoms, the tall-grass prairie, the high plain, over the Continental Divide, into Great Salt Lake Valley, across the desert, over the snow-covered Sierra Nevada, and into California. Even the sense of smell is involved. Special devices reproduce for the onlooker the dry desert air, mountain cold, even the smell of hay in the stable.

Other exhibits at the museum include photographs of the original riders, a replica *mochila,* blacksmith and wheelwright shops, an original mail envelope carried by an express rider, and a display that challenges the visitor to select the best breed of horse to use on such a high-speed ride.

Three blocks away the restored Patee House contains the re-created St. Joseph's office of the Central Overland, California, and Pike's Peak Express Company as well as other memorabilia of the famous Pony Express. When it opened in 1858 the Patee House was regarded as one of the finest hotels west of the Mississippi.

Kansas

Those who trace the Pony Express Trail today may follow U.S. Highway 36 across the northeastern corner of Kansas to Marysville, where the pony riders met the Oregon Trail as it crossed

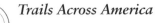
the Big Blue River. At Marysville is a sturdy old stone barn that once served as a home station. Preserved as a museum by a local historical organization, its dim interior appears much as it did when Johnny Fry and the other riders would stay for several days waiting to ride a return trip back to where they started.

Marysville Pony Express station; first home station after St. Joseph.

To one side, opposite where the horses were stabled, stands a crude, double-decked bunk covered with buffalo hides for blankets. In another corner is a forge used by a blacksmith to make instant repairs or to shoe a horse. Portholes in the thick stone walls provide the only fresh air. A museum next to the barn exhibits a *mochila,* a revolver carried by one of the Pony Express riders, and facsimiles of some of the most important express messages ever carried, such as the news of Abraham Lincoln's election in 1860.

Thirty miles away at Hollenberg, which is near Hanover and close to the Kansas-Nebraska border, stands a weathered ranch-style building that is the only unaltered Pony Express station remaining in its original location along the trail. Gerat Henry Hollenberg, a German immigrant, built this roadhouse on Cottonwood Creek in 1857–1858 to serve the increasing emigrant, freight, and stagecoach traffic along the Oregon Trail. Families looking for land to farm, men chasing visions of gold, teamsters hauling goods to the growing western population, all passed by. Many emigrants stopped to buy supplies for the trail, repair their wagons, or stay overnight.

Hollenberg was only too happy to add the Pony Express riders to his customers—he provided them with fresh horses and charged them 27 cents for a hot meal. Six downstairs rooms housed a store, unofficial neighborhood post office, tavern, and the family's living quarters. The upstairs provided a common sleeping room for the Pony Express men and stage line employees.

Each August the restored roadhouse comes alive as this Kansas state historical park celebrates a Pony Express Festival. Visitors enjoy living history demonstrations, purchase commemorative Pony Express re-ride letters, watch a wagon train arrive, and attend a church service presided over by a circuit-riding preacher.

Nebraska

Another carefully restored roadhouse still stands just across the Kansas-Nebraska border at Fairbury. Trail ruts left by the Oregon Trail, creating a depression up to five feet deep through the tall-grass prairie, greet visitors at the two ranches that were once owned by David McCanles and have been reconstructed by the Nebraska Game and Parks Commission. The West Ranch consisted of a log cabin, stables, and corral. McCanles then built the East Ranch across the creek, with its ranch house, barn, well, bunkhouse, and corral. He connected the two ranches with a toll bridge and rented out the East Ranch as a stage and Pony Express station.

But the Rock Creek station was clouded by tragedy. A stablehand named James "Wild Bill" Hickok treacherously ambushed and murdered McCanles at the East Ranch when the owner came by to collect a payment on the mortgage that was due him. Two other men were killed in the shooting as well. Even though McCanles's son was an eyewitness to the murder, as a minor he was not allowed to testify, and Hickok was acquitted. Hickok later had a checkered career as a gunfighter and was himself murdered during a card game. A contemporary visitor center offers a slide presentation on the area's history as well as various events, including a covered wagon ride.

In Nebraska the Pony Express riders took the Oregon Trail to Fort Kearny on the Platte River, where the various feeder trails from the east blended into the "Great Platte River Road," which followed the river across the state much as I-80 does now. The Pony Express riders kept to the south side of the river along with those on the Oregon and California Trails while the Mormons used the north side.

At Fort Kearny the Express riders changed horses at a relay station that was probably located just off the military reservation since the courier service was a privately run business, not a government operation. On the grounds of the fort today are a replica stockade and a reconstructed sod blacksmith shop where a Pony Express stationhand could have had a repair job done in a pinch. A slide show at the visitor center of this Nebraska state historical park tells the story of Fort Kearny and of the Pony Express.

Two towns within easy reach of I-80 have preserved cabins once used as Pony Express stations. At Cozad a rough-hewn log cabin, 40 feet by 20 feet, stands in a city park in the middle of town. A bronze plaque on its front wall attests to its authenticity. Those who peek in the windows see a table set with pewter plates, mugs, and utensils—as well as a can of chewing tobacco.

Ten miles to the west, at Gothenberg, is a similar cabin, which was moved from its original site south of the river in 1931 by the local American Legion post. Now located in a town park, the cabin displays artifacts of the trail days and includes a museum and gift shop that sells Pony Express memorabilia. It attracts some sixty thousand visitors each year.

Colorado

Pony Express riders continued on the well-used Oregon Trail along the Platte River across Nebraska until the river divided into two tributaries near Julesburg in what is now the northeastern tip of Colorado. A trading post, built by Jules Reni at this river junction, provided supplies to the emigrants as they reached the point where they had to ford the river in order to continue up the North Platte.

The mail couriers also had to ford the river, which posed a problem when the stream grew wider and rougher during the springtime runoff. Horse and rider often had to risk swimming these swollen streams. Once safely across the rider sped on past the buttes, spires, and mesas that dotted the landscape, grateful for the recognizable landmarks that showed him the way, landmarks such as Courthouse Rock, Chimney Rock, and Scotts Bluff. The pony route along the North Platte as far as Casper, Wyoming, is paralleled today by U.S. Highway 26.

The thrill of seeing a Pony Express rider beating a tattoo across the plain was once described by Mark Twain as he craned his neck out of a stagecoach window:

> Presently the [stagecoach] driver exclaims: "Here he comes!" Every neck is stretched further, and every eye strained wider. Away across the endless dead level of the prairie a black speck appears against the sky and it is plain that it moves. Well, I should think so! In a second or two it becomes a horse and rider, rising and falling, rising and falling—sweeping toward us nearer and nearer—growing more and more distinct, more and more sharply defined—nearer and still nearer, and the flutter of the hoofs comes faintly to the ear—another instant a whoop and a hurrah from our upper deck, a wave of the rider's hand, but no reply, and man and horse burst past our excited faces, and go swinging away like a belated fragment of a storm!

Wyoming

At Fort Laramie, like Fort Kearny, the Pony Express station was not on the military reservation itself but nearby. Such way stations were usually located near a spring or water source. Built hurriedly they often provided only primitive living conditions for the station keeper and the passing riders.

The company usually provided two men at each relay station, the station keeper and an assistant. Station keepers received a $50- to $75-a-month wage, and assistants, called "boys," averaged $25 to $50. Their primary duty centered on being ready for the next riders—two a day. Horses had to be constantly cared for and well shod. Life at a station was isolated, lonely, and actually more hazardous than the life of a rider.

Few reminders are left of these crude outposts that serviced the horsemen of the fast mail service as they followed the North Platte to present-day Casper, then made their way along the Sweetwater River to cross the Continental Divide with the emigrant caravans at South Pass. Although thirty-nine Pony Express stations were established across Wyoming, only a few faint traces of foundations are left today to punctuate the trail ruts of the

Oregon, California, and Mormon Pioneer Trails. But motorists who catch sight of the wild horses and pronghorn antelopes that still roam the landscape will sense the loneliness that must have come over these long-distance riders speeding across the treeless terrain.

Fort Bridger, where the riders left the Oregon Trail to head for Great Salt Lake, was a better-than-average station. Visitors to this colorful fort in the southwestern corner of Wyoming will note that the Pony Express stable is incorporated into a complex of buildings operated at the fort by the sutler, or concessionaire, for the U.S. Army.

Following ownership of the trading post and fort by Jim Bridger and later by the Mormons, the Army took it over and in 1857 built a greatly enlarged frontier fort to protect the continuing stream of settlers heading westward. It granted to Judge William A. Carter the right to provide services to the soldiers and emigrants. Those who go to Fort Bridger State Historical Site today will view a neat, white-walled sutler's complex that includes the post trader's store, the first schoolhouse built in the state of Wyoming, a milk house, wash house, warehouse, mess hall, carriage house, icehouse, and Pony Express stable. During the 1860s the complex served as a station both for the Pony Express and for the Overland stagecoach line operated by Russell, Majors, and Waddell.

Utah

When the pony riders reached the rugged Wasatch Mountains of present-day Utah they gratefully followed the wagon route that had earlier been cut through the mountains by the Mormons, a route that by then had been improved to allow emigrant parties from the East and from Europe an easier time making it to the Salt Lake valley. Moreover a single horseman had the advantage over a wagonload of emigrants in negotiating narrow Echo Canyon, where there was a relay station, climbing over Big Mountain Pass, and riding through Emigration Canyon to reach the expanding settlement known as Salt Lake City.

Motorists who approach today on I-80 might stop at the Utah welcome center, where exhibits describe the history of transportation through the Wasatch Range from the time of the Indians, trappers, explorers, and express riders to the modern-day motorist.

Beyond Salt Lake City the Pony Express rider faced more miles of desert. Here he left the established trails and headed out across the Great Salt Desert, where he faced the increased threat of Indian attack, few water sources, and isolation. Meanwhile, the California Trail swung north up the Salt Lake valley to the City of Rocks before continuing west along the Humboldt River.

Anyone who wants to share the feelings of the Pony Express riders should drive the 133-mile backcountry byway across western Utah that was designated by the Bureau of Land Management. This drivable gravel road begins at the town of Fairfield, west of Provo and Utah Lake, and closely follows the Pony Express Trail as far as Ibapah near the Nevada border.

Start this commemorative drive at Camp Floyd/Stagecoach Inn State Park near Fairfield. A two-story adobe and frame hotel has been restored with period furnishings. Erected in 1858 the hotel served both the Overland Stage and the Pony Express. Adjacent to the hotel Camp Floyd was established in 1858 as an Army encampment within the Mormon homeland.

Of the fourteen relay and home stations that existed on this segment of the Pony Express Trail, all have been identified but few original remains are left. Interpretive signs describe the most significant locations. At one overlook the trail follower on a clear day can look across the grass-covered rangeland and see the entire distance a rider had to cover to reach the next relay station. At Simpson Spring, one-third of the way along the byway, are a reconstructed stone station, a monument, and interpretive signs that underline the courage required of both the rider and the station keeper in this lonely landscape. At Boyd Station the visitor can see ledges that were cut into rock walls to provide primitive bunks for the Pony Express hands. To obtain more information about the backcountry byway write to the Bureau of Land Management Salt Lake District Office, 2370 South 2300 West, Salt Lake City, UT 84119.

Nevada

The trail continues across Nevada, crossing terrain almost as empty today as it was during a mail carrier's solitary ride. Evergreen ranges alternate with broad valleys, most of them desert dry, but a few, like the Ruby Valley, set with lakes or marshes fed by snowmelt streams.

Travelers can follow the approximate route of the Pony Express and see much the same scenery by tracing U.S. Highway 50 across the state. Most of the twenty-eight stations that once dotted the trail in Nevada have disappeared or crumbled into a scattering of stones, but waysides and interpretive markers tell their story. One of the few where anything more than rubble remains is near the town of Cold Springs and bears the name of the original Cold Springs station. One mile east of U.S. 50 visitors can see still standing the walls of this station, which bore the brunt of several Indian skirmishes.

Sir Richard Burton, a noted English explorer who traveled by coach along this part of the route in October 1860, described another Nevada station in these uncomplimentary terms:

> Sand Springs deserved its name ... with drifted ridges of the finest sand, sometimes 200 feet high and shifting before every gale ... . Behind the house stood a mound shaped like the contents of an hour glass ... . The water near this vile hole was thick and stale with sulphury salts: it blistered even the hands ... . The station house was no unfit object in such a scene, roofless and chairless, filthy and squalid, with a smoky fire in one corner, and a table in the center of an impure floor, the walls open to every wind and the interior full of dust.

The Indian war took its greatest toll in Nevada. In May 1860 the Paiutes, numbering perhaps five hundred, rose in holy war to chase the white man from what today is most of Nevada and a slice of Utah. War parties attacked ranches, wagon trains, and stragglers. Along 300 miles of trail about half the Pony Express stations came under attack; horses were stampeded, several were burned, and sixteen employees were killed.

In spite of the continuing danger to riders and station hands the mail went through—except for one four-week period when the company suspended operations. Never following exactly the same route twice in succession, and avoiding the normal mountain passes whenever possible, the riders continued to make their way across the desert, trusting solely in the speed of their mustangs.

To quell these attacks and protect the pony riders the U.S. Army built Fort Churchill along the Carson River a few miles east of Carson City. The ruins of the old fort are now preserved as Fort Churchill State Historic Park, located on U.S. Highway 95A eight miles south of U.S. 50. Interpretive signs among its crumbling walls relate the story of the frontier fort, while displays at the park's visitor center tell of the pony riders and the Indian uprising. Nearby Buckland Station was the site of a relay station; the original log cabin is gone, but an inn later built for the stage line remains. Samuel Buckland constructed the inn with surplus materials he purchased when the fort was abandoned in 1869.

California

For the final leg of the famous east-west mail run pony riders had to surmount the Sierra Nevada, where peaks soared a mile high and snow covered the mountaintops most of the year. By the 1860s the gold-hungry forty-niners and the emigrants who followed had defined and improved the Johnson Pass route, which skirted Lake Tahoe, climbed to Echo Summit (7,382 feet), and threaded its way through steep-sided valleys and along mountain streams as it twisted downslope to Sacramento. The Johnson Pass route replaced the earlier Carson Pass route to the south. The Carson Pass route was a more difficult route that reached as high as 9,500 feet before it passed over the crest and often retained its snowdrifts well into the summer.

The motorist who drives U.S. 50 from Carson City to Sacramento retraces much of the Johnson Pass route. If the traveler watches closely he will see along the roadside remnants of a century or more of transportation history across the Sierra: segments of the trail, fords, and rock retaining walls that buttressed the winding roadway that carried wagons, stagecoaches, and the hurrying horses of the Pony Express. In the 1930s the trail, then called the Placerville Road, provided the right-of-way for the famed Lincoln Highway, the first U.S. roadway to span the country from the Atlantic to the Pacific. In later years the route evolved into present-day U.S. 50.

Snow, wind, and rain often assaulted the riders in the high Sierra but rarely defeated them. On the inaugural ride eastward of the Pony Express on April 4, 1860, "Boston" Upson took over from the first rider as rain turned to snow. Ralph Moody wrote in *The Old Trails West:*

> Above the 4,000-foot level a raging blizzard was blowing, and gales at more than 60 miles an hour piled snow 15 to 20 feet deep. The trail was completely obliterated,

and visibility reduced to less than 100 feet, but "Boston" fought his way upwards from one isolated relay post to another. He made the last three miles to the summit relay post afoot, shouldering the mochila and leaving his pony bogged belly-deep in a snowdrift. Beyond the summit the blizzard was less severe, and at 2:18 in the afternoon he rode a staggering pony into Friday's Station on Lake Tahoe. In a storm that few men could have lived through, he had carried the first Pony mail 55 miles across the high hump of the Sierra Nevada in just eight hours, better time than the fastest stagecoaches could make in summer weather.

Each westbound rider ended his journey at Sacramento, at the terminus at the B. F. Hastings Building, a structure that has been restored as part of Old Sacramento. Old Sacramento State Historic Park preserves much of Sacramento's original downtown. Its restored historic buildings are alive with shops and exhibits, including, in addition to the Pony Express terminus, the first permanent home of the California Supreme Court, the first theater built in the state, and the extensive California State Railroad Museum.

Here the pony riders pulled up and delivered their mail. Wells, Fargo had the responsibility of delivering the letters to the addressees, putting some of the letters on packet boats to San Francisco.

In April 1861 Russell, Majors, and Waddell suffered a serious financial reverse when the federal mail contract they sought was awarded to their rival, the Butterfield Overland Mail, which then shifted its operations to the central route. Moreover the federal postal contract, which went into effect in July 1861, made the company's financial losses even greater. It cut the original postal rate from $5 to $1 per half ounce, with six pounds of government mail to be carried each trip by the Pony Express for free.

The loss of the government mail contract, questionable financial dealings to cover its losses, and completion of the telegraph sealed the Pony Express's fate. The Butterfield Overland Mail bought them out, leaving Russell, Majors, and Waddell to operate only the trail's western end as a subcontractor. Shortly afterward, when the telegraph linkage was completed across the country, the colorful Pony Express came to an abrupt halt. Although the Overland Mail continued to offer a slower mail service by stagecoach, the day of the fast, ten-day mail was over.

In the entire 18 months of the historic Pony Express experiment, a total of 120 riders rode 650,000 miles with only one scheduled run not completed on time. Only one *mochila* of mail was lost and one rider was killed by Indians. At the peak of its service the pony riders carried as many as seven hundred letters a week, each transmitted in a special government-stamped envelope.

"Farewell pony: Our little friend," wrote the *Sacramento Bee* newspaper in a final salute. "The Pony is to run no more. Farewell and forever, thou staunch, wilderness-overcoming, swiftfooted messenger. For the good thou hast done, we praise thee."

Newspapers as far away as Europe lauded the Pony Express. Pulp magazine writers made some of the riders famous, detailing their exploits as they won out over floods, snowstorms, buffalo stampedes, and Indian attacks with self-confidence and devotion to duty. This elite band of daring horsemen who sped the mail across the wildest miles of the continent had won the admiration and captured the hearts of people all over the world.

National Pony Express Association

Established in 1978 the National Pony Express Association is a non-profit group of more than seven hundred members, organized into divisions for each of the eight states the Pony Express Trail crosses, and is dedicated to creating a deeper appreciation of the historic Pony Express.

The association is perhaps best known for its annual re-ride, when members dress in historic garb and furnish their own horses to ride once again a segment of the historic trail. In addition its members sponsor school essay contests and take part in patriotic parades within the states where the historic trail lies.

The association also carries commemorative mail to communities holding celebrations and raises funds through the delivery of Christmas cards by Pony Express. In 1983 it stepped in when a mud slide near Lake Tahoe interrupted normal postal service. Saddling up to meet the emergency its members carried the mail cross-country around the slide area. The number of letters delivered increased during the two months of horseback delivery from some four hundred daily to three thousand.

For more information write the National Pony Express Association, P.O. Box 236, Pollock Pines, CA 95726.

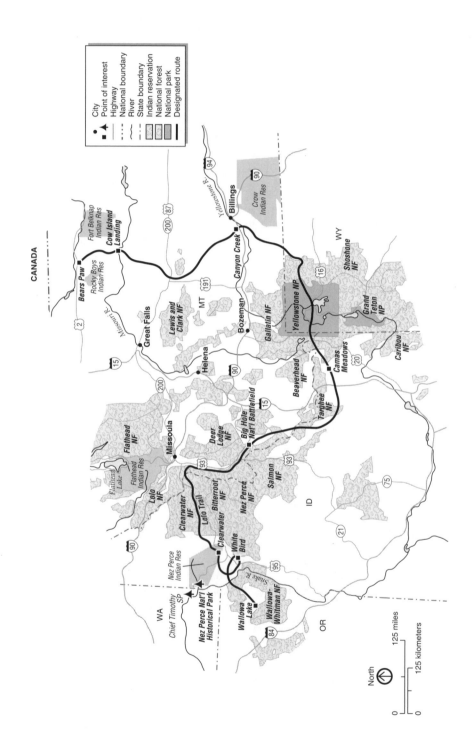

Chapter 17

NEZ PERCE NATIONAL HISTORIC TRAIL

THE NEZ PERCE (NEE-ME-POO) NATIONAL HISTORIC TRAIL WINDS across a series of mountain ranges, through deep canyons, along valleys, across rivers, and through forests and plains—even past a thermal geyser field—as it penetrates some of the most rugged and spectacular scenery of Oregon, Idaho, Wyoming, and Montana.

As is evident to anyone who seeks to follow it the route was not chosen for its convenience or ease of travel. Quite the opposite. This was an escape route, a pathway taken by a desperate people at a crucial time of the tribe's existence. It lies like a forgotten piece of string across America's last frontier.

Like the Trail of Tears of the Cherokee (see page 145) the Nez Perce Trail commemorates the route followed by an Indian people who were being forced by events beyond their control to abandon their homeland. Like the Cherokees entire communities—men, women, and children—were uprooted. Like the Cherokees it was the discovery of gold on their lands that provided the final impetus that forced them to move.

While the Trail of Tears was an organized migration to a known location, the Nez Perce Trail represents an unplanned, improvised flight from a threatening adversary toward an unknown destination. Whereas the Cherokee had reluctantly agreed to their own forced removal, the Nez Perce who had not agreed to the Treaty of 1863 had to either flee or be captured or killed by the pursuing U.S. Army.

257

By its very nature, the Nez Perce Trail is not a pathway made familiar by everyday use. Instead it is a route taken only once in its entirety, although the Nez Perce were familiar with much of the route from previous hunting and food-gathering forays into the plains. There is no existing trail, merely the landscape that the Nez Perce traversed in their desperate journey. The trail comprises a series of sites where events occurred that either helped or hindered the "non-treaty" group of Nez Perce as they fled from the U.S. Army while trying to preserve their traditional way of life. Because it is one of the later historic trails authorized by Congress, few roadside trail signs bearing the distinctive logo have been erected along public roads that cross or parallel the trail.

To aid the traveler in finding these disconnected historic sites the U.S. Forest Service, which administers the trail, publishes a free four-page folder, "The Nez Perce National Historic Trail" (USGPO 1992-694-859), which includes a map depicting the entire trail length. To obtain a copy write to Clearwater National Forest, 12730 Highway 12, Orofino, ID 83544. A 20-minute video on the Nez Perce Trail has also been released by the northern region of the Forest Service.

The best place to start to retrace the Nez Perce Trail by auto is the Nez Perce National Historical Park, located 11 miles east of Lewiston, Idaho. The national park is located on the Nez Perce Indian Reservation, two miles from Lapwai, the headquarters of the Nez Perce Tribal Council.

Here the traveler finds a contemporary visitor center and the remains of an early mission established among the Nez Perce in 1838 by the Presbyterian missionaries Henry and Eliza Spalding. A self-guiding trail leads past a meeting house and school as well as a gristmill and sawmill that were powered by water from the nearby Clearwater River. The missionaries distributed seeds to the Indians and taught them farming methods. Encouraged by the Spaldings a number of Nez Perce converted to Christianity and became farmers, but many others kept to their traditional way of life, fishing for salmon; gathering roots, berries, and herbs; and occasionally hunting bison.

Exhibits at the visitor center museum focus on a number of major facets of Nez Perce culture. The role of the horse is illustrated with handmade saddles, harness straps, and blankets as well as historic photographs showing the Indians using this tack.

Headdresses and beaded moccasins and gloves, for which the Nez Perce are well known, demonstrate the intricate workmanship of the tribesmen and women. Arrows and ceremonial pipes fill other cases.

A ranger at the visitor center can also provide a list of sites that are significant in the history of the Nez Perce. The 1965 legislation that created the national park included twenty-four sites in Idaho; later legislation added fourteen more sites in Oregon, Washington, Idaho, and Montana.

A film and publications give visitors additional information about Nez Perce history and culture. For thousands of years, visitors learn, the valleys, prairies, and plateaus of north-central Idaho and adjacent Oregon and Washington have been home to the Nez Perce people, who call themselves simply the Nee-Me-Poo—"the People." They were given the name Nez Perce ("pierced nose") by French trappers who mistakenly thought they wore ornaments in their nose.

The Nez Perce lived in the valleys of the Clearwater and Snake Rivers and their tributaries. They fished the streams, hunted in the woodlands, and dug the bulbs of the camas lily on the high plateaus. This bulb, a mainstay of their traditional diet, is high in protein and is eaten raw, cooked, or ground into meal.

Often several villages formed a loose confederation, or band, pooling their resources for a long hunting trip over the mountains to the plains or to fight a war. In the early 1700s the Nez Perce, along with many other Indian tribes, acquired horses; the increased mobility and range the horse gave them added new dimensions to their age-old ways and forged new ones.

Not until after the American Revolution did the Nez Perce begin to feel the impact of the wave of people who had settled in the country. Their first meeting with white men took place in September 1805, when Meriwether Lewis and William Clark and their "Corps of Discovery" entered Nez Perce country along the Lolo Trail (see page 170). The Nez Perce welcomed the explorers, gave them supplies, and described to them a feasible river route to the Pacific. Despite later persecution and pressure by white men the tribe's friendship and peaceful coexistence with early settlers would persist with few interruptions until 1877.

In the 1840s settlers began to make their way west along the Oregon Trail. By 1846 the Nez Perce found themselves surrounded by U.S. boundaries when the United States and Great Britain divided the Oregon country along the 49th Parallel. By this time the Nez Perce had also come under an influence that was to have a lasting effect on them: the Christian missionaries. The missionaries believed the Indians would be best served if they abandoned their traditional ways and adopted the white man's religion and culture, including his farming methods.

As these forces imposed change and new ways on the Nez Perce, political developments began to affect them as well. Washington Territory, which included all of Idaho and part of Montana, was formed in 1853. Its governor, Isaac Stevens, wanted to define the traditional Indian lands and draw boundaries for reservations. The lands not included within the reservations, he reasoned, could then be used by settlers, and the federal government could have a right-of-way on which to build a transcontinental railroad. To this end he called the Nez Perce leaders to a council at Walla Walla in May and June 1855. An agreement was reached between Stevens and the leaders of each of several independent Nez Perce bands to reserve the greater part of their traditional homeland as their exclusive domain while opening up other areas.

But white settlers and miners encouraged by the slogan of "Manifest Destiny," which envisioned a United States that would extend from the Atlantic to the Pacific Ocean, poured heedlessly into the area, ignoring the treaty boundaries. When gold was discovered on the Nez Perce Reservation in 1860, the illegal influx increased. Mining towns sprang up on Indian lands. Some miners, disdainful of Indian rights, killed any Nez Perce who resisted them.

Now the white settlers raised calls for an even smaller reservation that would exclude the goldfields. So in 1863 a new reservation, containing only one-tenth of the land set aside in 1855, was proposed to the tribe. A pro-American Christian Nez Perce leader, named Lawyer, and his followers accepted the plan and signed the treaty because the lands that belonged to their band were included in the proposed smaller reservation. Other Nez Perce leaders of bands whose tribal lands were not included in the proposed reservation rejected it. The Nez Perce who accepted the shrunken reservation were called the "treaty" band; those who did not accept the new boundaries were called the "non-treaty" bands.

U.S. government officials, conveniently claiming that Lawyer represented the entire tribe, asserted that the agreement was binding on all, but to the Nez Perce this was not true or even possible. Lawyer could only sign away his own tribal band's land, no one else's. After President Andrew Johnson ignored the protests of the non-treaty bands and signed the document in 1867, the U.S. government launched a campaign to move all the Nez Perce onto the greatly reduced reservation. The Nez Perce leaders who had not signed the treaty and who lived outside the new reservation paid no attention to the orders. Foremost among them was Old Joseph, who led a band that lived in Oregon's Wallowa Valley. Young Joseph, who succeeded his father, hoped that a peaceful solution could be found for he did not wish either to go to war or to leave his homeland.

Finally, in May 1877, the non-treaty Nez Perce were told that the U.S. Army would forcibly move them onto the reservation. Reluctantly, in early June, Chief Joseph and his people decided to comply rather than risk violence and the probable death of many of the tribesmen. In sadness they packed up, gathered their livestock together, and began to leave the lands of their forefathers.

White Bird Battlefield

Crossing the Snake River, the band camped near Tolo Lake near Grangeville, Idaho, preparing to move onto the reservation by the June 14 deadline. On the morning of June 13 three young men, angered by the decision to give up and bent on revenge for the murder of one of their fathers by a white man, rode out into the dawn. By midday of June 14 they had killed four settlers. Joined by seventeen more warriors, the group killed fourteen or fifteen white men in the next two days, spreading panic among the settlers.

Knowing that General Oliver O. Howard would certainly retaliate for this attack, the Indians headed for a familiar campsite at White Bird Creek. General Howard immediately ordered two companies of cavalry soldiers to ride to the area and called on the Army to send reinforcements. When the cavalrymen reached White Bird and discovered that the Nez Perce were camped nearby, they decided to attack.

At first light the Army's advance scouts came upon a Nez Perce peace party sent out under a white flag. A rifle cracked and the lead Army bugler fell dead. Then, forming a skirmish line, the Army attacked. With all of his other buglers also out of action the cavalry commander was left with no way to issue bugle commands to his forces during the rest of the engagement.

An Indian attack on one flank pushed the Army defenders off a knoll, enabling the Nez Perce riflemen to shoot with deadly accuracy down the line of skirmishers. Another Indian attack crumpled the opposite Army flank, and the Nez Perce followed this by stampeding a herd of their horses through the center of the cavalry line. Clinging unseen to the sides of the loose horses were several Nez Perce warriors armed with repeating rifles. Once past the center of the ranks they began firing on the harried troops from the rear.

Although outnumbered the experienced Nez Perce warriors turned the action into a rout, killing other troopers trapped in a canyon and pursuing the defeated cavalrymen for miles beyond the battlefield. The casualty figures told an incredible story. The Army had lost thirty-four men dead and four wounded. Not a single Nez Perce warrior had been killed and only two had been wounded.

Today a wayside exhibit shelter and a circular tour road at the White Bird battle site enable visitors to visualize this first action of the "Nez Perce War." To reach the battlefield site drive 80 miles south on U.S. Highway 95 from the visitor center at Spalding. A self-guiding folder of the battleground is available at the visitor center, at the Nez Perce National Forest office in nearby Grangeville, or at the beginning of the auto-tour route.

The 16-mile loop tour road takes the traveler past the sites of the engagement from the arrival of the troops at the battleground to their retreat along the same route. The folder describes the action that took place at each location. A wayside shelter provides an excellent view of the rolling landscape; displays illustrate the progression of the battle in which the Nez Perce soundly defeated a much larger force that possessed superior weapons.

Battle of Clearwater

The Battle of White Bird convinced General Howard that subduing the non-treaty Nez Perce was not going to be an easy task. The victorious Nez Perce added sixty U.S. Army rifles and a smaller number of pistols to their arsenal—all of them picked up on the battlefield. General Howard cautiously marked time until reinforcements arrived, then moved southward again with some five hundred soldiers and a hundred supply workers to intercept the Nez Perce.

In the meantime the five independent bands of non-treaty Nez Perce had consolidated into one group that numbered about 750—some 150 of them warriors, the remainder older men, women, and children. Whereas the troops could move unencumbered, the Indians had the much more complicated task of moving their whole community of tipis, supplies, and two to three thousand horses and cattle through a terrain of fast-flowing rivers, deep valleys, and wooded slopes.

On a hot day in July General Howard caught up with the non-treaty Indians camped beside the south fork of the Clearwater River, a high bluff protecting one side of their encampment. The Army attacked bringing to bear its greatly superior firepower of Gatling guns, a howitzer, and rifle-carrying cavalrymen. While an Indian skirmish line held off the Army's threatened advance at one end of the valley, the entire Nez Perce encampment pulled down its tipis, rounded up the cattle, and moved out the other end. After a full day of inconclusive fighting the Nez Perce made good an orderly withdrawal to the north.

An interpretive sign, one of a series of signs set out by the Idaho Historical Society to mark historic points along the trail, greets travelers at the Clearwater site. To reach it follow Idaho 13 north, 15 miles past the town of Grangeville.

Lolo Trail

On July 15 the chiefs of the five bands met to decide their future strategy. They could turn back to defend their traditional homeland in the Wallowa Valley, they could accede to the demands of the Army and agree to live on the much smaller reservation, or they could turn east where they might form a military alliance with some old tribal friends, the Crows. Chief Joseph, who favored returning to Wallowa, deferred to the principle of united action as the five bands became a single group of expatriate refugees and headed eastward toward Montana, then toward Canada, where they hoped to get safely beyond U.S. control as the Sioux Indians had done before them.

Seeking to avoid further bloodshed the Nez Perce—warriors, wounded, families, and herds—started up the Lolo Trail. They were thoroughly familiar with this ridgeline trail through the forest for they had used it for years to journey to the plains to hunt buffalo. The trail follows the ridge and not the river because steep cliffs and indentations along the riverbanks make a lower path impractical. It was this same trail over the Bitterroot Mountains where seventy years earlier the Lewis and Clark expedition had barely survived when winter storms impeded their progress and starvation threatened.

It was no less difficult for the Nez Perce, even though it was not wintertime. Tangled underbrush, jagged boulders, and trees uprooted by powerful winds blocked their way. General Howard later reported that the Indians "jammed their ponies through, up the rocks, over, and under, and around the logs and among the fallen trees ... leaving blood to mark their path," and abandoning livestock that could not make it. A one-lane marked forest road suitable for four-wheel-drive vehicles now traces this Nez Perce–Lewis and Clark route through the Clearwater National Forest.

Today passenger cars turn onto U.S. Highway 12 after the Clearwater Battlefield and follow the "Lewis and Clark Highway" along the middle fork of the Clearwater and the Lochsa Rivers. The actual 150-mile trail followed by the Nez Perce is up on the ridge above the roadway, but interpretive signs at pulloffs along the scenic road describe the historic actions for the auto traveler. Rapids whiten the river at many places along the route and waterfalls cascade over the cliffs.

Just past Lolo Pass at Howard Creek auto travelers may take a self-guiding foot trail that leads along the Lolo Trail. A small U.S. Forest Service visitor center at Lolo Pass offers exhibits and publications.

An annual trail ride in early summer on the Lolo Trail portion is popular with visitors as well as nearby landowners, historians, and members of the Nez Perce tribe. The trail ride usually ends with a salmon and buffalo feast.

In 1877, after only 11 days, the Nez Perce reached Montana and the end of their mountain trek—only to face another obstacle. An Army captain with thirty-five soldiers supplemented by two hundred volunteers from nearby settlements blocked their way. Chiefs Looking Glass, Joseph, and White Bird came forward under a flag of truce to negotiate, telling the troops and volunteers that they wished only to pass through the Bitterroot Valley and would promise to do no harm to the settlers who lived there. The captain wanted to prevent the passage of the Nez Perce, but the volunteers were unwilling to provoke Indian attacks on their vulnerable settlements. So the Nez Perce were allowed to bypass the roadblock and continue on. The barricade was disparagingly dubbed "Fort Fizzle" by the volunteers, who were prepared for the potential skirmish that never occurred. Visitors to the site today view a reconstruction of the barricade at a picnic area along U.S. 12.

Big Hole National Battlefield

True to their word the Nez Perce rode peacefully into Montana Territory and up the Bitterroot Valley, taking no hostile action and paying for the provisions they needed. Knowing that General Howard and his forces were many days behind they slowed their pace, little suspecting that another Army contingent under Colonel John Gibbon was approaching from another direction. The folder for the Bitterroot National Forest relates the story of this peaceful interlude between episodes of violence.

Crossing a high range over the Continental Divide they camped beside a creek in a meadow in the Big Hole Valley. Today U.S. Highway 93 follows this route through the Bitterroot Valley, then climbs the Beaverhead Range to Lost Trail Pass (6,995 feet). Montana 43 leads the motorist from U.S. 93, descending into the valley to Big Hole National Battlefield.

Once at Big Hole the Nez Perce let down their guard, failing even to post their usual scouts to keep watch. They spent valuable time cutting new poles for their tipis and roasting camas roots dug from the familiar meadows they had long known.

On August 8 Colonel Gibbon's advance patrol spotted the Indians in Big Hole Valley and the following night his main force moved into attack position barely two hundred yards from the fugitives' camp. The attack started prematurely when a lone Nez Perce, out in the predawn darkness to check the horses in the pasture, stumbled onto the concealed soldiers and volunteers and was shot and killed.

Immediately the troops waded through the waist-deep water, firing into the village. Taken by surprise some of the Nez Perce scattered quickly while others were slow to awaken. In the confusion of the faint predawn light men, women, and children were shot indiscriminately.

The soldiers soon occupied the south end of the camp while the Nez Perce warriors, urged on by Chiefs Looking Glass and White Bird, quickly took up sniper positions, some of them in the trees. Their deadly sniper fire eventually forced Gibbon's men to retreat back across the creek. For the next 24 hours the troops were pinned down and suffered many casualties. At one point a group of Nez Perce horsemen daringly galloped forward, captured a cannon that was about to fire into the camp, and dismantled it.

As the siege continued Chief Joseph and others cared for the Indian wounded and buried the dead, who tragically included Chief Joseph's own wife. Then they gathered the survivors, horses, and tipis and broke camp. While an Indian rear guard remained behind to keep the soldiers under fire, the main body of the Nez Perce headed south, leaving many of their belongings behind them. Finally, in the early morning of the second day of fighting, the remaining warriors fired parting shots at the soldiers, then galloped off to join the others. The Nez Perce had lost eighty of their people, many of them women and children,

A ghost village at Big Hole National Battlefield, Montana.

twelve of them warriors. The Army suffered thirty-one soldiers killed and forty wounded.

Exhibits at the visitor center at Big Hole National Battlefield contain photographic portraits, quotations, and personal belongings of some of the participants in the battle. A trail from the visitor center leads visitors to a "ghost village" of tipi poles that stands on the spot where the Nez Perce camp stood. The creek and the willow swamp that gave its watery protection to both the attacking soldiers and the Indian noncombatants still exist as they did a century ago.

Scattered among the ghost tipis are markers that show where soldiers and Indians alike fought on that fateful day. A feather symbol marks where a Nez Perce was positioned; a hat symbol marks where a soldier or volunteer stood. Trail folders are available to guide visitors as they walk both the Nez Perce Camp Trail to the ghost village and the Siege Trail to the Army's defensive positions. National Park Service rangers conduct interpretive walks and talks.

Yellowstone National Park

After losing so many of their people at Big Hole the Nez Perce desperately pushed east to reach their Crow allies. General Howard and his Army troops resumed the pursuit, following on the heels of the fleeing bands.

Since many of the Indians had been wounded, they had to be dragged behind the horses on travois, thus slowing the pace for others. Knowing they were a burden some of the old and ailing dropped out and wandered off into the forest to die alone. To buy some time Ollokut, Chief Joseph's brother, one night under cover of darkness raced back with twenty-eight warriors, raided General Howard's camp at Camas Meadows, and drove off 200 pack mules. Left without animals to carry his supplies and ammunition General Howard was delayed for three days until he could procure more pack animals.

That was long enough for the Nez Perce to evade another Army detachment that had been sent to look for them, surmount Targhee Pass, and descend into Yellowstone National Park. Here they met a complication they had not faced before—tourists. Yellowstone had been opened as a national park only three years earlier, and sightseers were beginning to come to enjoy it. Thus it was that in late August a number of visitors were in the park. To the embattled Nez Perce the visitors, some of them armed, posed a possible hindrance to their escape and might inform the Army of their whereabouts.

As they entered the park the Nez Perce captured a prospector and compelled him to guide them through the park. When they came upon ten tourists camping near the junction of the Madison and Firehole Rivers they captured them and took them along as hostages. After several tourists escaped and two were wounded and abandoned, the others were set free when the bands reached the eastern side of the park. In other confrontations two other tourists were killed and four wounded in the eight days the Nez Perce spent within the park.

By entering at the West Yellowstone entrance the motorist can trace the path taken by the Nez Perce, although the historic trail is as yet unmarked within the park. The Indians took the route now followed by the park road along the Madison River. Then, as now, the river teemed with fish. Elk grazed its banks. Two interpretive signs at road turnoffs tell the story of the forced march. A campground is located today near the spot where the Nez Perce captured the tourists.

Turning south at the Firehole River, travelers drive past thermal phenomena such as mudpots, hot springs, and geysers until they reach a creek and a trailhead known as the "Mary Mountain Trail." Here, if they wish, they may walk literally in the Nez Perce footsteps. The Indians followed the creek—now appropriately called Nez Perce Creek. The trail runs parallel to the creek and leads for 22 miles through lodgepole pine forest and meadows; much of the forest, however, was burned over by a forest fire in 1988. Bison are often seen in this area during the spring, and grizzly bears may be spotted during spring months.

The remainder of the historic route across Yellowstone is unidentified and unmarked, although historical accounts confirm that the Nez Perce went close to the northern end of Yellowstone Lake, then turned north through the Hayden Valley, before turning east through unpopulated wilderness valleys to move into Crow territory.

Bear's Paw Battleground

With bitter disappointment the Nez Perce learned that the Crows had no intention of giving them asylum or assistance, an action the Crows believed would jeopardize their relations with the U.S. Army. Flight to Canada—where the Sioux led by Chief Sitting Bull had earlier been given sanctuary—remained the only hope for the Nez Perce.

By September they had turned north. On September 13 they fought a successful running battle at Canyon Creek near Laurel, Montana, with soldiers who tried to prevent them from making their way through a canyon to the open prairie beyond. They crossed the Missouri River eight days later, pausing on Cow Island to fight for and seize some food from an Army depot (after local citizens had refused to sell it to them). Now a unit of Nez Perce National Historical Park, the battle site is marked with an interpretive sign. A Bureau of Land Management backcountry byway leads over a rough but scenic roadway to an excellent overlook at the Cow Island site.

Then they plodded north again as cold winds heralded the arrival of autumn. By the end of September the fleeing Nez Perce had reached the Bear Paw Mountains of northern Montana. They had now traveled 1,200 miles. Although within a scant 40 miles of the Canadian border, the Nez Perce were too weary to travel any farther. After holding a council of chiefs they decided to stay long enough to kill some bison that would provide nourishing food and warm robes for the cold weather. General Howard, they knew, was still several days behind them. What they did not know was that Colonel Nelson Miles was closing in on them from the east with a fresh cavalry troop.

When it came the fighting was fierce. One battalion had 53 casualties out of 115 men on its first charge. After the Nez Perce repelled a second charge, then a third, the Army settled into a siege of the Indian camp.

A two-day storm blew in bringing cold rain followed by swirling snow. All in the camp were suffering. Only two chiefs remained alive—Joseph and White Bird. In a council of warriors Chief Joseph, for the sake of his dying people, chose surrender. White Bird promised he would yield after supervising the roundup of his own band. But on the next day Chief Joseph stood alone in avowing that the Nez Perce would resist no longer. White Bird had slipped through the guard lines at night and made his escape to Canada taking with him fourteen warriors and more than a hundred women. Chief Joseph uttered the anguished words that have reverberated through the years: "Hear me, my chiefs! I am tired.

My heart is sick and sad. From where the sun now stands I will fight no more forever."

Today the site where the dwindling force of Nez Perce were subdued by a vastly superior Army contingent has been preserved as one of the extended sites of the Nez Perce National Historical Park. Visitors are welcomed to a storefront visitor center on U.S. Highway 2 in nearby Chinook in north-central Montana, then directed five miles south to the battle site. Here interpretive signs and a trail guide show the visitor the way along a trail that winds past the critical sites of the engagement. A marker stands near the spot where Chief Looking Glass fell—the last fatality of this heart-wrenching conflict.

Even then death and suffering did not end for the Nez Perce. Although General Howard had said they could return to Idaho, that promise was not kept until years later. Instead the Nez Perce were exiled for seven years to Oklahoma, where more of them perished of cold, disease, and starvation than had died in all of the fighting. Joseph and his band were placed on the Colville Reservation in Washington state—never to be allowed to return to his homeland in the Wallowa Valley.

A young member of the tribe stitches a pair of moccasins while explaining the stop on the Nez Perce Trail to travelers.

The heroic, fighting retreat of the Nez Perce has since been judged an epic of Indian warfare—a fight the Nez Perce did not seek and which they could not win. Some seven hundred fifty Indians, most of them women, children, and sick and old people, had withstood more than two thousand army regulars and as many volunteer militiamen in eighteen engagements, including four major battles and at least four fiercely fought skirmishes. In the words of the U.S. Army theirs was "one of the most extraordinary Indian wars of which there is any record."

Their route through four states, dictated by the geography with which they were faced and by their own strategy, was skillfully devised. They had lost approximately 65 men and 55 women and children and had killed approximately 180 whites and wounded 150. By the time the final tragedy played out at Bear's Paw their courage, tenacity, and skill at evading capture had earned them the sympathy of much of the American public. It will undoubtedly also earn them the respect of all those who seek and follow the Nez Perce National Historic Trail.

Nez Perce National Historic Trail Foundation

The Nez Perce National Historic Trail Foundation was formed in 1991 as an outgrowth of the advisory council that assisted the U.S. Forest Service, National Park Service, and Bureau of Land Management in the development and adoption of the Comprehensive Management and Use Plan for the trail.

Now numbering 120 members with addresses as far away as England and France, the members of the foundation help to promote and interpret the 1,170-mile-long trail that tells the sad saga of these Native Americans.

An important goal of the foundation is to inform its members of the condition of the trail and plans for future development and interpretation. The foundation makes an effort to gain rights-of-way along the trail route, especially those not on federal lands. In educational programs foundation members take the Nez Perce story to schools, historical societies, and the interested public. One feature unique to the Nez Perce National Historic Trail Foundation is its continuing effort to bring about greater cooperation and understanding between the treaty and non-treaty Nez Perce tribal members.

For more information write the Executive Director, Nez Perce National Historic Trail Foundation, P.O. Box 20197, Missoula, MT 59801.

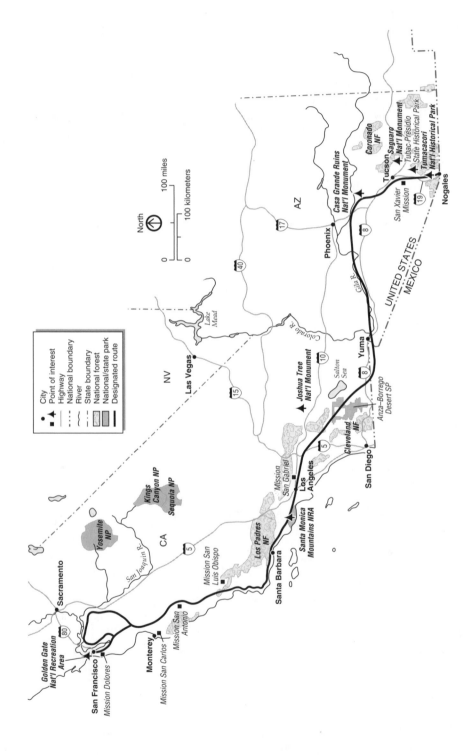

North

0   100 miles

0   100 kilometers

Legend:
- City
- Point of interest
- Highway
- National boundary
- River
- State boundary
- National forest
- National/state park
- Designated route

Golden Gate Nat'l Recreation Area

San Francisco
Mission Dolores

Sacramento

Monterey
Mission San Carlos

Mission San Antonio

Mission San Luis Obispo

Santa Barbara

Los Padres NF

Santa Monica Mountains NRA

Mission San Gabriel

Los Angeles

San Diego

Cleveland NF

Anza–Borrego Desert SP

Yuma

Joshua Tree Nat'l Monument

Salton Sea

Yosemite NP

Kings Canyon NP

Sequoia NP

San Joaquin R.

CA

NV

Las Vegas

Lake Mead

Colorado R.

Gila R.

Phoenix

AZ

Casa Grande Ruins Nat'l Monument

Coronado NF

Tucson

Saguaro Nat'l Monument

San Xavier Mission

Tubac–Presidio State Historical Park

Tumacacori Nat'l Historical Park

Nogales

UNITED STATES
MEXICO

Highways: 80, 5, 15, 40, 17, 10, 8, 19

Chapter 18

JUAN BAUTISTA DE ANZA NATIONAL HISTORIC TRAIL

Travelers who trace the Juan Bautista de Anza National Historic Trail through Arizona and California turn to a page in American history when Spain's rulers were devoted to the pursuit of "God, Gold, and Glory." In the New World Spain's empire in the eighteenth century extended from Central America and Mexico all the way into Alta (Upper) California.

The Anza Trail is a chapter in that pursuit of empire. The historic trail commemorates the route followed by a remarkable colonizing expedition that traversed some eighteen hundred miles during twelve months between 1775 and 1776. The result of this epic emigration was to link Spain's colony of New Spain (Mexico) with the developing chain of missions being established along the California coast as far north as the Golden Gate. What was needed was a safe and dependable overland route from Mexico to resupply and populate these new missions.

The Spanish viceroy in Mexico City also strongly desired to colonize what would later be known as San Francisco Bay, the spacious harbor that had been discovered by Spanish soldiers only a few years before in 1769. One of the few harbors that indents the rugged California coastline, this huge bay could provide protection for the procession of treasure ships that carried gold to Spain from the Philippines, gold that was critical to the financial health of the empire. A settlement here would also establish Spain's presence in the face of threats from Russian fur traders and English and French freebooters.

By coincidence at the very time the Spanish in the Southwest were thus extending their colonies northward, the American colonists on the East Coast were resorting to force to break the bonds that held their colony to the British Empire.

Juan Bautista de Anza, a third-generation frontier soldier, led the emigration, retracing the route across deserts, mountains, and valleys that he and other venturesome soldiers had blazed only a year before. Anza recruited emigrants willing to undertake this long trek from impoverished settlements in what is now western Mexico, gathering them together at a presidio in Horcasitas. He then led them 150 miles to Tubac, Arizona, the final staging area for the expedition.

He promised the colonists that they would get land of their own in Alta California, land a peasant could never hope to gain if he remained in Mexico, and could therefore start a new life for themselves and their families. As an additional incentive to take the risk of the cross-desert migration, the colonial government fully outfitted each volunteer family, providing each person everything from undergarments to guns and leather jackets for the men, to chemises and hair ribbons for the women. The prospective settlers were provided with bolts of cloth, kettles, and pots and pans for their future kitchens.

The emigrants were given cattle enough to slaughter one animal a day for food for the expedition on the trail and still have enough animals remaining to build up a herd when they reached their destination. Accounts of the journey add that the supplies for the expedition included three barrels of brandy and one of wine; thirty loads of flour; sixty bushels of beans; and modest amounts of ham, sausages, biscuits, cheese, spices, oil, and vinegar.

When the expedition assembled at the presidio of Tubac in present-day Arizona in October 1775, it consisted of almost three hundred persons. Among these were 39 women and no less than 127 children. Some five hundred horses and pack mules and more than three hundred head of cattle filled out the expedition. Thus began the most impressive migration yet undertaken on the continent by the Spaniards. With it went three friars: Francisco Garces, Tomas Eixarch, and Pedro Font, who kept a detailed diary of the journey and also served as its official astronomer.

The expedition made its way across the desert, moving at the slow pace set by the herd of cattle that the *vaqueros,* or cowboys, prodded along. The settlers faced a variety of hazards:

lack of accurate knowledge of the route, concern about the reception they would receive from the Indian tribes they passed, lack of water which forced them to dig holes in the dry river-beds. When cold winds blew they froze; when the sun burned hot they simmered.

By January 1776 Anza had guided the caravan across the southwestern deserts as far as a newly established mission at San Gabriel. From there the expedition followed what would become the Camino Real, the route that linked the California missions. Finally, on March 10, 1776, it reached its first goal of 300 miles up the coast at Monterey. There, after surviving the severe hardships of the trail, its members would find relief at Mission San Carlos Borromeo de Carmelo. The mission had been founded six years before by Father Junipero Serra, the pioneering priest who established many of the missions that constituted Spain's claim to Alta California. As a result of Anza's colonizing expedition these isolated California missions could thenceforth be resupplied by pack trains moving along this overland route instead of by an uncertain supply line of ships sailing up the coast from Mexico. Lack of adequate harbors, headwinds, and opposing currents had made supplying the missions by sea a difficult task.

The Beginning

The route taken by the Anza expedition reinforces the saying that "rivers are the highways of the desert." From his organizing point at Tubac and nearby Tumacacori, Arizona, Captain Anza led his emigrant caravan north along the Santa Cruz River, then west along the Gila River, a route long used by the Indians. Today's traveler can closely parallel the historic route as he or she proceeds north from Nogales on I-19 and I-10 through Tucson to Casa Grande Ruins National Monument, then west on I-8 to Yuma.

The traveler who traces the Anza Trail steps back into these Spanish colonial times at Tubac and Tumacacori. Tumacacori with its church was one of a string of missions the Spanish had established south of what is now Tucson; nearby Tubac was its presidio, or garrison. Friar Font, the chaplain of the expedition, stayed with his fellow priests at Tumacacori while Anza gathered the settlers, livestock, and supplies at Tubac.

Today at Tumacacori National Historical Park visitors see the remains of the large adobe church and outbuildings constructed to replace a smaller church that stood here at the time Anza came through. Such a church was the centerpiece of every frontier Spanish mission, a symbol of the efforts of the colonial power to convert the Indians to Christianity and encourage them to become tax-paying subjects of the King of Spain.

A self-guided walking tour takes the visitor into the dim interior of the 200-year-old church and associated mortuary chapel, the cemetery, and portions of the *convento,* or quarters. A handsome adobe visitor center built in the Spanish style provides an audiovisual presentation of the area's early Native American and Spanish colonial heritage. A mission garden features spice and herb plants, fruit trees, and native Sonoran Desert plants.

Between Tumacacori and Tubac is one of the few places on the Anza Trail where history buffs can follow the expedition's actual route on foot or on horseback. A 4.5-mile path that traces the historic route between the presidio and the mission runs through a steamside setting of cottonwood, mesquite, elderberry, and palo verde trees, twice crossing the usually dry bed of the Santa Cruz River. Along the way archeologists have unearthed the foundations of the original Tubac settlement. Pick up a trail map at one of the visitor centers at either end of the footpath.

At Tubac Presidio State Historic Park visitors can still see the surface outline of Anza's U-shaped fortified house, the outpost he commanded before he left to lead the historic expedition to the California coast. After viewing exhibits of artifacts at the small visitor center, visitors descend to an underground exhibit area where they peer through glass walls to see how archeologists peeled away layers of history at the site to unearth the pottery shards, knife blades, and sword points displayed in the visitor center.

From these bits of history the visitor can better visualize the day when the full expedition began its trek on October 23, 1775. Donald T. Garate of the National Park Service, in his booklet on the trail, describes the scene:

> As the march got under way, Father Font sang the *alabado* and everyone joined in, setting a precedent that would be followed the entire journey. A few scouts rode out in front to determine the best route. Lieutenant Colonel Anza led the

expedition, followed by Padre Font. Then came all the people with the Tubac escorts keeping a wary eye for Apaches. After the people came the mule train, followed by the *caballada*, or horse herd. The *vaqueros* and cattle brought up the rear of this mile-long traveling city.

Tragedy struck the expedition almost immediately. One of the women, Maria Manuela Pinuelas, died in childbirth. The body was taken for burial thirty miles farther to the next mission stop, San Xavier del Bac (pronounced san HAHV-yehr del bock). Founded in 1692 the mission still ministers to the Tohono O'odham people, formerly called the Papago.

The church that travelers now see miles away across the flat desert replaced an earlier mission church. Called the "White Dove of the Desert," the elaborate structure is an example of Spanish mission architecture with its six-foot-thick walls, twin towers, flying buttresses, domes, carvings, and arches. Murals on the interior walls and its altar glow with brilliant reds and golds. Busloads of tourists from Tucson arrive daily to see the ornate church, its cemetery, and its sunny courtyard.

San Xavier del Bac Mission near Tucson.

Anza followed the Santa Cruz River to its junction with the Gila River, a route that today skirts Tucson and is paralleled by I-10. While the expedition camped near the river junction Anza and Father Font paid a visit to the Casa Grande ruins, even then known to be a prehistoric Indian site. The Hohokam people ("those who have gone") inhabited the area up to the mid-1400s. These skilled farmers, who built a network of hundreds of miles of irrigation canals to water their crops, also had a well-developed knowledge and understanding of astronomy.

The Casa Grande, or "Great House," a four-story structure constructed of local caliche, a hard, cementlike combination of clay and limestone, has successfully weathered more than six hundred years; it is protected now by a roof. Around the main building stand the remains of the walled village. The visitor center at Casa Grande Ruins National Monument offers historical exhibits and walks guided by National Park Service rangers.

The Gila River led the way to Yuma, where the Gila meets the south-flowing Colorado River. I-8 now parallels the approximate route. Anza led the caravan through the lands of several Indian tribes, overcoming steadily blowing wind and sand. The sparse vegetation, then as now, consisted mostly of creosote bush, saltbush, and gnarled mesquite. The men had to look for lagoons or dig wells near the river to find water since the Gila was a dry riverbed at this time of year.

Thirty-seven days after leaving Tubac the Anza expedition reached the Colorado River. Here it was met by the friendly chief of the Yumas whom Anza had encountered on his earlier reconnaissance trip and had named "Captain Salvador Palma." The chief welcomed the weary travelers, Anza wrote in his diary, with "an abundance of beans, calabashes, maize, wheat and other grains which are used by them, and so many watermelons that we estimated that there must have been more than three thousand."

During the fall season of the year the Colorado, 200 yards wide, could be forded so rafts were not required. Scouting ahead Anza found a place where they could cut a rough road down the bluff to the riverbank. Visitors today can see this spot just north of where I-8 crosses the river near Yuma. Anza wrote:

> We began to cross the first branch of the river on the largest and strongest horses, leading by the bridles those on which the women and children were riding; and as a precaution, in

case anyone should fall, I stationed in front ten men on the downstream side. This branch was crossed in the main at a depth of five and a half palms of water and in the middle six ... . In these crossings we had no other mishap than the falling of a man who was carrying a child, but he was rescued immediately.

The Difficult Middle Part

The expedition now faced the most trying part of its long journey—wide stretches of desert with no river to guide them or to provide a source of water. The first hazard after they crossed the river into what is today the state of California was the shifting, sandy wasteland west of Yuma. Travelers see this forbidding terrain for themselves as they drive west on I-8 and skirt the Algadones Dunes. Offroad recreational vehicles now zoom up and down the dunes of this public-use area, tracing tire patterns on the same slopes that proved to be such an obstacle to the Anza emigrants. Water was scarce and the toll on the animals was great, but after nine days the lead party reached an oasis they called San Sebastian (later known as Harpers Well), where expedition members and livestock found water to drink after days of long desert marches.

Today the traveler sees a vastly different picture. Irrigation here in the Imperial Valley has transformed the barren desert into a lush patchwork of productive fields that grow tomatoes, cantaloupe, lettuce, sugar beets, alfalfa, and asparagus, one of the richest farming areas in the world.

Anza headed into the Anza-Borrego Desert, a region later named in his honor. A part of the region is now set aside as the Anza-Borrego Desert State Park, the largest in California. But first the emigrants had to struggle through an early winter snowfall for which they were unprepared. Most of the colonists, as natives of New Spain, had never before seen snow.

Anza reported on December 15 that "the snow which had fallen the day and night before was very hard ... . As a result of which six of our cattle and one mule died ... . Several persons were frozen, one of them so badly that in order to save his life it was necessary to bundle him up for two hours between four fires."

For the next seven days they made their way in bitter weather across the desert near the eroded Borrego Badlands. The pioneers undoubtedly did not know, nor would they have cared, that these badlands have since proved to be a paleontologist's dream. Some twenty thousand years ago these barren lands were a verdant savannah in which animals fed on lush plants along the edge of a giant lake. Since then the mud and clay deposits of the savannah have been solidified, uplifted by volcanic pressure, and sculpted by summer storms and sand storms. From beneath this eroded terrain the paleontologists have extracted the bones and shells that testify to the ancient savannah.

Travelers trace Anza's route today on California 78 toward Borrego Springs. In doing so they pass one of the expedition's campsites—Los Puertecitas ("little gateway" to the Borrego Valley) on the way toward park headquarters and its visitor center at the resort town of Borrego Springs. A bronze plaque set into a stone pillar marks the passing of the expedition.

The park visitor center is unique. Built partially underground, its roof is covered with earth in which specimens of desert plants grow. A pathway leads past these labeled specimens, introducing the visitor to the variety of plants that have adapted to this climate of extremes. Inside the center tells the story of its desert setting and acquaints the public with the many fossil remains from the Paleolithic era, such as mammoths, giant sloths, camels, mastodons, sabertoothed cats, vultures, and horses, which make Anza-Borrego one of the most fossil-rich areas of the country.

Hikers, equestrians, or those driving a four-wheel-drive vehicle can follow the Anza route across the park. It leads through San Felipe Wash, a sandy creekbed that is dry most of the year except when a thunderstorm brings a dangerous flash flood. An excellent park map defines the trail and identifies six marked expedition campsites along the way.

For those who would follow the Anza Trail during the hot summer months, a park folder offers this advice: "Because humans have neither the special body adaptation nor the instinctive behavior of desert animals, they must rely on their intelligence— careful planning, water, knowledge of desert survival skills—to survive in the desert." For that reason, hikers and horseback riders are warned to carry plenty of water, know their physical limitations in hot weather, and take along an accurate map on any cross-park hike or ride.

The Anza Trail follows the narrowing valley into Coyote Canyon. Coyote Creek flows as if by magic out of the surrounding rocks, as it did two centuries ago, providing a welcome water source in the torrid canyon. Bighorn Borrego sheep are sometimes seen on the mountain slopes. Spidery ocotillo, prickly pear, mesquite, and low shrubs like brittlebush dot the landscape. The expedition members gathered up mesquite branches to keep their fires going during their cold-weather march through the canyon.

On December 24 Anza's expedition, with its approximately eight hundred livestock, made its way upslope, past rocks and boulders, to the head of the canyon. It was Christmas Eve, Anza reported, when "we halted at the villages of the people who on our last journey [his exploratory trip in 1774] we called Los Danzantes, the stop being made necessary because a woman was taken with childbirth pains ... . At a quarter to eleven in the night our patient (Gertrudis Rivas) was successfully delivered of a boy (Salvador), which makes three who have been delivered between the presidio of Tubac and this place, besides two others who have miscarried."

Finally the expedition members surmounted San Carlos Pass through the Santa Rosa Mountains and began their gradual descent into the Los Angeles basin. Despite experiencing one of California's first recorded earthquakes conditions for the group improved. The unforgiving desert gave way to grass-covered hills, trees and flowers, and abundant springs. For those who had endured the freezing cold, sleet, and snow of the desert canyon it seemed that nature had suddenly turned benevolent.

El Camino Real

Three days' march brought the rejuvenated Anza expedition to the Mission of San Gabriel Arcangel, one of the five missions that had been established along the coast of California at the urging of the indefatigable priest Junipero Serra. Eventually this chain of missions—established conveniently a day's journey apart—would grow to twenty-one. The trail that connected them became known as El Camino Real—"the Royal Road."

Founded five years before, in 1771, San Gabriel was a welcome sight to the overland emigrants. So welcome, in fact, that most of them stayed at the mission for fully seven weeks, a postponement of the expedition brought about by an Indian revolt. Anza and a few of his soldiers volunteered to divert themselves from the task at hand and march south to San Diego to help put down an Indian uprising that threatened the mission there.

Travelers today find San Gabriel set amid the city streets of the southwestern sector of metropolitan Los Angeles. Architecturally the mission church is unlike any of its sister churches, its Moorish appearance reminiscent of a cathedral in Spain.

It later grew so prosperous that it was known as the "Queen of the Missions." Because of its location in a fertile valley with plenty of trees, grass for cattle, and water for irrigation it was soon producing abundant crops of corn and beans and building up great herds of cattle.

The mission, including the large church itself, an old winery where Indians trampled the grapes, the sacristy, the extensive garden, the cemetery, the kitchen complex where cooks fed many Indians, and a museum, is all open to the public. In the garden visitors view models of some of the other California mission churches. A baptismal font with a cover pounded out of copper is even older than the venerable old church itself.

Once done in San Diego Anza returned to lead the expedition once more toward its destination. The historic trail today leads through the metropolitan area, passing the restored plaza that marks the earliest days of the city, El Pueblo de Los Angeles. The landmarks visitors see include an old church, adobe dwellings, and Olvera Street, one of the oldest streets of Los Angeles, a street now transformed into a Mexican marketplace.

Making their way along the Los Angeles River the expedition camped at what is now Griffith Park, an expanse of recreation and forested wilderness that still hints at a good place for a campsite. The Gene Autry Western Heritage Museum, situated within the park, offers exhibits and artifacts that portray the history of the American West.

The traveler driving northward on U.S. Highway 101 traces Anza's approximate route and may visit other missions where the expedition stopped. Signs along the highway identify the route as the El Camino Real and indicate where to turn off to visit the nearby missions.

This string of missions, many of them founded in the years after the Anza expedition, are tangible reminders of the Spanish strategy of organizing missions for the purpose of laying claim to the territory for Spain and converting the native Indians to Christianity.

Next for the Anza expedition was San Luis Obispo de Tolosa, 160 miles up the coast from San Gabriel. At the time

Anza came through it was a struggling country mission endeavoring to convert the neighboring Chumash Indians. To this day the church remains a parish church, now ministering to the busy city of San Luis Obispo. The attractive plaza that surrounds the old mission provides a setting along a wooded creek where people relax on park benches. It is also the scene of outdoor activities—art shows, dramas, and musical festivals. A sidewalk cafe opens onto the plaza.

Inside the old mission, founded in 1772, the visitor may admire the restored church with its high beamed ceiling. Nearby is a museum that preserves stone points, bowls, and implements used by the Chumash before the Spaniards arrived. A walk through the carefully tended mission garden leads to a small room where Indians trampled grapes to make wine.

Seventy miles up the coast is Mission San Antonio de Padua, founded in 1771 by Father Serra. Though located 15 miles west of U.S. 101 in the midst of a military reservation, San Antonio spreads out in grand style like a miniature city in its oak-studded valley. The traveler coming upon it senses the spaciousness that characterized all the missions in their heyday.

The history of San Antonio is one of acceptance by the Indian population, prosperity, and goodwill. In its prime it was home to some thirteen hundred Indians who worked at a score of handicrafts, produced fields full of crops, and herded some seventeen thousand livestock.

On March 10, 1776, Anza and the expedition reached Monterey, the site of a presidio constructed by the Spanish to guard the coast and the home mission of Father Serra, the founder of the California missions. The settlers had by now been on the road 165 days since they left Horcasitas. Although soaked by rain the day they arrived, they were ecstatic to be so close to their goal.

The presidio was an unequal rectangle with workshops and living quarters surrounding its open central courtyard, a small chapel at one side. With the arrival of the new settlers it expanded into a community. A few of the emigrants were chosen to remain and settle at Monterey.

Later, in 1794, a new chapel replaced the initial structure of logs, brush, and mud. Today the Royal Presidio Chapel, the oldest structure in Monterey, is one of the treasured structures of this historic town. Monterey has the distinction of having served as the capital of Alta California under the Spanish, Mexican, and

American flags. Walking tours of the picturesque city leave daily from the visitor center of Monterey State Historic Park at the Custom House Plaza on the city's waterfront.

During the expedition's stay at Monterey Anza fell ill and was taken by Father Serra to Mission San Carlos Borromeo de Carmelo, which had been moved ten miles south to Carmel in 1771 from its original site at the presidio. Serra had chosen the new site for its fertile farmland and to separate the mission from the distractions of the fort and its soldiers.

This mission at Carmel was Father Serra's headquarters as father-president of the entire chain of California missions. He was seldom there, however, since he spent most of his time making the rounds of the spreading mission settlements, often walking long distances between missions. When he was at Carmelo he was equally at home to governors and Indians.

Visitors at the beautifully restored mission today see a replica of the tiny cell where Father Serra lived. Its only furnishings are a cot of boards, a single blanket, a table and chair, a chest, a candlestick, and a gourd. Father Serra is buried beneath the stone floor of the replacement church that was built at the spot in 1797, 13 years after his death. Thousands of people walk through the quiet basilica and through the colorful gardens each year, reliving the history of this mission that provided a haven near the end of the journey for the Anza settlers.

The End of the Trail

On March 28, 1776, Anza finally reached his destination, San Francisco Bay. Leaving the main group behind in Monterey he, Father Font, and an advance party of soldiers marched the remaining one hundred miles up the coastal peninsula. Upon reaching the highland that overlooks the Golden Gate, he erected a cross at a point high above the white cliffs that formed one side of the entrance into the huge bay. Beneath the cross, under some rocks, Anza left a message describing his arrival and his exploration of the area. Father Font wrote:

> This mesa affords a most delightful view, for from it one sees a large part of the port and its islands, as far as the other side, the mouth of the harbor, and of the sea all that the sight can take in as far as beyond the Farallones (offshore islands) ... . And I think that if it could be well settled like Europe

there would not be anything more beautiful in all the world, for it has the best advantages for founding in it a most beautiful city, with all the conveniences desired, by land as well as by sea, with that harbor so remarkable and so spacious, in which may be established shipyards, docks, and anything that might be wished.

This mesa the commander selected as the site for the new settlement and fort which were to be established on this harbor, for, being on a height, it is so commanding that with muskets it can defend the entrance to the mouth of the harbor, while a gunshot away it has water to supply the people, namely, the spring or lake where we halted.

After designating the place where he thought the presidio and the mission should be constructed, Anza and Father Font explored the southern and eastern reaches of the bay, confirming the existence of this 60-mile-long protected harbor that is fed by several rivers, a realization that had eluded other seaborne explorers for more than a century. Anza then left the expedition and returned to Mexico City, leaving his second in command, Lieutenant José Joaquín Moraga, the task of establishing the main group of settlers at their new settlement site.

In June 1776 Moraga led 192 colonists and their cattle north to the presidio site and to the nearby site that had been selected for the mission. A large group set up camp at the presidio site while a smaller number pitched their tents beside a small lake at the site of the mission, named San Francisco de Asis, although it was commonly called "Mission Dolores," named for a creek that ran into the lake.

As soon as additional supplies arrived by ship, the new arrivals and local Indians set about building the presidio, the third of four military garrisons the Spaniards constructed to guard their occupation of Alta California. This presidio eventually became the first in a series of fortifications to occupy this strategic point at the entrance to San Francisco Bay. The visitor to the famous Presidio today can see these layers of military history, which began with the Spanish fortifications and continued through installations used in the Mexican War, World War I, World War II, the Korean War, the Vietnam War, and for coastal and missile defense. Recently archeologists uncovered a section of the original Spanish presidio wall beneath the present-day parade ground.

These old stone rubble foundations of the original presidio are not the only reminders of the Anza expedition that visitors find at this military installation, now a 1,480-acre preserve administered by the National Park Service as part of Golden Gate National Recreation Area. They may walk, ride, or jog along a three-mile trail that follows the route taken by Anza's advance party. A bronze tablet set in a large rock near Mountain Lake identifies the party's last campsite. National Park rangers bring this expedition to life when they provide visitors with a guided tour, "In Anza's Footsteps."

The Presidio today is a study in contrasts. Travelers who drive or walk its winding roads and pathways see not only some eight hundred structures of the former U.S. Army base and abandoned fortifications atop the rocky sea cliffs, but also spectacular views of bay and ocean, shadowy forests, meandering creeks, and groves of cypress and eucalyptus trees. The post's colorful history is reflected in the Presidio Army Museum, with its exhibits and a collection of U.S. Army uniforms from various eras. The San Francisco National Military Cemetery holds the graves of fighting men from the Civil War to the present. Fort Point, a classic example of a mid-nineteenth-century coastal fortification, is situated literally beneath the Golden Gate Bridge.

Nearby Mission San Francisco de Asis, now tucked away among the urban streets of the city, is the northern terminus of the Camino Real. The present restored church, the oldest intact building in San Francisco, was constructed from 1788 to 1791, replacing the earlier mission church. Redwood roof timbers are still lashed together with rawhide. The altar is one of the most ornate among the missions. Visitors look through a glass cutaway in the wall to see some of the original adobe bricks that form its four-foot-thick walls.

Under the floor of the nave is the grave of José Moraga, who guided the settlers on the last lap of their long journey. A multicolored tile mosaic in the courtyard depicts the arrival of Juan Bautista de Anza and of Junipero Serra in San Francisco. A small museum displays old books, manuscripts, and mission relics.

There are those living in San Francisco today who trace their forebears to the courageous settlers who came with Juan Bautista de Anza to find a new home in California. It was a daunting feat both for the expedition's leader and for the settlers.

For the emigrants it was an ordeal from which there was no turning back. It meant leaving their homes, however poor, in New Spain for a future they could not foretell. It meant many months of exhausting trekking across the waterless desert and rugged mountains until they reached the path that linked the coastal missions. It meant seeing their first snow and enduring the cold of the mountains.

For Anza it was a triumph. The expedition had opened successfully an overland route of immigration and supply from Mexico to the growing chain of Spanish mission settlements in California, a route he proved to be feasible. He had demonstrated with his exploration of San Francisco Bay that this body of water was one of the world's great protected harbors. Above all he had performed the extraordinary feat of safely leading a contingent of men, women, and children—most of them women and children—across 1,800 miles of forbidding terrain with the loss of only one life. In fact the expedition ended with more members than when it started; three babies were born during the journey. The expedition, a complete success, established the first European settlement at this farthest outpost of New Spain.

Amigos de Anza

The *Amigos de Anza* (Friends of Anza), an organization of volunteers from nineteen counties along the route in Arizona and California, pursues objectives that will extend and improve the trail through the southwestern United States.

The organization works with the National Park Service, state agencies of Arizona and California, the government of Mexico, and tribal and local agencies, organizations, and individuals to preserve and enhance the historic, educational, and recreational opportunities of the national historic trail.

The Amigos develop informative materials for trail users; organize local volunteer chapters; identify, build, and maintain the trail; and point out areas threatened by conflicting land use. It fosters trail days activities, costumed events such as reenactments of the 1776 expedition, educational presentations to school students, and community awareness of the trail. The group secures rights-of-way for places where the trail is under private or corporate ownership. It publishes a quarterly newsletter, *Noticias de Anza,* for its members.

For more information write the *Amigos de Anza,* c/o Heritage Trails Fund, 5301 Pine Hollow Road, Concord, CA 94521.

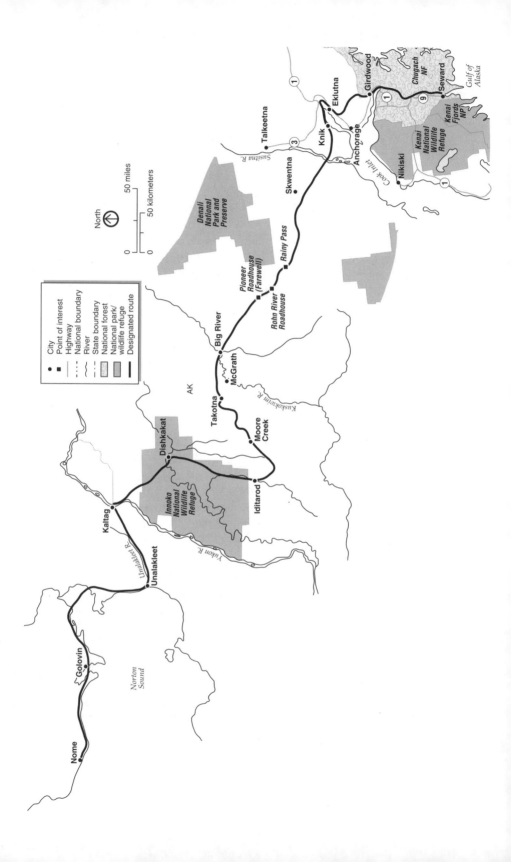

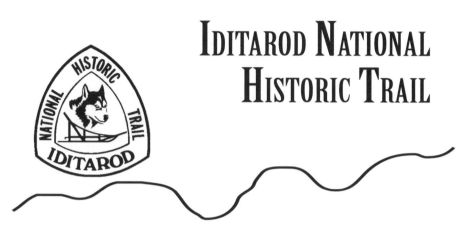

Chapter 19

IDITAROD NATIONAL HISTORIC TRAIL

O NE BY ONE EACH SLED DRIVER PULLS HIS OR HER TEAM OF POWERFUL dogs and a heavily loaded sled into position under the color-ful pennant that stretches across the street at the starting line in Anchorage. The pennant announces in bold letters: "Iditarod Trail Sled Dog Race."

Spectators crowd against the snow fences that line both sides of the street, clapping their mittened hands and shouting encour-agement to their favorite drivers. They have come to watch the start of the world's longest sled dog race, a race that each year sends competitors across the snow-covered tundra, mountains, and rivers of Alaska on a grueling 1,000-mile marathon from Anchorage to Nome on the Bering Sea.

Each driver, assessing the abilities and temperaments of his dozen or more dogs, has arranged them in pairs in front of the sled. At the head of the pack is the lead dog, the brains of the team, comparable to the steering wheel on a car. It is up to the lead dog to take the commands of "gee" and "haw" for right and left respectively, and keep the team on the trail. The lead dog also sets the pace and gets his harness mates up to speed so they keep the gang line taut. All good lead dogs show an uncanny ability to stay on the trail. When snow covers the route, the lead dog feels for the packed snow underneath; when the trail has been swept bare by the wind, it uses its sense of smell to remain on the trail; when the trail cannot be seen or felt or smelled, a good lead dog can find the way with its apparent sixth sense.

The two dogs behind the leader, called swing dogs, help steer by staying in the trail and forcing the rest of the team to turn in a wide arc that will bring the sled around a corner safely. Without trained swing dogs the dogs behind the leaders might jump off the trail to follow the leaders, creating a tangle of lines or even over-turning the sled.

The next several pairs of dogs, the team dogs, provide the muscle to pull the load and to maintain speed. Finally the last two in line are the wheel dogs. Usually the largest animals in the team, they have the added responsibility of being the first to feel the weight of the load as the team starts out or pulls uphill. The wheel dogs must be steady animals for the constant pounding of the runners close behind them can be unnerving.

Teams racing in the Iditarod have from ten to twenty dogs in a team. With a team of sixteen or more dogs the driver rides as far as 60 feet behind the lead dog.

Months before the start of the race on the first Saturday of March, the "mushers" assemble their equipment and train their dogs, running up to 60 miles a day. All sleds must carry snow-shoes, a sleeping bag, an ax, and booties to protect the dogs' feet from the snow and ice. Booties are usually made from a polar fleece fabric and are attached to the dogs' feet by Velcro. Food for the driver and team is loaded aboard. Additional food is forwarded to checkpoints along the race route where veterinarians stand by to assist any sick or injured dogs. Radio-equipped pilots help monitor the route to spot any teams in trouble.

Now the dogs are straining against the gang line, eager to be off, sensing that they must catch the teams that have already started. Race officials send the teams off in a two-minute staggered start, determining the winner by the total elapsed time on the trail. Handlers help the driver restrain the dogs as the race announcer counts: "Five ... four ... three ... two ... one. Go!"

Up the snow-covered streets of Anchorage they go, the driver standing on the sled's runners, trying to control the excited team until the dogs settle down and hit their stride on the open trail, once they are clear of the crowds and traffic.

This is the scene that each March brings action and excite-ment to the Iditarod National Historic Trail when these adven-turesome sled drivers set off on the grueling trans-Alaska race. It will take each driver and dog team ten days or more to battle their way to Nome, the elapsed time depending on ice conditions, winter storms, and mishaps that might occur to either a sled or a driver while on the trail. The Iditarod is the only one of the national trails that serves as the locale for such an annual competitive race.

The race was the idea of Joe Redington Sr., a native of Knik, a town 50 miles up the trail from Anchorage. He and other organizers felt that Alaska was losing its sled dogs to the new snowmachines and that only something the scope of such a cross-country race would keep an interest in dogsleds alive.

In 1973 thirty-four "mushers" entered and twenty-two finished in the first Anchorage-to-Nome race, a race route that closely follows much of the historic Iditarod Trail. The national historic trail actually begins at Seward, 100 miles south of Anchorage, but Anchorage was chosen as the starting point for the race because Alaska's largest city was better able to support the needs of the racers. In the years that followed interest in the race spread to other parts of the world. As the prize money increased mushers from other countries entered the competition. Today more than fifty drivers usually compete in the internationally known race for a first place prize of about $30,000. The race is normally televised and draws media attention worldwide.

The race has drawn renewed attention to a trail that was laid out in the early 1900s to permit gold-hungry prospectors to cross the snow-covered tundra to get to promising goldfields in the interior of Alaska.

Gold rush days began for Alaska in 1895, many years after the discovery and exploitation of the goldfields of California. In Alaska dogs and sleds took the place of the burro used in California, sourdough took the place of johnnycakes, and cigars replaced chewing tobacco (cigars deter the plentiful population of mosquitos in Alaska).

When gold was found in the fast-running streams of the Kenai Peninsula on Alaska's southern coast, fortune hunters from California and elsewhere could reach the new strike area only by steamship or sailing vessel. A few short local trails were built on the peninsula to connect the new mining camps with the trading posts they depended on for supplies.

Three years later three Swedish prospectors staked out what proved to be an even richer claim in the creekbeds of Cape Nome, far to the north on Alaska's west coast on the Bering Sea. Word of the gold discoveries in the beach sands of Nome caused Alaska's largest stampede. Once again the eager prospectors could get there only by ship. By the summer of 1900 an estimated 20,000 to 30,000 people had arrived by steamer to dig the "golden sands" of Nome. Miner's tents spread for miles along the coast. Nome became an instant city.

But from October to June every winter, Nome was ice-locked. Ships could not get into port through the frozen sea. No supplies or mail could come in. Nome was effectively isolated from the rest of Alaska and the world.

Iditarod Trail Blazed

To relieve this wintertime isolation and link Nome with the goldfields of the Kenai Peninsula and the year-round port at Seward on the south coast, a team of four U.S. Army engineers blazed the Iditarod Trail in 1908. Parts of the route they plotted followed dogsled trails used over the years by the native Indians and Eskimos as they hunted for game or traveled from one village to another. Russian fur trappers had also developed parts of what became the Iditarod Trail as a route to supply and provision their fur-trading outposts.

The Army engineers cleared and smoothed a trail that was approximately eight feet wide and had no grades steeper than 4 percent. They set out tripods to mark the route as it crossed barren stretches and ran above the timberline.

No sooner was the cross-Alaska trail route established and marked than more gold was discovered—on Christmas Day 1908. This new claim was in the Iditarod region in the interior; by great good fortune the find lay close to the new trail. The trail was quickly rerouted to include the new goldfields and adopted the Iditarod name. Dogsled runs along this Seward-to-Nome trail provided the only means during each winter of bringing in needed supplies and mail to the new Iditarod mining district.

Most travelers on the Iditarod did not go from trailhead to trailhead—Seward to Nome—as did the pioneers who followed the migration trails of the American West. Instead they guided their dogsleds from the ice-free harbor of Seward to the various mining districts or used segments of the trail to travel between mining camps and trade centers.

An assortment of travelers used the trail. The majority were prospectors, trappers, or natives who traveled—often without dogs or with only one or two to help pull a sledload of supplies—to isolated cabins. A surprising number walked in the summer or snowshoed in the winter along the southern portion of the trail.

Nevertheless the hero of the trail and inspiration for much of its lore was the dogsled driver and his team. These were the colorful and self-sufficient individuals who shrugged off the weather and pushed along the trail to carry fresh foods, mail, or express— or somebody's valuable shipment of gold. Among them was Frank Tondreau, known as the "Malemute Kid"; the famous racer John "Iron Man" Johnson and his Siberian dogs; the tireless Captain Ulysses Grant Norton; the Eskimo driver Split-the-Wind; and the wandering Japanese Jujira Wada. All the drivers were enthusiastically welcomed at each of the mining camps—their reputations burnished by the glowing newspaper accounts.

In the 1920s dogsled transportation gave way to the airplane for delivering mail and supplies to the Alaskan interior. But the Iditarod Trail had one last moment of glory in 1925, when an epidemic of diphtheria caught Nome without enough serum to inoculate the community.

An emergency call for help went out by telegraph but airplanes were unable to fly because of the limited hours of daylight during winter months. Instead a relay of dog teams picked up the serum at Nenana at the head of the Alaska Railroad and carried it down a trail along the Yukon River to the Iditarod trailhead. Mushers, urging their dogs through storms and darkness, carried the serum 674 miles in 127 hours. The dogsled drivers became heroes and were awarded medals for heroism by President Calvin Coolidge. Balto, the lead dog of the last team into Nome, was used as a model for statues of dogs that were raised in places as distant as Central Park in New York City.

Today portions of the trail are used by local residents who travel by snowmachine or dogsled from village to village in the roadless interior. Hunters use the trail as an access route through the Alaska mountains. At least one commercial operator offers 30-day dogsled tours along the Iditarod from Knik to Nome. Other groups take ski tours along the southern section of the trail. But hardly anyone uses the trail west of Knik in the spring, summer, and fall, when the route thaws into a quagmire of swamps, bogs, and wet tundra.

The trail crosses land owned by several native corporations, municipal governments, and the State of Alaska as well as federal lands managed by the Bureau of Land Management, U.S. Forest Service, U.S. Fish and Wildlife Service, and Department of Defense.

The Iditarod was designated a national historic trail in 1978. The Bureau of Land Management coordinates the management of the trail. Congress also established the Iditarod National Historic Trail Advisory Council, a group that represents both governmental and private land managers and users. The council provides guidance on all aspects of trail management such as the design of trail markers, cooperative agreements with landowners, and competitive events.

Seward to Rainy Pass

The Iditarod is the only national trail that is usable only part of the year—during the winter. It is when winter closes in, temperatures drop, and snow falls that the bogs and rivers along the route freeze over and provide trail users the firm footing on the snow they need for sleds or skis. The trail leads over the frozen surface of five major rivers (Susitna, Skwentna, Kuskokwim, Yukon, and Unalakleet) and even strikes out over sea ice at Norton Sound as it takes a shortcut across an arm of the Bering Sea as the trail approaches Nome.

From the ice-free port at Seward, with its spectacular fjords, the trail heads inland across the rugged Kenai Peninsula, an alpine terrain of mountains, glaciers, and lakes. It snakes through narrow valleys whose mountainsides are covered with spruce, hemlock, and hardwoods. Coastal Alaska weather is milder than in the interior, generating cool summer temperatures that average 55°F in July and comparatively mild winters. Winter brings temperatures that average 28°F in January and produce heavy snowfalls.

The trail heads northward through the extensive Chugach National Forest and Chugach State Park. The state park lies east of Anchorage, Alaska's major city. Nonexistent in 1910, Anchorage today has a population of more than two hundred thousand and is the regional trade, transportation, and service center of the state. Its population contributes most of the recreational users of the Iditarod.

This portion of the Iditarod is the only part of the trail where hikers can walk in the spring, summer, and fall; in the winter cross-country skiers and snowshoers use the trail. Wintertime users, however, need to beware of avalanches that from time to time sweep down the steep mountainsides and cover the trail. Signs along the route warn of places vulnerable to the snow slides. Cross-country skiers should check at the Eagle River visitor center at Chugach State Park near Anchorage or at U.S. Forest Service offices before setting out on a ski run along this portion of the trail.

These jagged mountains are also home to mountain goats and Dall sheep, while moose browse in the lowlands. Foxes, porcupines, and marmots are common.

At Eklutna, ten miles past Eagle River, the route passes the log structure of historic St. Nicholas Russian Orthodox Church with its brightly painted "spirit houses," built to house the spirits of the deceased. In the early summer the woods and meadows along the trail are ablaze with pink wildflowers.

After skirting the farthest inland reach of Cook Inlet the Iditarod turns west to go through the town of Knik. The main street of Knik recalls the early trail days when the town was a supply point for the dogsled teams. A museum in the town's old pool hall contains exhibits and photographs of early days along the trail as well as the "Dog Musher's Hall of Fame," with its colorful profiles of some of the famous sled drivers.

Crossing the Susitna River on the wintertime ice the trail traverses what is boggy tundra and swamp in the summer as it begins a slow climb to Rainy Pass (3,200 feet). Here it crests the Alaska Range, a mountain range that sweeps in a north-south arc across the state. Just to the north stands Mt. McKinley, at 20,320 feet the tallest peak in North America. The mountain is the centerpiece of Denali National Park, a park of four million acres that exemplifies interior Alaska's character as one of the world's last great frontiers for wilderness adventure.

As the trail heads inland the temperatures turn colder. Near Rainy Pass, for example, snowfall averages 86 inches a year, summer temperatures are cool (ranging from 37° to 63°F in midsummer), and winter temperatures range from −130° to 34°F.

Rainy Pass to Kaltag

After leading across the Alaska Range the Iditarod descends to sparsely vegetated tundra and barren ground as it crosses the numerous rivers and streams that drain the terrain. The trail winds across the Kuskokwim Mountains, then swings south to reach the former gold-mining town of Iditarod before it continues another 160 miles to the town of Kaltag, located on the banks of the Yukon River. The Yukon, following a curving course across the state from east to west, is a major geographic feature of Alaska. This is the river that enabled some of the gold rush miners to reach their destinations by boat.

There are no roads or railroads in this part of Alaska. The region is sparsely settled, primarily by Athabascan Indians. Trappers and hunters occasionally use the trail. The native Alaskans, with no roads or railroads to connect their villages, use it even more. The snowmachine, as Alaskans call the snowmobile, is the vehicle of choice here. In days past they would have hitched up a dog team. Now villagers jump into their snowmachine in the same fashion as people in the "lower forty-eight" hop in their cars. All the members of a village's basketball team, for example, will ride their snowmachines to a nearby village to play a game.

Few recreationists come to this region, except game hunters who fly in with bush pilots or come in overland by snowmachine. Wildlife is prolific, including moose, caribou, hare, lynx, black and grizzly bear, wolverine, beaver, Dall sheep, marten, land otter, muskrat, weasel, and mink. Moose can present a special problem to a musher because the powerful animal will often stand in the packed-down snow of the trail and refuse to move. Veterans say that the moose probably mistakes the sled dogs for wolves, its enemy. As a result a driver must often beat a detour around the threatening animal rather than challenge it.

When warm weather comes this part of the trail is next to impassable. Few bridges span the rivers. Only all-terrain vehicles (ATVs) can negotiate the boggy landscape. Most local travel is accomplished by boat on the rivers or by bush plane to more distant locations.

Although many historical reminders of the gold rush days have disappeared along the Iditarod Trail, you will still find some evidence of the cabins, trading posts, roadhouses, and mining settlements that once dotted the route. One of the outbuildings of the Pioneer Roadhouse, which welcomed travelers to the town of Farewell, still stands. Historically roadhouses were located along the trail about twenty miles apart, providing food and lodging for the mushers as well as needed rest and food for their dogs. After the airplane and the bush pilot replaced the dogsled and musher, most of the roadhouses fell into disuse. One of the few surviving examples is the Cape Nome Roadhouse, which was still used as a stopover for dog teams at the time of the 1925 diphtheria mercy mission.

At Iditarod and the nearby mining settlement of Flat is the largest concentration of intact historic structures on the Iditarod Trail and perhaps in Alaska: a store, warehouse, cabins, roadhouse, saloon, and mining structures such as shops, bunkhouses, and a dredge. Historians estimate that since the first strike some $30 million worth of gold has been taken out of the streams and mines of the region. Implements and memorabilia from these prospecting days have been removed from the buildings in these two ghost towns and are now displayed at museums in other Alaskan cities.

Kaltag to Nome

From Kaltag on the Yukon River the trail crosses a low divide, then runs along the riverbanks of the frozen Unalakleet River as it makes its way to Alaska's western coast. The trail then takes to the beaches of Norton Sound, leading across frozen lagoons, spits, and barrier beaches until it strikes out across the sea ice of the sound—when the ice is thick enough to hold a sled.

This portion of the Iditarod crosses the boundary between Athabascan Indian and Eskimo cultures. People of Eskimo descent make up the majority of the population of the villages along the route between Unalakleet and Nome.

Nome averages 82 inches of snow a year and has an average summertime temperature between 38° and 58°F. In the winter, temperatures are cold, averaging from –4° to –13°F.

Nome's name is said to be the result of a cartographer's mistake. On early maps the location was unknown and an anonymous cartographer penciled in "Name?" as a question to be answered. Instead an artist who did the finished map interpreted the word as "Nome" and lettered it in. A town of thirty-five hundred, Nome is the communication center of northwestern Alaska and the main supply point for nearby mining districts and Eskimo villages. The native Eskimo arts and crafts that are displayed and offered here for sale include ivory carvings, footwear, dolls, drums, and boat models. The Carrie McLain Memorial Museum typifies the lifestyle, architecture, and culture of the former gold camps. On display are examples of Eskimo art, archeological artifacts, and memorabilia from Nome's gold rush years.

And, of course, Nome is the finish line for the annual Iditarod sled dog race, the fame of which helped gain recognition for the cross-Alaska route as a national historic trail. Each year the race committee erects a big wooden archway on Front Street to welcome the trail-weary competitors. Visitors crowd in as the town triples in population at race time. Spectators noisily cheer and greet each team as it passes under the arch. They know that each of these plucky drivers has conquered a thousand or more miles of the Alaskan outback, spent weary days alone on the rugged trail, and brought his or her team successfully to the finish line in spite of wrong turns, mechanical breakdowns, injured dogs, freezing cold, and stinging snowstorms. Once again the epic race has reconfirmed the Iditarod Trail as one of the nation's most unusual national historic trails.

Iditarod Trail Associations

Although there exists no overall trail association for the Iditarod National Historic Trail, volunteers play an important role in maintaining and marking the route.

The Iditarod Trailblazers, a volunteer group organized in 1972, is composed mostly of recreational trail users from the Seward area who ski, run dogsleds, and operate snowmobiles. The Trailblazers provide maintenance and construction assistance on the Kenai Peninsula, the southern segment of the trail, and have laid out side and connecting trails to the Iditarod. Its members have taken part in the planning and designation of much of the historic trail.

The Iditarod Trail Committee, which plans the annual Iditarod Sled Dog Race, mobilizes an extensive group of volunteers at race time—veterinarians, marshals, hut attendants, pilots, and trail maintenance personnel. Volunteers clear the trail, repair rough spots, and mark the route for the racers.

Two other volunteer groups help maintain the northern portion of the trail—the Kaltag Sportsman Association and the Norton Sound Sled Dog Club.

For more information write the Iditarod Trailblazers, P.O. Box 1923, Seward, AK 99644, or the Iditarod Trail Committee, P.O. Box 870800, Wasilla, AK 99687.

Appendix

Federal Trail Administrators

Each of the nineteen national long-distance trails is managed by a federal agency. You may contact these agencies for specific site information and trail maps. General management plans for the trails are also under their jurisdiction. In addition the agencies are assisted and supported by working partnerships with the volunteer trail associations that are described at the conclusion of each trail chapter. Some of these groups also carry information and maps for their trails.

APPALACHIAN NATIONAL SCENIC TRAIL
National Park Service—
Appalachian National Scenic Trail
Project Office
c/o Harpers Ferry Center
Harpers Ferry, WV 25425
(304) 535-6278

CALIFORNIA NATIONAL HISTORIC TRAIL
National Park Service—Long
Distance Trails Coordinator
P.O. Box 45155
324 State Street, Room 250
Salt Lake City, UT 45155
(801) 539-4093

CONTINENTAL DIVIDE NATIONAL SCENIC TRAIL
Montana:
USDA–Forest Service,
Northern Regional Office
Federal Building
P.O. Box 7669
Missoula, MT 59807
(406) 329-3150

Wyoming:
USDA–Forest Service,
Intermountain Regional Office
Federal Building
324 25th Street
Ogden, UT 84401
(801) 625-5774

Colorado:
USDA–Forest Service, Rocky
Mountain Regional Office
740 Simms
Golden, CO 80401
(303) 275-5045

New Mexico:
USDA–Forest Service,
Southwestern Regional Office
Federal Building
517 Gold Avenue SW
Albuquerque, NM 87102
(505) 842-3236

FLORIDA NATIONAL SCENIC TRAIL
USDA–Forest Service,
National Forests in Florida
325 John Knox Road, #F-100
Tallahassee, FL 32303
(904) 942-9376

ICE AGE NATIONAL SCENIC TRAIL
National Park Service—Ice Age
National Scenic Trail
700 Rayovac Drive, Suite 100
Madison, WI 53711
(608) 264-5610

IDITAROD NATIONAL HISTORIC TRAIL
Bureau of Land Management,
Anchorage District
6881 Abbott Loop Road
Anchorage, AK 99507
(907) 267-1207

JUAN BAUTISTA DE ANZA NATONAL HISTORIC TRAIL
National Park Service
Planning, Grants, and
Environmental Quality Division
600 Harrison Street, Suite 600
San Francisco, CA 94107
(415) 744-3975

LEWIS AND CLARK NATIONAL HISTORIC TRAIL
National Park Service—Lewis and
Clark National Historic Trail
700 Rayovac Drive, Suite 100
Madison, WI 53711
(608) 264-5610

MORMON PIONEER NATIONAL HISTORIC TRAIL
National Park Service—Long
Distance Trails Coordinator
P.O. Box 45155
324 State Street, Room 250
Salt Lake City, UT 45155
(801) 539-4093

NATCHEZ TRACE NATIONAL SCENIC TRAIL
Superintendent, Natchez
Trace Parkway
R.R. #1, NT-143
Tupelo, MS 38801
(601) 680-4004

NEZ PERCE NATIONAL HISTORIC TRAIL
USDA–Forest Service,
Northern Regional Office
Federal Building
P.O. Box 7669
Missoula, MT 59807
(406) 329-3654

NORTH COUNTRY NATIONAL SCENIC TRAIL
National Park Service—North
Country National Scenic Trail
700 Rayovac Drive, Suite 100
Madison, WI 53711
(608) 264-5610

OREGON NATIONAL HISTORIC TRAIL
National Park Service—Long
Distance Trails Coordinator
P.O. Box 45155
324 State Street, Room 250
Salt Lake City, UT 45155
(801) 539-4093

OVERMOUNTAIN VICTORY NATIONAL HISTORIC TRAIL
National Park Service
Planning and Compliance Division
75 Spring Street SW
Atlanta, GA 30303
(404) 331-5465

PACIFIC CREST NATIONAL SCENIC TRAIL
Oregon, Washington:
USDA–Forest Service, Pacific
Northwest Regional Office
333 SW First Street, 1 Oak Plaza
Portland, OR 97204
(503) 326-3644

California:
USDA–Forest Service,
Southwest Regional Office
630 Sansome Street
San Francisco, CA 94111
(415) 705-2646

PONY EXPRESS NATIONAL HISTORIC TRAIL
National Park Service—Long
Distance Trails Coordinator
P.O. Box 45155
324 State Street, Room 250
Salt Lake City, UT 45155
(801) 539-4093

POTOMAC HERITAGE NATIONAL SCENIC TRAIL
National Park Service—National
Capital Region
1100 Ohio Drive SW
Washington, DC 20242
(202) 619-7025

SANTA FE NATIONAL HISTORIC TRAIL
National Park Service—Long
Distance Group
P.O. Box 728
Santa Fe, NM 87504
(505) 988-6888

TRAIL OF TEARS NATIONAL HISTORIC TRAIL
National Park Service—Long
Distance Group
P.O. Box 728
Santa Fe, NM 87504
(505) 988-6888

National Agencies

NATIONAL PARK SERVICE—RECREATION RESOURCES ASSISTANCE DIVISION
National Trails and
Recreation Branch
P.O. Box 37127
Washington, DC 20013-7127
(202) 343-3780

USDA–FOREST SERVICE RECREATION, CULTURAL RESOURCES, AND WILDERNESS MANAGEMENT
P.O. Box 96090
Washington, DC 20090-6090
(202) 205-1313

BUREAU OF LAND MANAGEMENT—HISTORIC TRAILS CONTACT
Special Areas and
Land Tenure Team
Department of the Interior
1849 C Street NW
Washington, DC 20240-9998
(202) 452-0325 or (202) 208-5213

INDEX

Index

Index